KT-131-331

Relationship Marketing
Theory and Practice

edited by

Francis Buttle
Manchester Business School

Selection and editorial material Copyright © 1996, F. Buttle
All other material © as credited.

All rights reserved

Paul Chapman Publishing Ltd
144 Liverpool Road
London
N1 1LA

Apart from any fair dealing for the purposes of research or private study, or criticism or review, as permitted under the Copyright, Designs and Patents Act, 1988, this publication may be reproduced, stored or transmitted, in any form or by any means, only with the prior permission in writing of the publishers, or in the case of reprographic reproduction in accordance with the terms of licences issued by the Copyright Licensing Agency. Inquiries concerning reproduction outside those terms should be sent to the publishers at the abovementioned address.

British Library Cataloguing in Publication Data

Relationship marketing: theory and practice
1. Marketing 2. Customer relations
I. Buttle, F.
658.8′12

ISBN 1 85396 313 5

Typeset by Dorwyn Ltd, Rowlands Castle, Hants.
Printed and bound in Great Britain

A B C D E F G H 9 8 7 6

15907

658.812/REL

Relationship Marketing

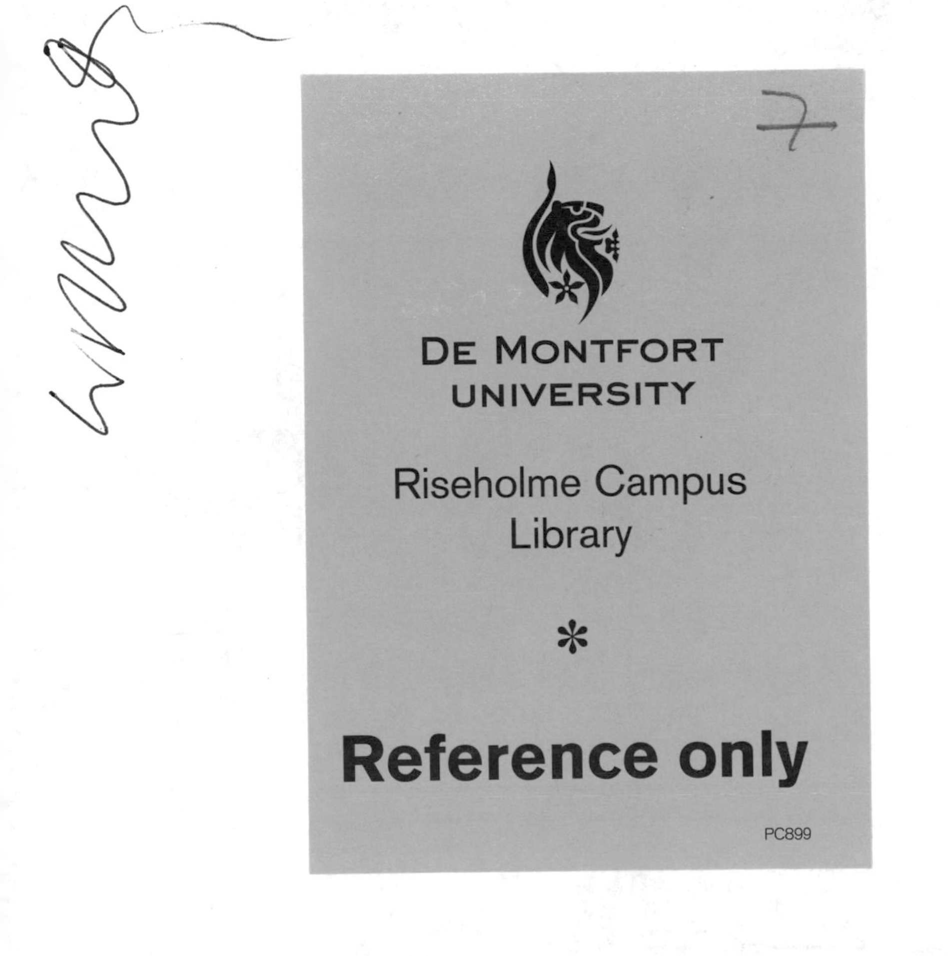

DE MONTFORT UNIVERSITY
LIBRARY
Date 16 · 10 · 96
Loc./Form Riseholme
Class 658 · 812
Suffix REL

Contents

Preface

Relationship marketing, the development of mutually beneficial long-term relationships between suppliers and customers, is being widely cited as the future of marketing. The traditional short-term focus on transactions has been criticised on two main grounds. First, short-termism has promoted a form of hit-and-run marketing in which the customer's best interests are not served. Second, short-termism has not served corporate self-interest either because it is more costly to attract new customers than it is to retain existing ones. Despite this, marketing theory is still resolutely transaction-oriented. Its focus is clearly on customer acquisition, rather than customer retention.

Slowly, however, a body of relationship marketing (RM) theory is developing, and companies are beginning to experiment with relationship marketing strategies. For example, theorists are examining relationships between customer retention and profitability, relational longevity and trust, customer defection and customer satisfaction. Practitioners have begun to segment customers according to their profit potential. According to one recent report (Hales, 1995), only 15% of bank customers are profitable. In the pursuit of a greater share of customers, these have become the focus of customer retention strategies and cross-selling efforts. Charitable fundraisers are striving to move individual donors up the ladder from casual gift-giving to legacy status. Companies are developing sophisticated customer databases to enable them to fine-tune offers.

In the light of this developing activity the main purpose of this book is to examine the association between relationship marketing theory and practice.

The opening chapter examines relationship marketing theory, reviews a number of RM definitions and reports on the economic arguments in favour of RM. It describes the nature and scope of marketing relationships, picking out characteristics such as concern for the welfare of customers, trust and commitment between partners, and the importance of customer service. Finally, it identifies a number of requirements for successful RM.

The next twelve chapters describe, analyse and critique RM practice in a number of organisational settings (supply-chain relationships, principal–agent relationships, business-to-business relationships, intra-organisational relationships) and industries (hospitality, air travel, retail banking, corporate banking, credit cards, financial advisory services, advertising agencies, not-for-profit organisations).

The final chapter reflects on the relationship between theory and practice. It does so by revisiting a number of questions raised in the first chapter.

Is there evidence of a shift from short-term to longer-term orientation?

Is there any evidence of mutual interests being served?

Do companies understand the concept of life-time value of a customer?

Is there evidence of trust and commitment between relational partners?

Is endorsement of RM reflected in high quality customer service?

Is internal marketing necessary for RM to prosper?

Are sophisticated information systems employed, enabling managers to meet or exceed customer expectations?

Do organisational structures and reward systems facilitate the achievement of RM goals?

The book has been written principally to meet the needs of the student reader. Students on MBA programmes, Masters students studying marketing, and Masters students on sectoral programmes examining financial services, hospitality, tourism, retailing, industrial and not-for-profit markets are the primary audience for this book. However, the clear link between theory and practice means that company directors and managers will also find much to interest them. Finally, upper level undergraduates on business studies and marketing courses will find the content challenges the traditions of marketing theory.

The book is the product of collaboration between editor and contributing authors. Grateful thanks are extended to all the contributors: Gary Davies, Neil Carruthers, Peter Naudé, Chris Holland, Javier Reynoso, Brian Moores, John Murphy, Charles Schell, Steve Worthington, Chris Ennew, Mary Hartley, David Gilbert, Sue Gilpin, Paul Michell and Tony Conway. Since the final decision on what to include and what to exclude lies with the editor, Francis Buttle is responsible for all errors of commission and omission. Apologies to all those offended.

Work continues to develop and refine RM concepts, and to promote better RM practice. The editor invites readers to join that effort. He may be contacted by e-mail at f.buttle@fs2.mbs.ac.uk or by writing to Manchester Business School, Booth Street West, Manchester M15 6PB, United Kingdom.

Reference

Hales, M.G. (1995) Focusing on 15% of the pie, *Bank Marketing*, Vol. 27, No. 4, April, pp. 29–34.

Contributors

Francis Buttle is Senior Fellow in Services Management at Manchester Business School. He has over 20 years experience in marketing management, research, consulting and education on three continents. Author of two books, he has contributed over 130 articles to academic and professional publications, as diverse as *European Journal of Marketing, International Journal of Advertising, Cornell Hotel and Restaurant Administration Quarterly*, and *International Boat Industry*. He teaches marketing management, customer service, and services marketing on MBA and executive courses. His PhD is from the University of Massachusetts.

Neil Carruthers is an ESRC Fellow in retailing at Manchester Business School. After completing an honours degree in Finance, his initial career involved him in large-scale corporate re-structuring programmes within the brewing and leisure industry. He then moved into the field of executive recruitment consultancy, ultimately becoming responsible for the successful launch and development of a new business venture. In 1991, he joined the full-time MBA programme at MBS, specialising in marketing and strategy. He is currently investigating the impact of inter-organisational relationships on performance outcomes for his Doctorate, as well as conducting research into the impact of governmental initiatives on entrepreneurial success.

Tony Conway is Principal Lecturer in Management at University College, Salford. He has produced a number of journal articles, text contributions and conference papers on public sector and general services marketing. He teaches Services Marketing, and Marketing Communications to a variety of postgraduate and undergraduate programmes and is involved in short course consultancies in Customer Care and Service Quality in both public and private sector organisations.

Gary Davies is POCL Professor of Retailing at Manchester Business School where he is also head of Marketing and Strategy and Director of the International Centre for Retail Studies. He has written over 200 articles and 10 books or monographs. His commercial experience includes employment with companies such as the Mars group and consultancy to organisations including retailers and manufacturers in Europe and North America. His current research interests involve a number of studies into supply-chain management.

Christine Ennew is Professor of Marketing in the School of Management and Finance at the University of Nottingham. She has been involved in a range of research projects relating to the marketing of financial services and published in a variety of journals including *Journal of Marketing Management, British Journal of Management* and *European Journal of Marketing*. She is co-editor of a leading text on financial services marketing and Associate Editor of the *International Journal of Bank Marketing*.

David Gilbert is Senior Lecturer in Marketing and Course Leader for Surrey University's Masters Degree Course in Tourism Marketing. He is the Research Director of the Thomas Cook Research Centre at the University of Surrey and carries out research for a number of leading UK companies. Other areas of interest include academic research related to tourism marketing and consumer behaviour. His specialist expertise has been sought for consultancy and the running of courses in many overseas countries and he has published over 50 refereed articles and papers.

Suzanne Gilpin is Senior Lecturer in Marketing in the Department of Hotel Catering and Tourism Management, the Manchester Metropolitan University. A graduate of Strathclyde University, she later gained her MA in Marketing at Kingston Business School. She has over eight years experience of operational, sales and marketing management in the hospitality, leisure and information technology industries. Prior to her present position, she has held posts at the former Oxford and South Bank Polytechnics. She has published in the area of international standardisation of leisure products and is currently researching branding within the business travel market.

Mary Hartley is a Graduate Teaching Assistant at the University of Nottingham. She is currently conducting doctoral research into relationship marketing and has co-authored a number of papers on this topic for conferences including MEG and EMAC. She has a BSc in Marketing and Organisational Behaviour from Lancaster University.

Christopher P. Holland graduated from the University of Warwick in Computer Systems Engineering. After working in product marketing for P&P, an information technology company, he was appointed ICL research associate at Manchester Business School. The focus of his research for ICL was on the effects of information systems on the organisation of supply chains and competitive advantage in the retail industry. He moved to Salford University's IT Institute as lecturer and developed his work on electronic data interchange and strategic information systems implementation. He is currently lecturer in Information Management at Manchester Business School where he gained his PhD in business administration. He has published articles in *Strategic Management Journal, Journal of Strategic Information Systems* and *Sloan Management Review* and regularly contributes to international strategy and IT conferences. He is director of the Master in Business Information Systems (MBIS) degree at MBS and is co-ordinator of the information systems in global business track for HICSS. His main research interests are globalisation, supply-chain management and the implementation of strategic information systems.

Paul Michell is Professor of Advertising and Marketing at Manchester Business School and Visiting Professor of Marketing at ESC Lyon Business School. He is a graduate of London, Boston and Brunel Universities. He has also worked at The Stern School New York University, and previously was in marketing management with United Biscuits and Procter and Gamble. He has published in *Journal of Marketing, Journal of Advertising Research, International Journal of Advertising, Journal of Marketing Communications*, among others.

Brian Moores undertook postgraduate research at UMIST into the efficacy of the work measurement process. He was awarded a Harkness Fellowship in 1964 and returned to UMIST in 1966. Brian Moores was appointed to a chair in Management in Cardiff in 1984 and he moved in 1987 to the chair of Management Science at Stirling where, amongst other activities, he created and directed the Scottish Quality Management Centre. He took up a chair at Manchester Business School in 1990. A less than satisfactory experience in a hospital Accident and Emergency Department led to him becoming involved in the development of methods for assessing inpatient perceptions of their hospital care and also triggered off a wider concern for quality assurance and customer service across all service industries. During his time at Manchester Business School he concentrated on the development of a portfolio of educational programmes across the full spectrum of specialised customer service issues. He has been involved, since its inception, with the SIGMA project in the Trent region.

John A. Murphy is the Abbey National Visiting Senior Fellow in Service Quality at Manchester Business School, prior to which he was Visiting Professor of Quality at the University of Ulster. He directs the Quality Master Class in Service Quality and teaches customer retention management on MBA and executive courses. He has over 15 years experience in senior management and is currently managing director of CRD International Ltd. He holds three professional fellowships and is a member of the International Academy for Quality, whose members are chosen from among the most active and experienced protagonists of quality in the world. He is the author of three books, the most recent of which – *Service Quality in Practice* – has also been published in several countries.

Peter Naudé did his undergraduate studies in marketing at the University of Cape Town, and subsequently completed his MSc in Operational Research at Sussex. He spent a number of years as a research officer with the Council for Scientific and Industrial Research and then as a consultant with the P-E Consulting Group. He moved into academia by joining the Department of Business Science at the University of Cape Town in 1983, and then moved to the Graduate School of Business at the same university in 1985. He joined the Doctoral programme at Manchester Business School in 1988, and became a faculty member there in 1990. His PhD studies were concerned with the statistical modelling of purchasing decisions in industrial marketing. His research interests focus on the general area of the application of statistical techniques for marketing analysis.

Javier F. Reynoso obtained a BSc in Industrial and Systems Engineering from Instituto Technologico y de Estudios Superiores de Monterrey (ITESM), Mexico. From 1983 to 1989 he worked as an internal facilitator in the design and implementation of quality management systems in major Mexican manufacturing industries. In 1987 he studied for a diploma in Total Quality Management in Osaka, Japan sponsored by the Japanese Government. From 1989 to 1991 he joined the ITESM faculty to work as a senior researcher and consultant in the Graduate and Research Division. From 1991 to 1995, he studied for a PhD in Services Management at Manchester Business School sponsored by The British Council, ITESM and the Mexican Government. During this period, he conducted research in service organisations, including the hotel industry and the health service. He is currently Assistant Professor at the faculty of the Graduate School of Business Administration at ITESM, Monterrey, Mexico.

Charles Schell is a Fellow in Banking at Manchester Business School and lectures on the MBA and executive programmes in the areas of finance, banking and business strategy. He is a regular contributor to executive training programmes for a number of UK banks and insurance companies and has undertaken consulting and research contracts for some of the UK's best-known institutions. His recent publications include *Corporate Credit Analysis* (with Nick Collett, now in its 2nd edition) and *Project and Infrastructure Finance in Asia*. Prior to joining MBS Charles worked as a consultant in Asia and the Pacific Islands and was employed as a financial and market analyst for Dun & Bradstreet, Canada.

Steve Worthington is the Britannia Building Society, Professor of Marketing of Financial Services at Staffordshire University Business School. He specialises in the issues surrounding the distribution of financial services via plastic cards and in the organisation and control of the payment systems through which these cards are used. He has previously lectured at Manchester Business School, the University of Stirling, and Trent University, Nottingham. Before returning to academic life in 1992, he worked as Marketing Group Head within Co-op Brand, the own label of the Co-operative Wholesale Society. Prior to that he was Head of Marketing and Planning with the Co-operative Bank, a subsidiary of the CWS. He also has business experience with ManuLife Insurance and Kodak. He was published widely both in academic journals such as *Journal of Marketing Management, International Journal of Retailing* and the *International Journal of Bank Marketing*, and in more practitioner focused publications such as *The Financial Times, European Card Review, Retail Week* and *Point of Sale Terminal News*.

1

Relationship marketing

Francis Buttle

> Harley-Davidson, whose Harley Owners club has 200,000 members worldwide, has an insurance programme, travel agency, emergency roadside service, two magazines, member competitions and 750 local chapters.
>
> In two years from launch, British Airways' worldwide executive club grew from 100,000 to 1.3 million members. Starting as a lounge at Heathrow airport, the club is now based on card ownership and the provision of multiple benefits. The cards are linked to BA's customer database which tells the airline which seat is preferred by the customer, whether the customer is a smoker and the customer's flying history.
>
> Renault's relationship marketing programme is mediated by the car firm's dealership network. Notes thanking owners for buying Renault, service reminders and special offers are printed on dealers' headed notepaper and personalized. Renault's UK market share rose from 3.5% in 1988 when the scheme was introduced to 5.5% in 1994.
>
> Nestlé's French baby-food marketing programme invests heavily in relationship marketing. The firm regularly mails offers and information to young mothers. It employs qualified dieticians to operate its customer service lines and it runs a chain of baby cafés to cater for families away from home. In 1985, Nestlé's market share was 20%; in 1992 it was 40%.

These stories are indicative of the changing nature of marketing. Marketing is no longer simply about developing, selling and delivering products. It is progressively more concerned with the development and maintenance of mutually satisfying long-term relationships with customers. If the 1950s was the era of mass-marketing, and the 1970s the era of market segmentation, then the 1990s represent the genesis of personalized marketing, in which knowledge about individual customers is used to guide highly focused marketing strategies. This change is driven by several conditions: more intense, often global, competition; more fragmentation of markets; a generally high level of product quality which is forcing companies to seek competitive advantage in other ways; more demanding customers; and rapidly changing customer buying patterns. Enduring relationships with customers cannot be duplicated by competitors, and therefore provide for a unique and sustained competitive advantage.

The expression most widely used to describe this new form of marketing is relationship marketing (RM). Other terms have been used, either as substitutes for RM or to describe some close parallel – micromarketing, database marketing, one-to-one marketing, loyalty marketing, wrap-around marketing, customer partnering, symbiotic marketing and interactive marketing.

Although the shift to RM is widespread, it is occurring more rapidly in some sectors and industries than others, facilitated by fundamental cultural shifts within organizations, powerful databases and new forms of organizational structure.

Redefining marketing

Marketing's leading international professional bodies are the Chartered Institute of Marketing and the American Marketing Association. They offer the following definitions of marketing:

> Marketing is the management process of identifying, anticipating and satisfying customer requirements profitably.
>
> (CIM)
>
> Marketing is the process of planning and executing conception, pricing, promotion and distribution of ideas, goods and services to create exchanges that satisfy individual and organizational objectives.
>
> (AMA)

Both these definitions reflect a traditional, transaction-orientated view of marketing. They contain no explicit recognition of the long-term value of a customer.

Theoreticians have begun to develop alternative definitions which capture the nature of the new marketing. Grönroos (1990; 1991; 1994, p. 355), for example, offers the following: 'Marketing is to establish, maintain, and enhance relationships with customers, and other partners, at a profit, so that the objectives of the parties involved are met. This is achieved by a mutual exchange and fulfilment of promises.' This definition attempts to incorporate both the transactional and the relational qualities of marketing. All marketing strategies, Grönroos (1991) tells us, lie on a continuum ranging from transactional (e.g. fast-moving consumer goods) to relational (e.g. services). Relational marketing, he claims, is characteristically different from transactional marketing. For example, rather than routinely employing the marketing mix's four Ps, it focuses on interactive marketing with the four Ps in a supporting role. (The four Ps (product, price, promotion, place) are the traditional tools that marketers use to manage demand. Known as the marketing mix (Borden, 1964), the four Ps have become a staple organizing construct of marketing texts since the early work of E.J. McCarthy (1975).) Rather than employing market share to assess marketing success, relational marketing measures customer retention.

Others have sought not to redefine marketing *per se* but more precisely to define the character of RM. Some have examined RM from sectoral perspectives. Berry (1983, p. 25), the first to publish work on RM, takes a service sector perspective: 'RM is attracting, maintaining and – in multi-service organizations – enhancing customer relationships.' Jackson (1985, p. 2) writes from an industrial marketing perspective: 'RM concerns attracting, developing and retaining customer relationships.' Others have attempted to characterize RM more broadly. Dwyer, Schurr and Oh (1987, p. 12) describe RM as 'longer in duration [than transactional marketing], reflecting an ongoing process'. Christopher, Payne and Ballantyne (1991) see RM as a synthesis of marketing, customer service and quality management. Sheth (1994, p. 2) describes RM as 'the understanding, explanation and management of the ongoing collaborative business relationship between suppliers and customers'. Evans and Laskin (1994, p. 440) suggest: 'RM is a customer centred approach whereby a firm seeks long-term business relations with prospective and existing customers.' Morgan and Hunt (1994, p. 22) offer the broadest definition of RM, taking neither a sectoral perspective nor specifying the need for there to be a 'customer'. Rather, 'RM refers to all marketing activities directed toward establishing, developing and maintaining successful relational exchanges'.

Some critics of the new RM have suggested that it is really no more than a series of transactions over time, and that it has no special character. However, Czepiel (1990, p. 13) retorts that a relationship possesses 'mutual recognition of some *special* status between exchange partners' (emphasis added), to which Barnes (1995, p. 1394) adds: 'a succession of interactions does not necessarily lead to a relationship any more than repeat purchasing constitutes loyalty.'

Finally, as Gummesson (1994, p. 7) has rightly observed: 'RM is currently seeking its identity. Gradually, a more general approach to marketing management, based on relationships, is gaining ground.' It may be that RM will not be firmly entrenched as standard business practice until the millennium.

Whose relationships?

As indicated by these definitions, there is some debate about the focus of RM. The older definitions suggest that RM's focus is the external customer. The newer contributions widen its scope. Morgan and Hunt (1994) identify ten discrete forms of RM (see Table 1.1). Gummesson (1994, p. 12) goes even further. He lists 32 relationships in defining RM as 'marketing seen as relationships, networks and interaction'. Companies clearly have relationships with many different persons and organizations.

Traditionally, marketing strategies have been developed both to push product through distribution channels (trade marketing strategy) and pull consumers towards the point of sale (consumer marketing strategy). A third form of marketing strategy has gained currency recently – the internal marketing strategy. Internal marketing focuses on employees. It recognizes that every

Table 1.1 The relational exchanges in RM

Supplier partnerships	Lateral partnerships	Internal partnerships	Buyer partnerships
Goods suppliers Services suppliers	Competitors Non-profit organizations Government	Business units Employees Functional departments	Intermediate customers Ultimate customers

person in an organization is both a customer and a supplier. An organization's final output, be it a good or a service, is almost always the product of operations and processes performed by people in series. A principal purpose of internal marketing is to ensure that the final outputs of the organization are of suitably high, external-customer-satisfying quality. For this to happen, each operation in the series must be performed to high standards. It is therefore helpful for employees to view the next person in the series as a customer. Internal marketing is also concerned with ensuring all employees buy into the organization's mission and goals and successfully develop and execute strategies.

These three relationships – company/intermediary, company/consumer and company/employee – are at the heart of most RM practice, although the dominant focus is on external customer relationships.

New words are being employed to describe these relationships. Customers are now *associates* or *partners* enmeshed in *alliances* or *partnerships* with companies. Levitt (1983a) and Dwyer, Schurr and Oh (1987) both employ a marriage metaphor to describe the new marketing. Levitt (1983a, p. 111) wrote: 'the relationship between a seller and buyer seldom ends when the sale is made . . . the sale merely consummates the courtship. Then the marriage begins.' Dwyer, Schurr and Oh (1987) incorporate dating and divorce into the metaphor when they observe that supplier–customer relationships are marked by five stages: awareness, exploration, expansion, commitment and dissolution.

Marketers are now beginning to talk about share of customer (in addition to share of market), economies of scope (as well as economies of scale) and customer loyalty (instead of brand loyalty). Share of customer, a reference to the percentage of an individual's annual or lifetime purchases that is won by a company, is employed as a measure of RM performance. Economies of scope are cost savings owing to the complementarities of products. Cross-selling related services generates these economies. Customer loyalty emphasizes the interactive nature of RM, unlike brand loyalty; it is an acknowledgement of the personal nature of the commitment of the customer to the firm and/or its employees. Brand loyalty, in contrast, suggests that the commitment is to the product.

Christopher, Payne and Ballantyne (1991) have developed the idea that there is a relationship 'ladder of customer loyalty'. Initially the company's relationship is with a prospect. The relationship progresses up several rungs – customer, client, supporter and, at the top, advocate. Accordingly, the job of RM is to advance relationships to advocate status. Advocates are so deeply enmeshed in the organization that they are not only very loyal long-term purchasers but they also influence others through positive word of mouth.

Having claimed that the goal of RM is to identify and nurture mutually satisfying long-term relationships with customers, there has been an argument that RM need not necessarily focus on the long term. Grönroos (1990, p. 3), for example, stresses that

> marketing can be considered as revolving around relationships, some of which are like single transactions, narrow in scope and not involving much or any social relationship (e.g. marketing soap or breakfast cereals). Other relationships, on the other hand, are broader in scope and may involve even

substantial social contacts and be continuous and enduring in nature (e.g. marketing hospitality or financial services).

He argues that 'every single customer forms a customer relationship with the seller', but that 'the emphasis should be on developing and maintaining enduring, long-term customer relationships' (p. 4).

The economics of relationship marketing

The impetus for the development of RM has been a growing awareness of the long-term financial benefits it can convey. RM is not philanthropic. It is a means to an end, and it is based on two economic arguments. One: it is more expensive to win a new customer than it is to retain an existing customer. Two: the longer the association between company and customer the more profitable the relationship for the firm.

Theodore Levitt once said that the job of marketing is to create and keep customers. Historically the focus has been on creating customers; less attention has been paid to their retention. RM reverses the emphasis.

It has long been claimed that it is between five and ten times as expensive to win a new customer than it is to retain an existing one (e.g. Rosenberg and Czepiel, 1984). While the factor will differ between industries and companies, it is evident that recruiting new customers is a costly business. Not only are there the direct costs of the successful conversion of a prospect into a customer (selling costs, commission, product samples, credit-checking costs, administrative costs, database costs) but there are also the costs of unsuccessful prospecting. Some industries experience a very low conversion ratio of prospects to customers. These costs of failure also have to be recovered.

There is now a growing awareness of the lifetime value of a customer. A transaction-orientated view of the customer would consider the sales value and margin earned from a single sale. A relationship-orientated view of the customer considers the revenues and contributions earned from a long-term relationship with a customer.

Reichheld and Sasser (1990) argue that companies should attempt to improve their customer-retention performance. They have observed a cross-industry trend: sales and profits per account rise the longer a relationship lasts. As customers become more satisfied with the service they receive, the more they buy. As purchases rise, operating costs decline, because companies climb the experience curve and become more efficient. Profits therefore improve. They provide illustrative data from the credit-card industry: it costs $51 to win a new account; profits earned grow annually from $30 in year 1, through $42, $44, $49, to $55. Clearly, a customer relationship must last into the second year before break-even (profits equal to the cost of winning the account) is reached. The pattern of annually increasing profits is commonplace, and it emphasizes the benefits of retaining customers into the long term. Heskett *et al.* (1994, p. 164) estimate that the lifetime revenue stream from a loyal pizza customer can be $8,000; from a Cadillac customer it can reach $332,000; and in the case of 'a corporate purchaser of commercial aircraft literally billions of dollars'.

Reducing customer defection rates is critical for retention rates to improve. As defection rates fall the average customer-relationship lifespan increases. According to Reichheld and Sasser (1990, p. 107), 'as the credit card company cuts its defection rate from 20% to 10%, the average lifespan of its relationship with a customer doubles from 5 years to 10 and the value of the customer more than doubles – jumping from $134 to $300.'

When customers defect they not only take margin from current transactions with them but all future margin also. Additionally, if customers defect angry or dissatisfied, they are likely to utter negative word of mouth about the company, thereby reducing the prospect pool for the firm.

Several authors have therefore suggested methods of measuring the profitability of relationships (Reichheld and Sasser, 1990; Grönroos, 1992; Buck-Lew and Edvinsson, 1993; Petrison, Blattberg and Wang, 1993; Pitt and Page, 1994; Payne and Rickard, 1994; Storbacka, 1994; Storbacka, Strandvik and Grönroos, 1994; Wang and Splegel, 1994; Hughes and Wang, 1995; Keane and Wang, 1995). Any attempt to compute the lifetime value of a customer requires the following data: cost of winning the customer; periodic cost of retaining the customer; gross margin earned from the first, second, third, fourth . . . *n*th sale to the customer; probabilities that the customer will buy a second, third, fourth . . . *n*th time; required rate of return for the company (in order to compute net present value); and numbers of purchases made by the customer from the company. These data can be used to compute the lifetime value of individual customers, segments of customers or of the 'average' customer. They can serve as benchmarking data and are useful to monitor the impact of customer-retention strategies.

Other authors have suggested strategies to improve customer retention rates (Hart, Heskett and Sasser, 1990; Reichheld and Sasser, 1990; Fornell, 1992; Pitt and Page, 1994; Reichheld, 1993; Rust and Zahorik, 1993; Rust, Zahorik and Keiningham, 1994). There is widespread agreement that the root causes of customer defection must be addressed, and that recovery programmes should be in place to prevent the defection of at-risk customers.

Customers have been shown to defect for a number of reasons (DeSouza, 1992 – see Table 1.2). Since not all these causes can be eliminated, there will clearly be some defections whatever actions companies take. Furthermore, companies realize that not all customers are worth retaining. Not all relationships are equally profitable. For example, Storbacka, Strandvik and Grönroos (1994, p. 32) claim that 'it is not uncommon for approximately 50% of the customers in a retail bank's data base to be unprofitable'. Neither is it always

Table 1.2 Reasons for customer defection

Type	Description
Price	Defections to a lower-priced alternative
Product	Defections to a superior product
Service	Defections owing to poor service
Market	Customers who leave the market, but not to a competitor
Technological	Defections to a product from outside the industry
Organizational	Defections owing to internal or external political considerations

possible to know whether a currently unprofitable account would generate a future profit stream given investment in that customer's satisfaction. One way of dealing with this problem is the use of customer profiling. This involves constructing a profile of existing profitable accounts and searching the prospect or light-user database for customers of similar profile. A close match indicates significant future potential.

Mutual satisfaction?

Traditional marketing theory places mutual satisfaction at the heart of marketing exchanges. Companies achieve their profit targets by virtue of satisfying customers. This is explicit in the CIM, AMA and Grönroos' definitions presented earlier.

As already noted, it is corporate economics that are forcing the pace of adoption of RM. The needs, wants and expectations of customers have not been of paramount importance. Indeed there is very little evidence that customers want to enter into long-term partnerships and alliances with suppliers (Barnes, 1995; Blois, 1995). There are some exceptions: clothing retailers, for instance, are building alliances with manufacturers to ensure the timely supply of goods of specified quality and design. Manufacturers are enjoying the long-term security and profitability that such relationships bring.

It is evident that customers generally seek quality, value and convenience in their transactions with suppliers. What is not clear is what else customers would expect if they were to enter into a longer-term relationship. In a close relationship customers could reasonably expect suppliers to have a better appreciation of their circumstances and requirements; customers in turn should develop more realistic expectations of their suppliers. However, we do not even know whether all customers value the formation of relationships with suppliers. It is entirely possible that markets may be segmentable against some sort of 'relationship-proneness' variable. Neither do we know whether relationship-building is contextualized, i.e. is valued more highly in some sectors than in others. It would seem reasonable to hypothesize that relationship building would be seen as offering significant benefits when transaction costs are high.

Finally, we do not fully understand the motivations of relationship-seekers. We have some indications from research into shopping motives (Tauber, 1972; Buttle, 1992) that some shoppers value and seek out social contact. How deeply this phenomenon extends into other parts of customers' lives is unknown. Other than seeking social contact, it may be that relationship-prone customers seek to reduce risk and avoid unduly stressful arousal.

Whether entering into a discrete transaction or ongoing relationship with a supplier, customers will experience what economists call transaction costs (Milgrom and Roberts, 1992). For example, there may be search costs, negotiation costs and legal costs. These costs may be higher when a customer is selecting a supplier with whom to have a long-term relationship. The search may be more extensive and more information may be acquired and processed in order to reduce the financial and other risks associated with a long-term commitment. However, once incurred, these costs do not recur in a relationship. In contrast, where a customer switches suppliers frequently, transaction costs may be significantly higher in the long term. RM therefore does offer customers an important benefit – the control, reduction and potential elimination of transaction costs.

In sum, Grönroos (1991, p. 10) noted that 'in a transaction marketing strategy there is not much other than the core product, and sometimes the image of the firm which keeps customers attached to the seller'. The implication is that in RM there will be much more.

The character of a marketing relationship

Relationships between customer and supplier have traditionally been characterized as confrontational or adversarial. The literatures on distribution-channel management and industrial marketing are typical. They have focused on issues of power, conflict and control (see, for example, O'Neal, 1989; Rosenbloom, 1991; Stern and El-Ansary, 1992). Only recently has the introduction of the concept of supply-chain management produced a more harmonious view of the relationships between retailer and supplier. Young and Wilkinson (1989) note that this emphasis in the literature has been on sick rather than healthy relationships.

RM is about healthy relationships which are characterized by concern, trust, commitment and service.

Concern

Relationship marketers are concerned for the welfare of their customers. They want to meet or, preferably exceed customer expectations, producing satisfaction or delight. KwikFit and American Express are two companies who claim to be dedicated to producing customer delight by exceeding customer expectations. The key is to understand intimately the expectations of customers. Since expectations are the product of personal needs and experience, word of mouth and marketing communications (Parasuraman, Zeithaml and Berry, 1994; Zeithaml, Parasuraman and Berry, 1994) they are dynamic. Dynamism means that it is no simple matter to understand, or to track, change in expectations. Marketers can to some degree mould expectations through mediated and interpersonal communications with customers, but only in very rare circumstances is it likely that they will be able to determine expectations.

Trust and commitment

Trust and commitment are the focus of much of the published research into RM. Moorman, Zaltman and Deshpande (1992), Gamesan (1994), Morgan and Hunt (1994) and Geyskens and Steenkamp (1995) focus on the role of trust in developing successful relationships. Morgan and Hunt (1994, p. 22) argue that

> commitment and trust are 'key' because they encourage marketers to (1) work at preserving relationship investments by cooperating with exchange partners, (2) resist attractive short-term alternatives in favour of the expected long-term benefits of staying with existing partners, and (3) view potentially high risk actions as being prudent because of the belief that their partners will not act opportunistically. When commitment and trust – not

just one or the other – are present they produce outcomes that promote efficiency, productivity and effectiveness.

Morgan and Hunt (*ibid.*) describe commitment as an enduring desire to maintain a relationship, and trust as the confidence that one partner has in the other's reliability and integrity. Confidence is associated with the partner's consistency, competence, honesty, fairness, willingness to make sacrifices, responsibility, helpfulness and benevolence. Trust, they argue, is the cornerstone of relationship commitment; without it commitment flounders. Geyskens and Steenkamp (1995) conclude that there is a consensus emerging that trust encompasses two essential elements: trust in the partner's honesty and trust in the partner's benevolence. Honesty refers to the belief that the partner stands by its word, fulfils promised role obligations and is sincere. Benevolence reflects the belief that one partner is interested in the other's welfare and will not take unexpected actions to the detriment of the partner. Trust brings about a feeling of security, reduces uncertainty and creates a supportive climate.

Morgan and Hunt (1994, p. 25) provide empirical data which support the role of commitment and trust in RM success: 'First, acquiescence and propensity to leave directly flow from relationship commitment. Second, functional conflict and uncertainty are the direct results of [lack of] trust. Third, and most importantly . . . cooperation arises directly from both relationship commitment and trust.' Co-operative behaviours, they claim, are necessary for RM success whatever the context. Relationship marketers have attempted to bond customers to their companies in a number of ways (Storbacka, 1994). Social, technological, legal, economic and cultural bonds all serve as exit barriers, discouraging customers from seeking alternative suppliers. Customers may therefore remain ostensibly loyal, even though they are not satisfied with the service they receive. Bonding which is not based on trust and commitment is unlikely to persist.

The challenge for RM managers is to demonstrate their commitment to the relationship and to inculcate trust in their partner. In a service marketing context this can be particularly challenging because of the relative absence of tangible clues, and because services cannot be examined before they are produced/consumed.

Service

The outcome of this concern for customers, in an environment of relationship commitment and trust, is a desire to provide excellent service. RM requires an organization-wide commitment to providing high-quality service which is reliable, empathic and responsive.

Since RM is a means to a profitable end, relationship marketers must believe that excellent service produces improved profitability. This has been the focus of a stream of research (e.g. Rust and Zahorik, 1993; Heskett *et al.*, 1994; Rust, Zahorik and Keiningham, 1994) which broadly supports this view. Recently, for example, Storbacka, Strandvik and Grönroos (1994, p. 23) have proposed a model which hypothesizes a number of connections between service quality and profitability. Their framework incorporates this basic sequence: 'service quality leads to customer satisfaction which leads to relationship strength, which leads to relationship longevity, which leads to customer relationship profitability.'

Where is relationship marketing found

Although 'relationship marketing' has entered the management lexicon only recently (Berry, 1983) the practice of RM has a long history. Historical research indicates that merchants in the Middle Ages recognized that some customers were worth courting more seriously than others. Richer customers would be offered credit terms; the poor paid cash.

Industrial marketers, particularly those selling high-priced capital goods, have long known that they must take a long-term view to make a sale. Team-selling, with multiple levels of contact between seller and customer organizations, is commonplace. Sales are only closed after protracted periods involving many people, and after-sale follow-up is the norm.

Manufacturers of fast-moving consumer goods (FMCG) have also attempted to climb on the RM bandwagon. Businesses which are dependent on large numbers of customers, high sales volumes and low margins tend to have more difficulty adopting RM. Frequently, their customer databases are inadequately disaggregated; they know little about their customers at a personal level. Heinz has computed that RM is not financially worthwhile if a customer spends less that £10 on Heinz products per annum (Treather, 1994). Until the costs of communicating with customers fall, it is likely that FMCG manufacturers will be slow to move to RM.

It is, however, in the services marketing area that RM is practised most widely. Services provided by banks, hotels and healthcare organizations are particularly suitable for RM initiatives because they supply multiple services deliverable over several contacts, in person. Because of their participation in the production of services, customers come face to face with employees and are able to form an interpersonal relationship with the service provider.

Research into RM has been produced from a number of perspectives. Relationships between members of the marketing channel have been examined by several authors (Dwyer, Schurr and Oh, 1987; Anderson and Narus, 1990; Spriggs and Nevin, 1992). Dwyer, Schurr and Oh (1987) found that channel relationships exist on a continuum, ranging from discrete to relational. Channel members whose relationships take the relational form have expectations that the relationship will persist over time, exhibit mutual trust and make plans for the future.

In an industrial marketing context, RM has been studied by many authors (Håkansson, 1982; Jackson, 1985; Gummesson, 1987; Spekman, 1988; Anderson and Narus, 1991). Switching costs associated with changing supplier may be immense; manufacturing technology and processes represent long-term commitments for most producers. Hence, suppliers of critical inputs are rarely changed. Often, relationships are made more secure through joint product-development programmes.

The service marketing context provides the setting for most research (Berry and Gresham, 1986; Crosby, 1989; Crosby, Evans and Cowles, 1990; Czepiel, 1990; Grönroos, 1990; 1991; 1994). According to Ellis, Lee and Beatty

(1993), published service sector research has taken two forms: those studies which focus on the individual service encounter and those which focus on the ongoing relationship between buyer and seller. Long-term relationships are composed of encounters in series and, according to Czepiel (1990), are developed in a number of stages: 1) the accumulation of satisfactory encounters; 2) active participation based on mutual disclosure and trust; 3) creation of a double bond (personal and economic); and 4) psychological loyalty to the partner. Frenzen and Davis (1990) characterized RM relationships as enduring sequences of encounters that involve indebtedness, embeddedness and rules of reciprocity.

Although Crosby, Evans and Cowles (1990) found that salesperson behaviours such as contact intensity, disclosure and co-operative intentions had a positive impact on the customer's level of satisfaction and trust, in general little is known about employee behaviours that foster long-term relationships (Ellis, Lee and Beatty, 1993).

The literatures of psychology, social psychology and communication theory have not infiltrated deeply into the marketing literature, although there is some evidence that they could contribute significantly to our understanding of RM. Martin and Sohi (1993), for example, found that trust, frequency of communication, quality of communication and relational norms impacted on the length of a relationship. Their work supports that of Heide and John (1992) who found that norms such as flexibility (mutual expectation of willingness to change), information exchange (mutual, proactive provision of information to the relationship partner) and solidarity (mutual expectation that a high value is placed on the relationship) facilitate relationship duration. Martin and Sohi (1993) also note that certain seller characteristics influence the duration of a relationship: dependability, competence, likeability and customer orientation. Dependability implies that the customer can predict how the seller will behave/perform; competence refers to the technical skill and knowledge required to satisfy customer expectations; likeability helps build rapport; and customer orientation refers to the seller's empathy towards customer needs, and willingness to prioritize those needs. These characteristics bear a remarkable resemblance to the generic dimensions of service quality identified by Parasuraman, Zeithaml and Berry (1985; 1988; 1991): reliability, responsiveness, empathy, assurance and tangibles.

An additional question concerns the locus of the relationship. Can customers develop relationships with organizations or must relationships always be interpersonal?

Requirements for successful relationship marketing

There appear to be a number of requirements for the successful implementation of RM programmes.

First, a supportive culture is necessary for RM to flourish. Several commentators have noted that RM represents a paradigm shift from the older, transactional way of doing business (Levitt, 1983b; Shapiro, 1991; Webster, 1992). Paradigm shifts inevitably pose threats to, and demand changes of, existing corporate culture. RM is typified by mutual co-operation and interdependence between customer and supplier (Sheth, 1994). Under a transactional regime, the relationship is better characterized as 'manipulation of customers, exploiting their ignorance' (Gummesson, 1994, p. 9). At its extreme, transactional marketing reflects P.T. Barnum's contemptuous observation: 'There's a sucker born every day.' Under RM, salespeople are likely to be replaced by relationship managers; customer retention is likely to be rewarded more highly than customer acquisition; customer satisfaction data will receive billing equal to that of financial data in management meetings; and the CEO will spend as much time with customers as with department heads. These are not the priorities in exploitative marketing settings.

Internal marketing is a second prerequisite for successful RM (Gummesson, 1987; Grönroos, 1990). The goal of internal marketing is to convert employees to the new vision of RM, to promote the development of the new culture, to persuade them that it is sensible to buy into the new vision, and to motivate them to develop and implement RM strategies. The internal market's expectations and needs must be satisfied. 'Unless this is done properly, the success of the organization's operations on its ultimate, external markets will be jeopardized' (Grönroos, 1990, p. 8). If the organization is unable to meet its employees' needs, it is likely that they will defect to other jobs before being able to build long-lasting relationships with customers.

It is also clear that the firm must understand customer expectations. This means that there must be a continuous flow of information into the business; continuity is required because expectations change over time. Work by Parasuraman, Berry and Zeithaml (1991) suggests that managers do not always have a clear understanding of customer expectations. This is a product of an inadequate marketing information system, too many levels of management between the front line and management, and communication difficulties.

A fourth requirement for successful RM is a sophisticated customer database which provides information in actionable format for the development and monitoring of RM strategy and tactics. Petrison and Wang (1993) claim that database technology is fundamental to allowing companies to get to know their customers as individuals. An example is provided by the US retail chain, Service Merchandise. Their point-of-sale system captures 100% of customers' identities and transactions down to the individual SKU (stock-keeping unit) level. The database contains over 20 million records and each household record has over 100 fields of information. The company uses these data to communicate highly focused offers to customers, and to monitor the impacts of any RM initiatives. Relationship managers are increasingly able to use databases to track retention rates longitudinally, conduct root-cause investigations of defections, segment their markets and establish retention objectives.

Finally, new organizational structures and reward schemes may be required. The traditional marketing and sales function is organized around products or geographic markets. Under the influence of RM, organization around customers becomes more sensible. Customer, or account, managers are better placed to build long-term relationships with clients, more deeply understanding their expectations and constructing financial, social and structural links to the firm. IBM, for example, has a team of customer relationship managers. The logic of RM would suggest that the people allocated to customer acquisition should differ from those dedicated to customer retention. Different knowledge, skills and attitudes are deployed. Through their combined efforts these account managers should be able to acquire, migrate (from light-user to heavy-user status) and retain customers. Companies will also need to reconsider how they reward employees. At present, sales and marketing management is widely rewarded with a mix of basic salary and performance-related bonus or commission. Common performance criteria include sales volume and customer acquisition. Under the RM regime, customer managers are more likely to be rewarded by customer profitability, account penetration and customer retention.

Summary

RM is a term which has yet to acquire uncontested status and meaning. For some, RM is simply transactional marketing dressed up in new clothes; for others, it represents a significant change in the practice of marketing. For some, RM refers to all types of internal and external organizational relationships; for others, RM is focused clearly on external customer relationships.

Companies, particularly in the service sector, are increasingly finding ways of building close, long-term relationships with external customers. These companies know that winning new customers is significantly more costly than retaining existing customers, and that when customers defect they take with them all future income stream. Their reason for practising RM is customer retention. However, the more advanced relationship marketers also know that not all customers are worth retaining. Not all contribute positively and equally to company performance.

The voice of the customer is absent from much RM. Indeed, it is not known whether customers want, in significant numbers, to enter into relationships with their suppliers. Companies routinely communicate more frequently and make special offers to their more valued customers. Whether this is seen by customers as adding value is a moot point.

At its best, RM is characterized by a genuine concern to meet or exceed the expectations of customers and to provide excellent service in an environment of trust and commitment to the relationship. To be successful relationship marketers, companies must develop a supportive organizational culture, market the RM idea internally, intimately understand customers expectations, create and maintain a detailed customer database, and organize and reward employees in such a way that the objective of RM, customer retention, is achieved.

References

Anderson, J and Narus, J. (1990) A model of distributor firm and manufacturer firm working partnerships, *Journal of Marketing*, Vol. 54, pp. 42–58.

Anderson, J. and Narus, J. (1991) Partnering as a focused market strategy, *California Management Review*, Vol. 33, pp. 95–113.

Barnes, J.G. (1995) The quality and depth of customer relationships. In M. Bergadaà (ed.) *Proceedings of the 24th EMAC Conference*, ESSEC. Cergy-Pontoise.

Berry, L.L. (1983) Relationship marketing. In L.L. Berry, G.L. Shostack and G.D. Upah (eds) *Perspectives on Services Marketing*, American Marketing Association, Chicago, Ill.

Berry, L.L. and Gresham, L.G. (1986) Relationship retailing: transforming customers into clients, *Business Horizons*, Vol. 29, pp. 43–7.

Blois, K. (1995) Relationship marketing in organizational markets – what is the customer's view? In M. Bergadaà (ed.) *Proceedings of the 24th EMAC Conference*, ESSEC. Cergy-Pontoise.

Borden, N.H. (1964) The concept of the marketing mix, *Journal of Advertising Research*, June, pp. 2–7.

Buck-Lew, M. and Edvinsson, L. (1993) *Intellectual Capital at Skandia*, Skandia, Stockholm.

Buttle, F.A. (1992) Shopping motives: a constructionist perspective, *Service Industries Journal*, Vol. 12, pp. 349–67.

Christopher, M., Payne, A. and Ballantyne, D. (1991) *Relationship Marketing: Bringing Quality, Customer Service and Marketing Together*, Butterworth-Heinemann, Oxford.

Cowles, D. (1989) Putting the relations into relationship banking, *Bank Marketing*, April, pp. 38–9.

Crosby, L.A. (1989) Building and maintaining quality in the service relationship. In S.W. Brown and E. Gummesson (eds) *Quality in Services*, Lexington Books, Lexington, Mass.

Crosby, L.A., Evans, K.R. and Cowles, D. (1990) Relationship quality in services selling: an interpersonal influence perspective, *Journal of Marketing*, Vol. 54, pp. 68–81.

Czepiel, J.A. (1990) Service encounters and service relationships: implications for research, *Journal of Business Research*, Vol. 20, pp. 13–21.

DeSouza, G. (1992) Designing a customer retention plan, *Journal of Business Strategy*, March–April, pp. 24–8.

Dwyer, F.R., Schurr, P.H. and Oh, S. (1987) Developing buyer–seller relationships, *Journal of Marketing*, Vol. 51, pp. 11–27.

Ellis, K.L., Lee, J. and Beatty, S.E. (1993) Relationships in consumer marketing: directions for consumer research, AMA Marketing Educator's Summer Conference.

Evans, J.R. and Laskin, R.L. (1994) The relationship marketing process: a conceptualisation and application, *Industrial Marketing Management*, Vol. 23, pp. 439–52.

Fornell, C. (1992) A national customer satisfaction barometer: the Swedish experience, *Journal of Marketing*, Vol. 56, pp. 6–21.

Frenzen, J.K. and Davis, H.L. (1990) Purchasing behaviour in embedded markets, *Journal of Consumer Research*, Vol. 17, pp. 1–11.

Gamesan, S. (1994) Determinants of long-term orientation in buyer–seller relationships, *Journal of Marketing*, Vol. 58, pp. 1–19.

Geyskens, I. and Steenkamp, J.–B. (1995) An investigation into the joint effects of trust and interdependence on relationship commitment. In M. Bergadaà (ed.) *Proceedings of the 24th EMAC Conference*, ESSEC. Cergy-Pontoise.

Grönroos, C. (1990) Relationship approach to the marketing function in service contexts: the marketing and organization behaviour interface, *Journal of Business Research*, Vol. 20, pp. 3–11.

Grönroos, C. (1991) The marketing strategy continuum: towards a marketing concept for the 1990s, *Management Decision*, Vol. 29, pp. 7–13.

Grönroos, C. (1992) Facing the challenge of service competition: the economies of services. In P. Kunst and J. Lemmik (eds) *Quality Management in Services*, Van Gorcum, Maastricht.

Grönroos, C. (1994) Quo vadis, marketing? Toward a relationship marketing paradigm, *Journal of Marketing Management*, Vol. 10, pp. 347–60.

Gummesson, E. (1987) The new marketing – developing long-term interactive relationships, *Long Range Planning*, Vol. 20, pp. 10–20.

Gummesson, E. (1994) Making relationship marketing operational, *International Journal of Service Industry Management*, Vol. 5, pp. 5–20.

Håkansson, L. (1982) *International Marketing and Purchasing of Industrial Goods: An Interaction Approach*, Wiley, New York.

Hart, C.W.L., Heskett, J.L. and Sasser, W.E. jr (1990) The profitable art of service recovery, *Harvard Business Review*, July–August, pp. 148–56.

Heide, J.B. and John, G. (1992) Do norms matter in a marketing relationship? *Journal of Marketing*, Vol. 56, pp. 32–44.

Heskett, J.L., Jones, T.O., Loveman, G.W., Sasser, W.E. jr and Schlesinger, L.A. (1994) Putting the service profit chain to work, *Harvard Business Review*, March–April, pp. 164–74.

Hughes, A. and Wang, P. (1995) Media selection for database marketers, *Journal of Direct Marketing*, Vol. 9, pp. 79–89.

Jackson, B.B. (1985) *Winning and Keeping Industrial Customers*, Lexington Books, Lexington, Mass.

Keane, T.J. and Wang, P. (1995) Applications of the lifetime value model in modern newspaper publishing, *Journal of Direct Marketing*, Vol. 9, pp. 59–71.

Levitt, T. (1983a) *The Marketing Imagination*, Free Press, New York.

Levitt, T. (1983b) After the sale is over . . ., *Harvard Business Review*, September–October, pp. 87–93.

Martin, M.C. and Sohi, R.S. (1993) Maintaining relationships with customers: some critical factors. Unpublished paper, University of Nebraska, Lincoln.

McCarthy, E.J. (1975) *Basic Marketing: A Managerial Approach*, Irwin, Homewood, Ill.

Milgrom, P. and Roberts, J. (1992) *Economics, Organization and Management*, Prentice-Hall, Englewoods Cliffs, NJ.

Moorman, C., Zaltman, G. and Deshpande, R. (1992) Relationships between providers and users of market research: the dynamics of trust within and between organizations, *Journal of Marketing Research*, Vol. 29, pp. 314–28.

Morgan, R.M. and Hunt, S.D. (1994) The commitment-trust theory of relationship marketing, *Journal of Marketing*, Vol. 58, pp. 20–38.

O'Neal, C. (1989) JIT procurement and relationship marketing, *Industrial Marketing Management*, Vol. 18, pp. 55–63.

Parasuraman, A., Berry, L.L. and Zeithaml, V.A. (1991) Perceived service quality as a customer-based performance measure: an empirical examination of organizational barriers using an extended service quality model, *Human Resource Management*, Vol. 30, pp. 335–64.

Parasuraman, A., Zeithaml, V. and Berry, L.L. (1985) A conceptual model of service quality and its implications for future research, *Journal of Marketing*, Vol. 49, pp. 41–50.

Parasuraman, A., Zeithaml, V. and Berry, L.L. (1988) SERVQUAL: a multiple-item scale for measuring consumer perceptions of service quality, *Journal of Retailing*, Vol. 64, pp. 12–40.

Parasuraman, A., Zeithaml, V. and Berry, L.L. (1991) Refinement and reassessment of the SERVQUAL scale, *Journal of Retailing*, Vol. 67, pp. 420–50.

Parasuraman, A., Zeithaml, V. and Berry, L.L. (1994) Expectations as a comparison standard in measuring service quality: an assessment of a reassessment, *Journal of Marketing*, Vol. 58, pp. 132–9.

Payne, A. and Rickard, J. (1994) *Relationship Marketing, Customer Retention and Service Firm Profitability*, working paper, Cranfield Business School, Cranfield.

Petrison, L.A., Blattberg, R.C. and Wang, P. (1993) Database marketing: past, present and future, *Journal of Direct Marketing*, Vol. 7, pp. 27–36.

Petrison, L.A. and Wang, P. (1993) From relationships to relationship marketing: applying database technology to relationship marketing, *Public Relations Review*, Vol. 19, pp. 235–45.

Pitt, L.L. and Page, M.J. (1994) *Customer Defections Analysis and Management: A Graphic Approach*, working paper, Henley Management College, Henley on Thames.

Reichheld, F. (1993) Loyalty-based management, *Harvard Business Review*, March–April, pp. 64–73.

Reichheld, F. and Sasser, W.E. jr (1990) Zero defections: quality comes to services, *Harvard Business Review*, September–October, pp. 105–11.

Rosenberg, L.J. and Czepiel, J.A. (1984) A marketing approach to customer retention, *Journal of Consumer Marketing*, Vol. 1, pp. 45–51.

Rosenbloom, B. (1991) *Marketing Channels: A Management View*, Dryden, Hinsdale, Ill.

Rust, R.T. and Zahorik, A.J. (1993) Customer satisfaction, customer retention and market share, *Journal of Retailing*, Vol. 69, pp. 193–215.

Rust, R.T., Zahorik, J.A. and Keiningham, T.L. (1994) *Return on Quality – Measuring the Financial Impact of your Company's Quest for Quality*, Probus, Chicago, Ill.

Shapiro, B. (1991) Close encounters of four kinds: managing customers in a rapidly changing environment. In R. Dolan (ed.) *Strategic Marketing Management*, Harvard University Press, Boston, Mass.

Sheth, J.N. (1994) The domain of relationship marketing. Unpublished paper, Second Research Conference on Relationship Marketing, Center for Relationship Marketing, Emory University, Atlanta, Ga.

Spekman, R. (1988) Strategic supplier selection: understanding long-term buyer relationships, *Business Horizons*, Vol. 31, pp. 75–81.

Spriggs, M.T. and Nevin, J.R. (1992) *A Relational Contracting Framework for Understanding Exchange Relationships*, working paper, University of Oregon.

Stern, L.W. and El-Ansary, A. (1992) *Marketing Channels* (4th edn), Prentice-Hall, Englewood Cliffs, NJ.

Storbacka, K. (1994) *The Nature of Customer Relationship Profitability*, Swedish School of Economics and Business Administration, Helsinki.

Storbacka, K., Strandvik, T. and Grönroos, C. (1994) Managing customer relationships for profit: the dynamics of relationship quality, *International Journal of Service Industry Management*, Vol. 5, pp. 21–38.

Tauber, E.M. (1972) Why do people shop? *Journal of Marketing*, Vol. 36, pp. 46–9.

Treather, D. (1994) Souped-up for direct attack, *Marketing*, 29 September, pp. 18–19.

Wang, P. and Splegel, T. (1994) Database marketing and its measurements of success, *Journal of Direct Marketing*, Vol 8, pp. 73–83.

Webster, F. (1992) The changing role of marketing in the corporation, *Journal of Marketing*, Vol. 56, pp. 1–17.

Young, L.C. and Wilkinson, I.F. (1989) The role of trust and cooperation in marketing channels: a preliminary study, *European Journal of Marketing*, Vol. 23, pp. 109–22.

Zeithaml, V., Parasuraman, A. and Berry, L.L. (1994) The nature and determinants of customer expectation of service, *Journal of the Academy of Marketing Science*, Vol. 21, pp. 1–12.

2

Supply-chain relationships

Gary Davies

Introduction

Relationships between those who make products and those who sell them to the general public (retailers) have been central to a free-market economy since the beginning of time. The Industrial Revolution created a clear separation into those who specialized in manufacturing and those who concentrated on the business of distribution. These new manufacturers who did not sell directly to consumers needed to ensure that they had an effective channel of distribution to market their wares. The very term 'distribution channel' evokes an image of a passive route to the shopper, one that can be managed or even controlled. Such was the reality in all free-market economies until the second half of this century.

A number of changes have helped promote a shift in who holds power in the marketing channels for consumer goods. The most obvious change has been the increase in concentration in many retail sectors. In grocery retailing throughout the western world it is commonplace for the largest five retailers to account for more than 50% of the market. In western Europe, by way of contrast, there are few grocery manufacturers who account for more than 5% of grocery sales in any one country. The general situation is, then, that the typical manufacturer needs the large retailer as much if not more than the retailer needs the manufacturer's brands.

As with all generalizations the reality for any one product or any one market can be very different. Car retailing in most countries, for example, is still dominated by manufacturer franchises. In 1995 the right for manufacturers to insist that their retailers sell only their brand of cars had yet again been approved as an exemption to free competition policy within the EC (the so-called block exemption). In Britain the Net Book Agreement had made it possible for book publishers of this and any other book, newspaper or magazine to insist that retailers do not sell at other than the price set by the publisher. Such legislation is intended to make it easier for small retailers to compete with large multiples who would otherwise offer discounts. In the USA Robinson–Patman legislation makes it illegal for a retailer to demand a preferential discount from a supplier unless it can be shown that there is a cost saving to justify the lower price. In Italy, planning legislation is such that it is particularly difficult to build new and large shops. As a consequence retail concentration is relatively low and the number of shops is high. The effect of legislation in each of these areas, car retailing in Europe, book retailing in Britain, Robinson–Patman in America and the planning process for all retailing in Italy, tends to favour the supplier as well as the smaller retailer, somewhat to the detriment of the larger retailer. Legislation has a marked effect on retail concentration and retailer power worldwide (Davies and Whitehead, 1995).

Though there are still many exceptions, the long-term trend is, nevertheless, for retailer power to grow and for supplier power to decline. The use of the word 'power' raises an issue which is central to this book. One way of managing a marketing channel is to use power to get a third party to do something they might not otherwise have done. Inherent in such an approach to channel management is the notion of two parties at war, each vying to benefit at the expense of the other. It is still a valid perspective to adopt as it explains much of the behaviour between retailer and supplier. To understand why, let us examine the relationship between the two by seeing who makes what revenue and profit from the money the shopper pays for a product in a retail outlet.

The supply-chain perspective

A supply-chain cost structure in its simplest form looks like an office block (Figure 2.1). The higher the building the more expensive it is to buy the product. The basement and one or two of the lower floors represent the costs and profit of the raw material supplier. For a branded product the largest part of the building represents the costs and profit of the brand manufacturer. If there is no wholesaler in the chain the top floors represent the third and only other major element in the supply chain, the retailer's costs and profit. The line between each of the three main zones represents the price charged as the goods are transferred from one member of the supply chain to the next.

The average margin the retailer makes in Britain is around 25% of the selling price to the shopper (CSO, 1994). The typical percentage of raw material costs in a product is of the same order of magnitude. For most

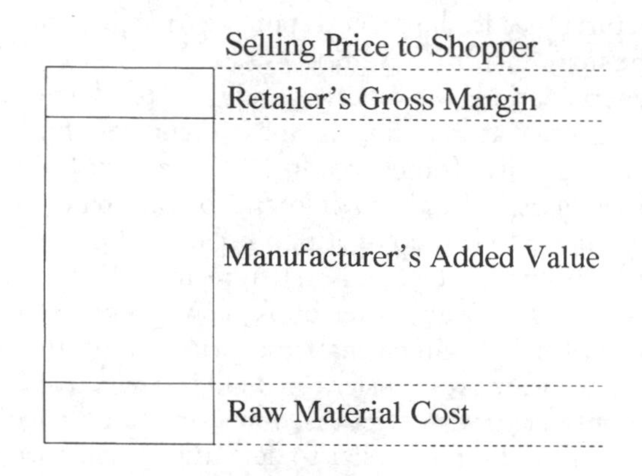

Figure 2.1 Supply-chain cost structure

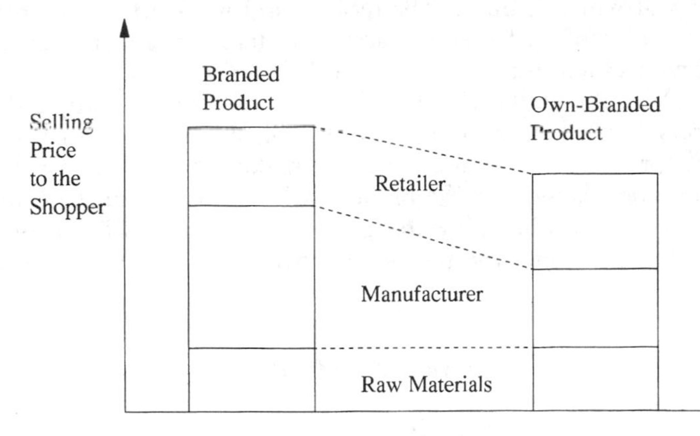

Figure 2.2 Typical brand and own-brand supply-chain cost structures

branded goods therefore the manufacturer accounts for about half of the office block; about half of the money the shopper pays lands up in the manufacturer's business. The supply-chain cost structure can be rather different in the case of an own-brand product (Figure 2.2). The overall selling price of the product tends to be lower but the proportions kept by manufacturer and retailer of the shopper's money also change. This time the retailer tends to keep a higher proportion.

The roles differ markedly in the two different types of product. In the case of a manufacturer's brand the product is presold to the shopper through the manufacturer's advertising. In the case of the retailer's own brand, the product is often an imitation of the manufacturer's brand and, if there is any real branding present, it comes from the retailer's name or from one it controls.

Manufacturers quite justifiably complain that many own-brand products do not have to carry the same research and development costs that they need to incur to develop new and innovative lines. They view them as parasitic products and many refuse to supply own-brand products to retailers on principle. There are, however, a large number of manufacturers who specialize in supplying own-brand products. In addition, many retailers employ their own development teams who are quite capable of creating innovative products themselves. Figure 2.2. illustrates some of the tensions between retailers and their suppliers. The issue is simply one of who gets the largest share of the shopper's money.

There are other pressures on the retailer that affect how much of the customers' money stays with the retailer. When the product is a 'known value item' (KVI), in other words, a product where the selling price is one that the shopper is well aware of and therefore sensitive to, a retailer may also have to cut the price to the shopper so as to appear price competitive in the market. It is far from unusual for the retailer to sell some products at a loss to encourage people to use its store. A retailer also needs to be careful not to stock high gross-margin products just because they appear attractive because they have a high gross margin (the difference between the price at which the retailer sells and the price at which it buys). The retailer still needs to sell the product to make money. It is often better to carry a different product with a smaller margin but with a high rate of sale than a product with a high margin but a low rate of sale. Manufacturers of branded products frequently argue that while their products do not have such high margins as own-brands, because they are more heavily promoted and sell better, they make more money for the retailer overall. The other danger for the retailer, who is dissuaded from stocking a leading brand because it has a low margin, is that shoppers will go elsewhere to make their purchases because the retailer isn't stocking the product(s) they want.

The power paradigm

The traditional way that marketing channels operate is for one member of the channel to be in charge, or put another way, to hold power over other channel members so that the channel operates in an orderly way. For power to be a relevant approach in channel management there are certain preconditions. For power to exist the other channel members have to be dependent upon the channel leader (Emerson, 1962; Gaski, 1984). There has to be a direct relationship (Gattorna, 1978), and the potential to use power is increased the higher the exit costs from that relationship (Porter, 1980). Power can be exerted in a number of ways, for example by coercing the other channel member, perhaps by threatening to stop supplying a product, or power may exist just because the other channel member has confidence in the expertise of the other to act in the interests of both.

When and if manufacturers' brands are all-powerful the manufacturer holds power over the retailer because of the consumer franchise possessed by the brand. The retailer needs customers and customers can be choosy about which products they buy to the point where they will shop elsewhere if the retailer is out of stock of their favourite line. If the franchise is weak, that is, the shopper is willing to accept another leading brand or even the retailer's own brand, this basis for power is reduced. Where the retailer is large, it may account for a sizeable proportion of the manufacturer's sales. This provides it with the

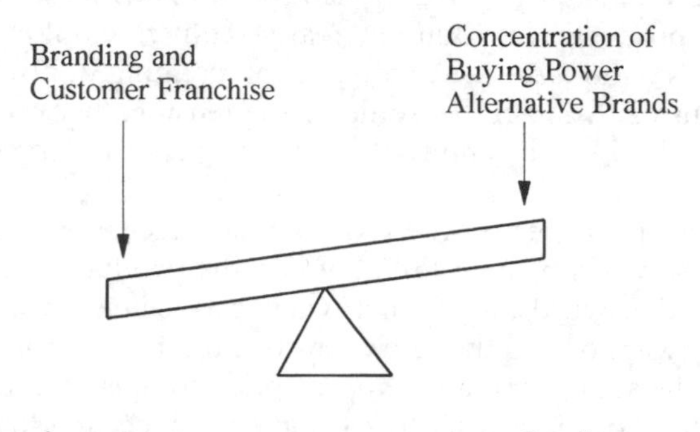

Figure 2.3 The power paradigm

ability to pressure the manufacturer into conceding on price, promotional support, delivery service and the supply of own-brand. It can be pictured as a see-saw, with each side seeking to use their sources of negotiating power to push down to their advantage (Figure 2.3). The manufacturer uses its branding and the consumer franchise this produces, the retailer uses its buying power and the threat of switching to other brands. Unless one side or the other is willing to be pushed around by the other the two sides will struggle for control until one or the other wins. While this may be fun in the playground, in business it can be damaging to both.

The partnership paradigm

The power paradigm precludes any true notion of partnership. One side makes the important decisions, the other agrees or acquiesces. The main issue in the relationship is one of negotiation by threat and counterthreat, where the objective is to gain at the other's expense. An alternative is to identify objectives that both the two key members of the supply chain have in common, to focus on these and the benefits to be achieved by co-operation. One such over-riding goal, shared by both retailer and manufacturer, is to sell more product. Another is to reduce the total cost of the supply chain particularly by reducing those costs associated with distribution.

The approach is fundamentally different from that traditionally taken in managing relationships between manufacturer and retailer. In the past the emphasis by manufacturers was on selling to and selling through the retailer. The main, in fact sometimes the only, point of contact between the two was between the salesperson and the buyer. The new approach requires far broader contact between the two organizations to create, in effect, a quasi-organization that spans both businesses and other businesses such as transport companies that operate at the interface between the two. Graphically, the difference between the two approaches can be represented by Figure 2.4. The traditional model involves one point of contact, the relationship approach requires that there are many. Distribution, information technology and forecasting management must work

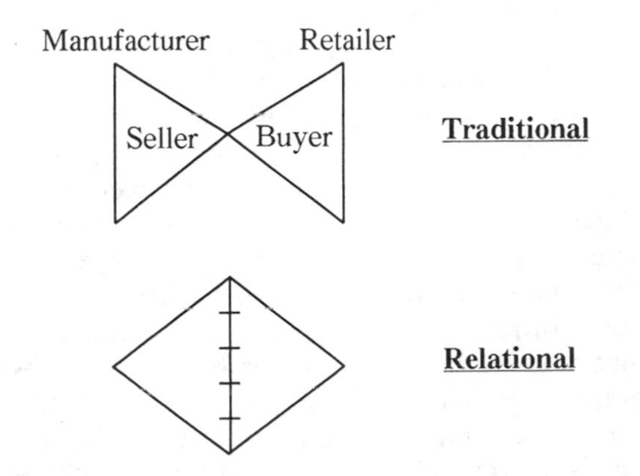

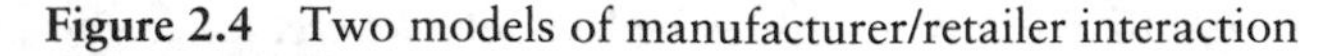
Figure 2.4 Two models of manufacturer/retailer interaction

together across their corporate boundaries for the relational model to work (Davies, 1994a).

The manufacturer needs to create a new role, that of national account manager (NAM) to replace or to complement that of the salesperson. In a number of businesses the NAM's role excludes price negotiation and focuses solely on reducing supply-chain costs and improving sales. Such businesses see day-to-day price negotiation as incompatible with this relational role. The NAM role is more that of a business development manager, an expert in the marketing of the product type and someone who is able to work *with* the retailer to develop the volume and profit from the product to the mutual benefit of both sides.

Managing the relationship

While the concept of developing the market for the product is easy to understand, implementing the concept is far more difficult. The first problem for the manufacturer to overcome is that the typical retail buyer is usually not well informed about the profitability of the products he or she buys for resale. The gross margin is well known but the true profit, the net margin, is not because it is difficult to allocate the retailer's costs to each product line. The costs of retailing sugar, for example, will be very different from those of retailing ice-cream. Yet both are sold in the same retail outlet. The handling and distribution costs are different, the capital costs and the running costs of the fixtures needed to store and display each product are different. Even within a product type such as ice-cream the costs of carrying one line, a family pack of vanilla ice-cream, will be different from those for a small tub of lemon sorbet. The rate of sale of each will also differ, so the stock-holding costs for each will be different.

Retailers are becoming both more sophisticated and more analytical in their attempts to allocate costs to individual products. They are aided by computer software which responds to changes in sales volume indicating how the profitability of each product line changes over time. Yet buyers appear to be assessed as much on the gross margin and sales volume their products make as their net margin (Swindley, 1992).

The problem for retailers of clothing is even more complex. Retailers who sell products that can be stacked on to shelves (grocery, DIY, chemists) can use the space occupied by the product as an indicator of the cost of carrying the product. Each product pays a 'rent' for being in the shop. The space occupied by an individual product is less easy to define for a jacket or a suit on a hanging rail. Other techniques such as gross margin return on investment on inventory or residual income analysis can be used but the evidence is that few retailers use any of these techniques to do more than help their decision-making.

Selecting products for resale is not, and cannot be, a totally objective process. Customers are not always attracted to shops because of individual products; rather they go for the range and selection on offer. Retail buyers use their market judgement to construct a range of products to attract the shopper to make a purchase decision. Too large a choice and the shopper might be confused. Too small a range and the shopper may feel it necessary to look elsewhere.

The second problem facing the manufacturer is that it is easier to convince an individual retail buyer to reduce the space allocated to a slow-moving line in favour of another more attractive line than to convince the retailer as a whole that more space should be given to one entire product range than to another. For example, Coca Cola realized that the invention by ICI of a new plastic that could be used to make large bottles for carbonated drinks in the 1970s would create a rapid growth in sales of such products via the grocery sector. Their problem was to convince retailers to allocate far more space to carbonated drinks in general and to theirs in particular, by reducing the shelf space given to other, unrelated products in the store. No one buyer could agree to such a proposition; Coca Cola needed to convince more senior managers in the organization of their ideas (Davies, 1994a).

The cost of such a relational approach to marketing to retailers can be high unless the retail sector is concentrated. But, owing to the increase in concentration and centralization of buying in retailing internationally, the typical manufacturer's salesforce has decreased in size allowing manufacturers to allocate more than one individual to handle each key account.

Informing the relationship

A supply chain contains many flows, the flow of product from manufacturer to retailer and on to the customer, and an equally important counterflow of information. The generation of information starts when the customer makes a purchase – the fact that a purchase has been made and data on what has been purchased are recorded in many, but by no means all, retail businesses by an electronic scanner. Most, but yet again by no means all, products carry a barcode or a similar device containing a unique number identifying precisely the product line.

Once captured, this information can be used to drive the supply chain. The supply chain 'knows' when it is necessary to replenish stock. It knows when to make more. By analysing any trends in the sales data a forecast can be made of what needs to be produced in the future. The benefits from such knowledge include a reduction in the amount of stock in the supply chain and a reduction in the level of out of stocks in the retailer's premises. Each 'stock out' or 'I'm sorry madam we don't have your size in stock, but we are expecting a delivery next week' risks a lost sale and perhaps a lost customer. A more frequent replenishment of stock can reduce the level of stock in the supply chain significantly. Instead of ordering large amounts infrequently, small amounts can be ordered regularly. No one needs to hold 'safety stock' to ensure that, if there is an unexpected increase in demand, there will be stock available.

Despite these obvious benefits, retailers and manufacturers rarely exchange sales data and forecasts. This remarkable fact is probably the result of the retail buyer's reluctance to concede the power that might be lost by being open about sales levels. Gone will be the demand for better discounts or advertising support because the product needs promotion 'because of its poor sales in one part of the country'. Some retailers even sell sales data to their suppliers. Other retailers and their suppliers are more open with their information, realizing the mutual benefits of being so. Some have been experimenting with automatic

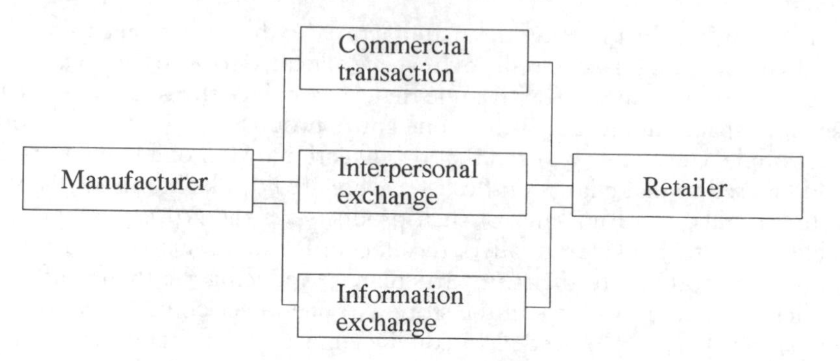

Figure 2.5 Linkages between manufacturer and retailer

reordering, thus removing any intervention by a buyer in the flow of major product lines. Electronic data interchange (EDI) is still very much in its infancy as a business tool. The principle is in place, all it needs is the will to employ it.

Maintaining relationships

Much research has been conducted into the criteria retail buyers use when making decisions. No clear or simple picture has emerged as decision criteria vary too much with the context for the buying decision – a new purchase with a new supplier versus a repurchase from an existing supplier, fashion goods versus grocery, imports versus home production. Maintaining a relationship with a retailer is nevertheless one particular context, and understanding what correlates with the relationship becoming unstable could be useful.

The relationship between supplier and retailer can be thought of as three distinct linkages (Figure 2.5). There is a commercial transaction, a relationship between people (the interpersonal exchange) and an information exchange. Problems in any one could cause the relationship to dissolve. Strength in any one could compensate for a weakness elsewhere.

In research with 102 British retailers (Davies, 1994b; 1994c), 125 buyers were interviewed about the circumstances surrounding their decision to delist or deselect a particular product and any subsequent decision to end their relationship with the retailer completely. Delisting for the purposes of this

Table 2.1 The importance of factors in deciding to delist a product (%)

	Unimportant 1	2	3	4	Very important 5
Sales volume too low	20.3	6.6	6.9	9.0	57.2
Gross margin too low	57.9	8.6	15.5	6.6	11.4
Net margin too low	56.2	8.3	13.8	7.6	14.1
Poor delivery	74.5	6.2	7.6	4.1	7.6
Wrong price point	63.4	10.0	6.9	6.9	12.8
Poor quality	76.2	4.1	5.9	4.5	9.3
Potential sales (too low)	45.2	3.4	10.3	13.4	27.6
Price too high	59.0	9.0	7.6	8.6	15.9

Table 2.2 Interpersonal exchanges

How well do the following words generally describe your relationship with the supplier? (1 = not at all; 5 = perfectly)

		1	2	3	4	5	Total
Businesslike	No.	15	20	63	82	41	221
	%	6.8	9.0	28.5	37.1	18.6	
Businesslike (still a supplier)	%	2.7	8.7	26.8	38.3	23.5	149
Businesslike (no more a supplier)	%	15.3	9.7	31.9	34.7	8.3	72
Co-operative	No.	52	19	59	56	34	220
	%	23.6	8.6	26.8	25.5	15.5	
Co-operative (still a supplier)	%	22.3	4.7	26.4	26.3	20.3	148
Co-operative (no more a supplier)	%	26.4	16.7	27.8	23.6	5.5	72
Social	No.	115	38	39	16	12	220
	%	52.2	17.3	17.7	7.3	5.5	
Social (still a supplier)	%	48.6	23.0	14.9	7.4	6.1	148
Social (no more a supplier)	%	59.7	5.5	23.6	6.9	4.2	72
Open	No.	50	11	44	71	43	219
	%	22.8	5.0	20.1	32.4	19.6	
Open (still a supplier)	%	23.6	1.4	19.6	31.1	24.3	148
Open (no more a supplier)	%	21.1	12.7	21.1	35.2	9.9	71

study was defined as removing a product even though it was still on sale in other retailers' outlets. Together the 125 buyers provided data on 290 examples of delisted products. A third led to, or coincided with, the ending of the relationship completely. The main aim of the research was to understand what accounted for termination of the relationship. Each delisted product represented a threat to the relationship. What, though, led to its being ended?

Buyers were first asked about their reasons for delisting (Table 2.1). By far the most important reason was low sales level, not (notice) that the net profit margin was too low. Future or potential sales was the second most important factor. The most important element in the commercial transaction for the retail buyer is having a product that sells well. If sales are lower than expected or fall, the buyer will consider delisting. Buyers were also asked about their relationships with suppliers. Table 2.2 presents the results of their views for those criteria where the responses were found to correlate with whether the supplier was delisted. The number of products is lower than 290 as the data in Table 2.2 are only for those retailers who claimed a relationship with the product's manufacturer (rather than just with a wholesaler). Where the relationship was described as more businesslike, co-operative, social and open there was less chance that the relationship ended. This is strong evidence that the nature of

Table 2.3 EDI links with multiple retailers

Did you have an EDI link with the retailer?

	Yes	No
Number	25	91
%	21.6	78.4
Still a supplier %	26.7	73.3
No more a supplier %	6.7	93.3

the interaction between buyer and salesperson has an effect on the stability of the business relationship. How frequently the two met was also significantly different indicating, not surprisingly, that the more frequently the supplier met the retailer the less likely it was that the relationship would end.

The importance of exchanging information was tested by asking whether the two exchanged market data, whether they had any forecasting and whether they had an EDI link. There were no differences correlated with whether the two exchanged market data but the level of exchange was remarkably low. Only 27.9% of retailers gave their suppliers' sales data. The only information the supplier could gain access to was therefore the retailer's own purchases from them. Whether there was an EDI link appeared to be important particularly with the large retailers (Table 2.3). Those who had EDI appeared far more likely to retain their retailer as a customer. (The difference is significant at the 0.05 level, using a chi-squared test.) Despite this the most significant factor was the interpersonal relationship between supplier and retailer. Note that the descriptor 'social' in Table 2.2 distinguishes between the two delisted groups even though most buyers did not describe their relationships with suppliers as 'social'. There would have been a reluctance to do so, as this may imply getting too close to one's suppliers. That said, having a social dimension to the relationship is still important in customer retention.

A picture emerges of a relationship where the retail buyer is inclined to make decisions on other than totally objective grounds. In fact, few buyers *can* make totally objective decisions owing to their lack of data for the cost of retailing individual products. It is essential therefore for suppliers to be close enough to their main retail customers to ensure that they can present a favourable view of both their products and themselves as suppliers.

Supplying own-brands

The relationships between suppliers of branded products and multiple retailers and those producing own-brand products and retailers can be expected to be different. The results of the survey were reanalysed differentiating between products which were own-brand and those which were not. The main difference was found to be in the frequency and nature of contact. Own-brand suppliers contacted their retailers *far* more frequently. They were more likely to receive and to provide sales forecasts and to receive sales data. The links between the two parties appeared to be more stable and to fit the model of a relationship approach. Branded suppliers were less likely to have achieved a relationship approach.

The retailer as a 'customer'

A significant change has taken place over the last decade or so in the way manufacturers and retailers treat each other. Gone are the days in many countries where manufacturers could dominate a fragmented retail sector, safe in their knowledge that brand loyalty was enough to ensure that retailers needed to carry their brands to attract sufficient customers to their stores. These days retailers are brands in their own right. The name on the product and the name above the store are often the same. The prices charged for own-brands are sometimes higher than those charged for manufacturer's brands. Certain fashion retailers such as Benetton would be good examples, as would Marks & Spencer in food retailing. Indeed, it is time we stopped differentiating between own-brands and brands; most shoppers do not make the same separation as those who make their living from the retail sector.

The potential for retailers to hold power in marketing channels was recognized by theoreticians as long ago as the 1930s. For them to promote products to shoppers is far cheaper than for manufacturers who need to spend proportionally more of their turnover on advertising. A manufacturer such as Kellogg's will spend more than 5% of its turnover on advertising. A retailer such as Sainsbury's will spend less than 1%. This one advantage alone can be used by the retailer to offer a similar product at an appreciably lower price. The one protection the manufacturer has is to ensure that its product cannot be matched in taste or quality. If this ever happens the advantage held by the retailer's own-brand is ultimately irresistible.

One way to ensure the retailer's own-brand doesn't match the real quality of an established brand is continuously to improve the product. But only some products can be improved. Protecting a brand such as Mercedes is easier than protecting Coca Cola. The Coca Cola formula is now virtually an open secret. As Coke found to its own near undoing, the public do not want a modified version of the traditional product. The logo and the pack design can change but not so the taste. By way of contrast a car has to change and develop as design and technology advance. The own-label car is a valid concept but copying this year's market leader is no way to market a new car! An own-label Cola is a different proposition as Sainsbury's demonstrated in Britain in 1995.

As the structural weakness of a heavily branded strategy becomes clearer, manufacturers will turn increasingly to a more relational model of dealing with retailers. Conceptually this means treating the retailer as a customer not as a distributor. For the retailer this also means a change in philosophy, seeing the supplier less as an adversary and more as a partner.

The last point may seem to be somewhat naive, as most of this chapter has been about how powerful the large modern retailer has become. But nothing remains static for long in today's marketplace. Home shopping is making significant inroads into the insurance and banking markets. Thus far home shopping for goods has been less successful but as it becomes more sophisticated it is likely to take more market share from the fixed shop. The electronic shop does not need to be operated by a retailer. Even in the grocery sector where there are few large suppliers, the larger ones could market directly to the shopper's home or collaborate with other suppliers in doing so, thus bypassing the fixed shop retailer. In fashion retailing the benefits of going direct for the manufacturer are even greater as the retail margins are higher, allowing more room for the cost of delivery to be borne by the manufacturer. In the future the balance of power could shift back to the manufacturer. It is in the retailer's interests to create strong links with suppliers almost as much as it is in the manufacturer's interests to create better relationships with its retailers.

References

CSO (1994) Retailing, *Business Monitor SDA25*, HMSO, London.

Davies, G. (1994a) *Trade Marketing Strategy*, Paul Chapman, London.

Davies, G. (1994b) The delisting of products by retail buyers, *Journal of Marketing Management*, Vol. 10, pp. 473–93.

Davies, G. (1994c) Maintaining relationships with retailers, *Journal of Strategic Marketing*, Vol. 2, pp. 189–210.

Davies, G. and Whitehead, M. (1995) The legislative environment as a measure of attractiveness for internationalisation. In P.J. McGoldrick and G. Davies (eds) *International Retailing: Trends and Strategies*, Pitman, London.

Emerson, R.M. (1962) Power-dependence relations, *American Sociological Review*, February, pp. 31–41.

Gaski, J.F. (1984) The theory of power and conflict in channels of distribution, *Journal of Marketing*, Vol. 48, pp. 9–29.

Gattorna, J. (1978) Channels of distribution conceptualizations: a state of the art review, *European Journal of Marketing*, Vol. 12, p. 470.

Porter, M. (1980) *Competitive Strategy*, Free Press, New York.

Swindley, D.E. (1992) Retail buying in the United Kingdom, *The Services Industries Journal*, Vol. 12, p. 533.

3

Principal–agent relationships

Neil Carruthers

Introduction

Business-to business relationships exist within many marketing channels. While the strategic focus for any channel should be on the external customers, it is essential that the internal channel members market to each other. Where the channel members are organizationally and contractually independent, as is the situation in most manufacturer–distributor–retailer relationships, the manufacturer is normally responsible for ensuring that positive relational interactions occur. However, in a franchise or agency relationship, the management of the channel-member interaction differs, since the organizational architecture is more formalized and there is a greater emphasis on role segmentation. This increases the reliance of either party to the relationship on the other channel member's successful performance.

This chapter examines the complex nature of the relationship that exists between a principal and its network of agents. While there are many companies that have successfully utilized this organizational format, the focus here is on one specific firm, Post Office Counters Ltd (POCL).

Background

In 1986, following a major organizational restructuring of the British Post Office, POCL became a separate, wholly owned subsidiary. This change was part of a wholesale public sector liberalization designed and orchestrated by the Conservative government to provide the bedrock for the anticipated increase in commercial flexibility that would enhance both the efficiency and competitiveness of the publicly owned sector. POCL's stated mission was to be the 'leading (national) provider of benefits distribution, postal services, banking and bill payment facilities'. It would achieve this by acting as the main distribution and collection agency for a number of governmental services through its national network.

Behind POCL's unified corporate image lies an innovativeness not normally found in quasi-governmental institutions. It has, for many years, successfully operated a vertically integrated marketing channel which is predominantly populated by legally independent retail agents. All the channel participants have gained from this situation. POCL's adopted strategy of 'outsourcing' the majority of the human resource and capital investments has enabled it to maintain a massive retail network when the trend among its competitors was towards a reduction in the number of customer outlets. The agents have acquired a ready-made business with an established and instantly recognizable brand-name, often allowing them to piggy-back a second business on to their core business. POCL's clients (organizations who use POCL as a distribution channel for their services) have benefited from negotiating with a 'unified' entity that gives them access to the single largest retail channel in the UK, while their customers (the general public and businesses) have ease of access to the facilities and services.

Technology has been instrumental in the concentration of the British financial service sector. This sectoral aggregation has been underpinned by the rationale that scale economies would enhance efficiency and combat the increasing pressures being exerted on corporate profits; thus, organizational rationalization and centralization have followed the wave of mergers and acquisitions. The net result may have benefited the banks and building societies, but the radical reduction in their high-street presence has not been well received by the majority of customers. POCL has gone against this trend, maintaining its retail network of around 19,000 outlets. Its customer-orientated approach is not some short-term public-relations exercise that has been crafted to win over the angry consumers of its faceless competitors, but one which reflects its social responsibility to operate at the heart of communities up and down the country.

However, the governmental ties were not completely severed, since the Department of Trade and Industry continued to set financial performance targets and operational parameters for the three newly created subsidiaries – the Royal Mail and Parcelforce being the other two companies formed in the reorganization. These targets took the form of a return on capital (expressed as a percentage of profit before tax on capital employed), a reduction in real unit costs (index-linked price target) and a negative external financing limit (the financial contribution that POCL have to make to the government's coffers). The Post Office as a whole has not only remained free of government subsidies for the last 19 years. It has actually contributed £235 million to the government during that time. POCL itself has also exceeded the set financial targets during this period. Its turnover and profit figures are shown in Table 3.1.

The effectiveness of any interdependent relationship requires explicit strategic goal congruence and a willingness for both parties to co-operate (Rosenberg and Stern, 1970). More specifically, agreement must be attained on the

Table 3.1 POCL's recent performance trends

	1995 £m	1994 £m	1993 £m	1992 £m	1991 £m	1990 £m
Turnover	1,118	1,089	1,061	1,028	959	875
Profit before tax	30	25	25	26	28	22

Source: Post Office Annual Report and Accounts.

operational methodologies (Robicheaux and El-Ansary, 1976), and on the functional specialization of the partners. In other words, partners in a collaborative venture must agree and adopt complementary roles to maximize the relational synergy. The desire for operational autonomy and pursuance of personal goals must be subjugated for the agreed superordinate goals of the relationship (Wiener and Doescher, 1991). If this occurs, any disparity in organizational size between the partners should not adversely affect their satisfaction levels (Etgar, 1979) or their performance expectations. This being said, the co-ordination of a huge marketing channel that is not fully incorporated within the boundaries of a single organization is fraught with many practical problems, as this case demonstrates.

Future threats to POCL's continued growth

Although POCL has surpassed its performance targets, the future may not be as rosy as Table 3.1 would suggest. Table 3.2 gives an analysis of POCL's core business, demonstrating that POCL derives the majority of its income from managing the transactions of three 'clients'.

This high dependency could be tolerated were it not for the fact that each of the main clients is facing rapidly changing markets, forcing them to re-evaluate their operations in a way that could radically reduce the business throughput for POCL. For instance, the Benefits Agency commissions POCL to pay cash for old-age pensions, income support, unemployment benefit and child allowances to the public. While POCL processes the majority of the agency's transactions, an increasing proportion is paid via automated credit transfer into the recipients' bank accounts. This trend is likely to continue for two reasons: first, it is cheaper for the client (and could, therefore, be incentivized in the future); and, secondly, the change in the attitude of the agency 'customer' base – the public who are more likely to have utilized computers and automated transfer-payment systems in both a work and personal capacity and who are far more likely to have a bank account. The UK government could even emulate the Australian government's policy decision to insist on all benefit payments being automatically paid into the bank accounts of any recipient.

The second largest clients of POCL are Royal Mail and Parcelforce. POCL acts as a collection point for parcels and letters, also deriving an income from

Table 3.2 Sources of business (transaction) volume

Clients	Business volume (%)
Benefits Agency	30
Royal Mail	23
Girobank	16
DVLA	6
British Telecom	6
BBC	4
Other	15

Source: POCL.

the sale of postage stamps. While this interorganizational trade has been beneficial for all parties concerned, these 'clients' are coming under increasing competitive pressures from the liberated foreign post offices, and from the private firms now operating in its arena. The increasing demands of the external financing target imposed by government have resulted in the Post Office (inclusive of POCL) reducing its direct capital investment in its operational and technological architecture by £100,000 p.a. The medium to long-term effect on the efficiency, and therefore profitability, of the Royal Mail cannot be underestimated; the knock-on effect could be deleterious to POCL's performance.

The picture is not all bad for POCL. Girobank, now part of the Alliance and Leicester Building Society, works with POCL, transacting over 1.5 million personal accounts through the latter's outlets; the joint venture could also carve out a niche in the profitable corporate banking sector. POCL has the exclusive rights to retail postal orders, vehicle licences and television licences, and acts as a payment point for National Insurance stamps, utility bills and telephone bills. However, a government green paper, presented in the autumn of 1994, could be the key to POCL's future success. This stated that the government were committed to preserving a national network of post offices, and to increasing the commercial freedom of the various Post Office subsidiaries. The aim of this liberation is to allow new ventures with private businesses in order that the client base can be diversified. So, for instance, POCL has been able to act as a collection point for the National Lottery (becoming the leading retailer), has started to operate a *bureau de change* and is looking at selling travel insurance in conjunction with General Accident, and life insurance for Sun Alliance. POCL has also examined the possibility of a joint venture with a private company, who will invest in and manage a high-tech swipe-card system that will combat the threat posed by automated banking and plastic cards, reinforcing the huge competitive advantage that POCL gains from its massive high-street presence.

The reduction in POCL's dependency on a client base (whose business was, in real terms, declining), is the minimum requirement that should be imposed on the future strategy of the organization. Maximizing the competitive advantage of being able to access 28 million customers per week using a single channel requires not only the retention of existing clients but also new business development in segments that are compatible with POCL's strengths. Bill Cockburn, while Chairman of the Post Office Group, stated that 'the provision of high quality, competitively priced services . . . is a key requirement for sustaining future business success'.

Organizational structure

National headquarters

Figure 3.1 illustrates an organizational structure that has existed since June 1993. At the national level, the business is split into four main segments: agent and client support are attempting to identify the needs of these two groups in order that POCL can continue to service them; market research reviews the consumer end of POCL's market, attempting to identify new areas of business; and central services provides expertise to both HQ and the seven regions on an internal consultancy basis.

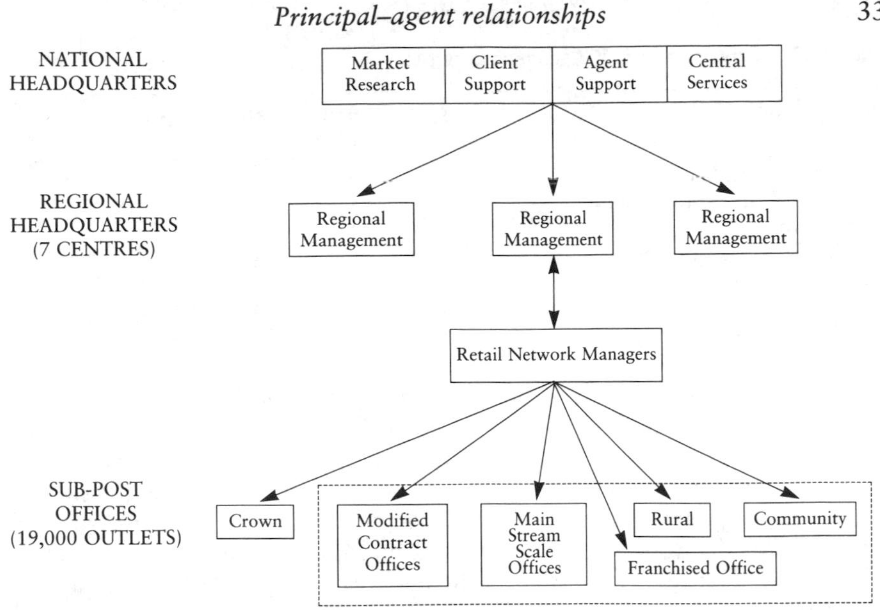

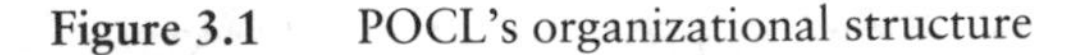
Figure 3.1 POCL's organizational structure

Regional headquarters

A reorganization in the early 1990s had a significant impact at the regional level; while there were 30 districts in the old organizational structure, in 1993 there were only seven regions under the new structure. This rationalization allowed POCL to reduce the amount of administrative duplication in the system and has ensured that corporate policy evaluation and implementation at the regional level are more consistent. The relationship between the regional HQs and the retail network is managed in a number of ways, but an innovation introduced in 1993 was the introduction of the retail network manager whose role was seen as the proactive management of the relationship with individual agents. However, the retail network managers have to oversee between 30 and 70 retail outlets each (the number depends on the latter's business volume).

The agency network

POCL has more retail outlets than any other organization in the UK; in fact, it has a larger high-street presence than the combined networks of the top four major banks and all the building societies in the country. Figure 3.1 illustrates the variety of sub-post offices that exist, each of which are governed by a different type of contract with POCL. Table 3.3 shows that there is a definite skew towards independent agents within POCL's estate.

The flagships of the organization are the Crown offices; these tend to be the largest in size, are mainly located at the centre of major conurbations, offer the widest range of products and services, and are wholly owned and staffed by POCL employees. The other sub-post offices all fall within the broad generic grouping of agency contracts and, while they are all run by independent

Table 3.3 Typology of POCL's agent network

Outlet typology	Total estate (%)
Main-stream scale offices	82.5
Community and rural offices	9.5
Crown offices	5.0
Modified contract offices	2.0
Franchised offices	1.0

Source: POCL.

agents, they differ markedly in operational and contractual structures. Modified contract offices are generally ex-Crown offices that have been converted to agency status and continue to offer the full range of services. Franchised offices are relatively new additions to POCL's estate. They are generaly situated within existing retail outlets such as supermarkets and POCL charges a franchise 'fee' for their operation (usually by a multiple retailer).

The vast majority of the outlets in the network are operated by independent subpostmasters who often combine the post office with a second business which will benefit from the increased footfall generated by the post-office business, e.g. confectioners, tobacconists and newsagents (CTN), stationery or grocery. The largest type of outlet in this category is the main-stream scale payment office. A monthly payment is made to the subpostmaster based on the number and type of transactions that occurred at the outlet during the previous 12 months (converted to an index called a business transaction hour, or BTH, reflecting the time taken to do the transaction not the profit to POCL). This payment structure is an issue of contention between POCL and the agents who are remunerated under the scheme, and we will return to this issue later in the chapter. Rural and community offices are small, often part-time agencies, frequently run at a loss to POCL, in order to provide a social service for geographically remote communities. The agents are remunerated via a base salary plus an additional payment for any extra hours worked above the agreed amount.

The absolute number of retail outlets in the network is considered to be too great by POCL's management and has been declining. However, they continue to abide by a rough rule of thumb that states that no customer in an urban area should have to walk more than half a mile to get to one of their outlets. As yet, the rationalization of retail outlet numbers has not been substantial enough to impact on customer perceptions of service levels or retail presence. However, if this programme gains momentum, this situation could change.

The nature of the relationship between POCL and its agents

As mentioned in the introduction to this chapter, the underlying ethos of this relationship is fairly traditional in terms of buyer–seller interactions: POCL obtains a huge competitive advantage over its rivals by having the largest national retail network, but without having to institutionalize the development and maintenance costs of such an infrastructure; in exchange, the agents are theoretically captains of their own ship, but with the added security of an extra ballast just in case they encounter rough conditions. In other words, the relationship is apparently both synergistic and mutually symbiotic. If we break down the various aspects of the interaction, it will become clear that one does not automatically follow the other for both parties in the relationship. By analysing various operational aspects of the relationship, such as the locus of operational control, policy-making, performance target-setting, communication patterns and investment profiles, we should be able to determine whether the two parties have adopted a truly constructive and complementary exchange pattern. Some of these will be contractually defined by POCL, but others will be determined by the structural architecture of the organization, the corporate culture and, to a limited extent, the personality of the agent involved.

Goals

For the relationship to be an effective collaborative effort, or partnership, there should be a high degree of goal congruence concerning the major issues between the parties. This requires participation in both goal planning and setting, and therefore agreement on roles and responsibilities. Dwyer and Oh (1988) state that this is the minimum requirement for partnership success. Driscoll (1978) found that participation in decision-making increased satisfaction with a relationship; this should engender greater levels of trust between the parties, enhancing the willingness to collaborate (Pruitt, 1981), thus increasing the propensity towards relational adaptability and flexibility in the face of common adversity (Williamson, 1985). Given the number of agents, one would expect to find a variety of personal or peripheral goals, but even these should not diverge too radically from the common objective, or superordinate goal. In other words, one would expect that the stated aims or objectives would be beneficial to both parties in the long term. The expectation of mutual benefits arising from the co-ordinated efforts of the partnership should compensate for the loss of autonomy (Cummings, 1984), so long as the expectations are met. This future-orientated commitment balances the short-term problems against the long-term goals (Angle and Perry, 1987).

If we look at the performance targets as the first example of the direction of the relationship, they are defined by POCL. For example, POCL or other clients determine the acceptable percentage of transactional efficiency (error rates), define the customer service levels (quality-of-service measure incorporating queuing times) and stipulate the outlet presentation standards (in terms of cleanliness and general upkeep). Although these targets are imposed by POCL, the majority of the agents would not disagree that they were in the best interests of all concerned. For instance, minimal waiting time (perceived or real) is one of the key priorities for the customers of POCL and it is doubtful that a dirty or run-down outlet would induce new customers to enter in order to sample the 'ambience'. The agents do not disagree with the fact that transactional accuracy is essential, especially given that the 'clients' impose financial penalties for errors, but they do disagree with the way error rates are calculated.

Other stipulated performance 'targets' are not quite as conducive to fostering the partnership. The agent, as an independent business person, will be interested in the bottom-line profit that his or her operations generate. POCL is remunerated by its clients on the volume of transactions that the outlets process. Herein lies the classical dilemma of competing business agendas when growth and profit are the stated aims of the various stakeholders. The agents want a product portfolio that is dominated by high-margin, low-volume business or at least want the lion's share of the transactional profit, whereas POCL is targeting high-volume, low-margin business which allows it to exploit its competitive advantage and traditional business linkages (this obviously does not pre-empt it from contracting other high-margin business).

One of the major problems concerning 'performance' within the context of POCL is the fact that, thus far, no precise volume targets are set or communicated to the agents. They have advance knowledge of the forthcoming year's remuneration (given that it is based on last year's business volume and transaction types), but they do not have a clear idea of the future expectation of their performance. Schmidt and Kochan's research (1972) illustrated that goal incompatibility would manifest overt conflict, while other studies have specifically indicated that differences in economic objectives would lead to conflict in relationships (Assael, 1968).

The cost of mismanaging a valuable partnership is huge: communication can go some way to avoid this by engendering trust, a sense of mutual commitment and a willingness to work together (Mohr and Spekeman, 1994).

Granovetter (1973) indicated that relational strength is a function of the amount of time both parties devote to the partnership, the intimacy between them (directness and ability to be open and honest) and the level of reciprocity (the extent both parties contribute resources to the relationship – both tangible and intangible). The formal operationalization of a communication network could be construed as a form of reciprocity, since frequent formal or informal contact requires a substantial investment of time and resources, especially for face-to-face contact. Closer and stronger relations will result from more frequent, more relevant information exchange (Huber and Daft, 1987).

Roles

As indicated by previous channel research, a partnership should involve the acceptance of clearly defined and delineated roles. In the typical principal–agent relationship there is a significant power imbalance. This is clearly true in the case of POCL. The contribution of any one sub-post office to POCL's turnover is small, while the contribution of POCL's business to the subpostmasters' business, even if there is a buoyant private business, is critical. POCL's contract gives it significant power over the subpostmaster. For example, the contract with a new subpostmaster may specify a capital investment requirement such as a refurbishment of the business, but when the business is sold on to the next incumbent, POCL receives a payment similar to that of a franchise fee.

The underlying issue here is, whose business is it? In a full franchise the issue is clear: the franchisor has developed a business that the franchisee pays to use. In the case of an agency agreement the situation is less clear.

POCL is responsible for the national, corporate image of the network, but the image locally and to the customers of a sub-post office can be determined by the outlet. Whose customer is the person buying a TV licence or being paid a pension? Whose role is it to generate new business and, if the responsibility is to be a shared one, how much responsibility does the network manager have in such an activity?

Communication

Communication between the partners is important both in terms of what is communicated and how. Communication can be overt or the manifestation of more subtle, yet fundamental partnership attributes such as trust and commitment (Anderson, Lodish and Weitz, 1987). It can be used to instil feelings of commitment and participation into the relationship and thus becomes one of the strongest conflict-avoidance and resolution techniques. Conflict itself can affect performance if it is allowed to exceed a certain threshold (Lusch, 1976). However, conflict is not necessarily a bad thing as conflict to some degree indicates a willingness to resolve differences of view.

Trust

In any relationship trust is both an essential ingredient and a measure of the strength of the relationship. Trust is essential if partners are to develop their exchange of information (Zand, 1972), a key issue if the retail network manager is to understand the full extent of the agents' problems and requirements. Agents appear to rely on their regional network manager on matters specific to POCL but are reluctant to let them intervene in their private businesses, even where there is clear synergy between them. Yet again the agency relationship falls short of that which would be normal in a full franchise.

POCL's future

POCL's operating arena has changed from a relatively stable, predictable environment, to one where flexibility is required to reflect the change in the customer base and rapid increase in competition. This situation is further complicated by the fact that POCL is not completely the master of its own destiny; to a certain extent, it has to react to and work within exogenously imposed restrictions, i.e. the government's current and future policy concerning its commercial autonomy. If the government expands POCL's ability to work with large private organizations as well as the governmental organizations, it will be in the key position to continue to co-ordinate the network activities. This centrality, coupled with its financial resource base, means that it makes more economic sense for POCL to expand rather than reduce its influence over the channel-decision structures, thus ensuring that the POCL 'brand' continues to grow.

The reorganization of its corporate architecture in 1993 actually put in place a structure that is more than capable of coping with the demands that it is now facing, from both within and outside its network of agents. The boundary-spanning link, retail network managers, between the agents and corporate POCL should enable two-way communication to occur between the two parties. However, before the benefits of this link can be completely released, a number of changes are implied from research into channel relationships generally.

In order for the channel to enhance its efficiency, POCL needs to agree with its agents mutual goals, and the specific roles that each will need to adopt to achieve these. Interestingly, the management of POCL and the agents would benefit from re-evaluating the perception that both their 'clients' have about their channel system: the linkage between the clients and the end customer is POCL, acting as a 'unitary' organization – i.e. both clients and customers perceive POCL to be a unified company, centrally controlled – not a fragmented organization consisting of a large number of small, independent business people acting as agents for a 'middle man'. Thus, both clients and customers perceive the main benefit to be locational proximity; that is, high-street presence. In other words, the internal relational dyad between POCL and its agents is less important than the external channel–customer dyad (both 'clients' and end-users being classed as customers of the channel in this definition).

The way forward could be easily defined. POCL should manage the corporate relations and national brand strategy, while the agents should manage the locally centred marketing campaigns. This complementary role specialization is the current officially stated version of the strategy that is said to be operating. However, the strength of the relationship seems to have been weakened by the lack of clarity in detailed operational procedures and policies. This can be put down to the gap between the communication strategy and reality, and some of the objectives of POCL which are incompatible with the objectives of the agents.

The preferred option for both POCL and its existing network would then appear to be to develop a more balanced partnership where roles were more clearly defined and accepted and where there exists an ability to share views on what these roles are and how they can develop.

There is a second option and that is to move towards a more formal franchise. POCL used the term 'franchise' in the early 1990s to refer to its shop-within-a-shop concept where a sub-post office was located inside the premises of a multiple retail business and run by them. The franchise fee reflected the benefit to the retailer of having an enhanced customer flow. In 1995 POCL began a more formal franchise activity where the traditional agency *plus* a package of other products were offered as a full retail franchise to independent entrepreneurs under the name Trading Post operating as a CTN. Significantly, the branding of this form of franchise became the responsibility of POCL leaving only the operation to the franchisee. It remains to be seen whether this format will be more successful than the traditional sub-post office. In this new approach the relationship between POCL and franchisee will be quite different: the franchisee will sacrifice independence in exchange for the purchase of a fully developed business. The type of individual this format attracts may well be different – the relationship certainly will be.

References

Anderson, E., Lodish, L. and Weitz, B. (1987) Resource allocation behaviour in conventional channels, *Journal of Marketing Research*, Vol. 24, pp. 85–97.

Angle, H. and Perry, J. (1987) An empirical assessment of organizational commitment and organizational effectiveness, *Administrative Science Quarterly*, Vol. 26, pp. 1–14.

Assael, H. (1968) The constructive role of interorganizational conflict, *Administrative Science Quarterly*, Vol. 14, pp. 573–82.

Cummings, T. (1984) Transorganizational development, *Research in Organizational Behaviour*, Vol. 6, pp. 367–422.

Driscoll, J. (1978) Trust and participation in organizational decision making as predictors of satisfaction, *Academy of Management Journal*, Vol. 21, pp. 44–56.

Dwyer, F.R. and Oh, S. (1988) A transaction cost perspective on vertical contractual structure and interchannel competitiveness strategies, *Journal of Marketing*, Vol. 52, pp. 21–34.

Etgar, M. (1979) Sources and types of interchannel conflict, *Journal of Retailing*, Vol. 55, pp. 61–78.

Granovetter, M. (1973) The strength of weak ties, *American Journal of Sociology*, Vol. 78, pp. 1360–80.

Huber, G. and Daft, R. (1987) The information environment of organizations. In F. Jablin *et al.* (eds) *Handbook of Organizational Communication: An Interdisciplinary Perspective*, Sage, Newbury Park, Calif.

Lusch, R. (1976) Channel conflict: its impact on retailer operating performance, *Journal of Retailing*, Vol. 52, pp. 3–12.

Mohr, J. and Spekeman, R. (1994) Characteristics of partnership success: partnership attributes, communication behaviour, and conflict resolution techniques, *Strategic Management Journal*, Vol. 15, pp. 135–52.

Pruitt, D.G. (1981) *Negotiation Behavior*, Academic Press, New York.

Robicheaux, R. and El-Ansary, A. (1976) A general model for understanding channel member behaviour, *Journal of Retailing*, Vol. 52, pp. 13–30.

Rosenberg, L.J. and Stern, L.W. (1970) Towards the analysis of conflict in distribution channels: a descriptive model, *Journal of Marketing*, Vol. 34, pp. 40–6.

Schmidt, S.M. and Kochan, T.A. (1972) Conflict: towards conceptual clarity, *Administrative Science Quarterly*, Vol. 17, pp. 359–70.

Wiener, S.L. and Doescher, T.A. (1991) A framework for promoting cooperation, *Journal of Marketing*, Vol. 55, pp. 38–47.

Williamson, O. (1985) *The Economic Institution of Capitalism*, Free Press, New York.

Zand, D. (1972) Trust and managerial problem solving, *Administrative Science Quarterly*, Vol. 17, pp. 229–39.

4

Business-to-business relationships

Pete Naudé and Christopher Holland

Introduction

Marketing in a business-to-business context has undergone a number of changes in perspective over the years. At first, attempts to understand such marketing relied on extending the prevailing (predominantly American) view of consumer marketing. This was a fairly simplistic black-box or input/output approach that relied on the marketer manipulating a set of variables (i.e. the four Ps) in order to maximize the desired return from the marketplace. The perspective of the buyer–seller relationship was overwhelmingly an adversarial and short-term one. In the 1980s, largely through the pioneering work of the Industrial Marketing and Purchasing (IMP) group (Håkansson, 1982), it was appreciated that this did not sufficiently reflect the complexities of how business-to-business markets operated. Rather, it was argued, such marketing was often long term, and involved buyers and sellers interacting to their mutual benefit, which in turn required levels of trust and commitment that could not be accommodated in the simpler adversarial model. This new perspective involved a fundamental change in the unit of analysis in researching business-to-business markets. Initially, the approach adopted was to study the buying centre or the selling process (Robinson, Faris and Wind, 1967; Webster and Wind, 1972; Sheth, 1973). What evolved was a wider model, expanding the unit of analysis from studying the behaviour of the buyer(s) *or* the seller(s) to the relationship between them (see, for example, Ford, 1980; Håkansson, 1982; Campbell, 1985). Naturally, the people and the personal interrelationships between them form a crucial part of this model.

In this chapter we argue that a new perspective is emerging. It seems to us that a new paradigm is required: not one that rejects the IMP framework, but one that builds upon it. We believe that it is increasingly common for relationships in business-to-business markets to be based not on human interaction but on information exchange. The existence of these new relationships is being made possible by fundamental technological changes in the power of IT and the creative ways in which these changes are being harnessed by the innovative marketer. With the advent of powerful ITs and their application to marketing problems the exchange of information becomes the central activity of most marketing processes. It is therefore more appropriate to view marketing primarily as an information-handling problem in order to analyse and understand IT-based marketing innovations. One example of where these changes are acute is the fundamental effect of how IT affects the formation and dissolution of relationships within market networks. We present a combination of theoretical arguments which are illustrated with three case vignettes from different industries. The chapter is therefore a theoretical one supported by cases which ground the core ideas in empirical data in order to show their general applicability. The case analyses indicate the extent to which the IT industry is becoming a key driver in determining relationships within markets. It is having a dramatic effect in both adapting existing relationships and forging new ones, and hence also in affecting how markets are structured. We conclude with the proposition that marketing needs to be redefined as an information-handling problem, and that traditional views of marketing should be reformulated in information terms (e.g. marketing structures need to be viewed as information paths) so that the effects of IT on marketing can be better understood.

It has long been accepted that marketing is about exchange: predominantly the exchange of goods or services, and the IMP framework has gone a long way towards changing the more classical view of marketing as a process of adversarial exchange. In this chapter we argue that the conceptual problems involved in managing such physical exchanges have largely been identified and solved. They are no longer sufficient to ensure success, only prerequisites to such success. Increasingly, what predicates the exchange of goods or services is an exchange of information. It is therefore argued that marketing problems should be transformed into the information domain and treated as information-handling problems.

The basic tenet of the IMP literature, that 'the relationships between buying and selling companies are frequently long term' (Håkansson, 1982, p. 16), has been built around a number of cornerstones. Among the most basic of these are the interaction between the parties involved, and the atmosphere surrounding that interaction. This early model has been widened more recently to encompass the networks that result from a linkage between several interacting parties (Thorelli, 1986; Håkansson and Snehota, 1989).

The IMP approach: interaction

The interaction between parties consists of particular episodes that, when viewed longitudinally, make up the relationship. These episodes between the buyer and seller involve the exchange of products or services, information, finance and social aspects. While we do not ignore the role that the others play, we posit here that it is the exchange of information that is having a fundamental effect on how markets develop and are structured. The exchange of products and/or services is, we believe, increasingly a generic function – all commercial relationships, of whatever kind, involve such exchange. The physical delivery of products or services has not really been an area of innovative change. The same is true of financial exchange – this is a natural consequence of any commercial relationship, and has remained essentially static for generations. Social exchange may or may not occur, depending on the level at which the parties decide to interact over time. We accept that each of these three elements is important to the formation of relationships, and that relationships may be formed out of the routinization of such exchange. But it is the exchange of information which has developed radically over the past decade, and which in turn is changing the way in which relationships are formed.

Håkansson (1982, p. 16) argues that the information exchange is characterized by its content (which may vary in width and depth), going on to say that 'impersonal communication is often used to transfer basic technical and/ or commercial data. Personal channels are more likely to be used for the transfer of "soft data".' We consider that this view, in the face of recent changes in the IT industry, is too simplistic. Rather, recent changes in the IT industry have led to the situation whereby it is increasingly likely that such 'impersonal' channels of communication are becoming the very cornerstones of new strategic relationships between firms. This, in turn, creates the possibility for new networks to exist.

In addition, the IMP literature has argued that it is the ongoing nature of the exchange episodes that leads to the formation and formalization of relationships between buying and selling firms. This occurs through the exchange episodes becoming 'institutionalised to such an extent that they may not be questioned by either party and may have more in common with the traditions of an industry or a market than rational decision-making by either of the parties' (*ibid.*, p. 17). We believe that this is changing, and that the situation is arising whereby relationships are not the result of the internalization of episodes, but rather that the changes in IT are shaping relationships in a fundamental way, to the extent that they are being formed on the basis of what information can be exchanged between companies, rather than the more traditional view which held that the relationships would be the result of such information exchange. We argue, therefore, that increasingly the situation is to be found where the relationship is based on the kind of information that can be and is transferred between parties. It is not the episodic exchange of information that results in a relationship emerging. Rather, it is the preplanned, formalized decision to embark upon the exchange of strategic information which has, as its consequence, the formalization of relationships between companies. Thus the basis of relationships is changing: no longer is it true that a series of episodic exchanges of information, products, etc., would be the building blocks supporting the developing relationship. Increasingly we are finding that a different pattern exists: that episodic exchanges are not prerequisites for a relationship to exist. Rather, it is an analysis of the information flows that either are possible or else are required that determines the form that the relationship will take. Such information flows, however, do not just determine the nature of the relationship between buyer and supplier. They are far more fundamental than that – they often determine the very structure of how markets operate, acting as the backbone of the channel of distribution.

The implication of this is that personal relationships may become less important, not more so. The argument that 'at the core of these exchange processes between suppliers and customers is the person-to-person dyadic relationship involving a salesman and a buyer' (Cunningham and Homse, 1986, p. 3) may have been true in the past. Increasingly, however, we believe that it is the exchange of information, through non-verbal, automated processes, that is at the core of the exchange process. We accept that this may not be true for all types of IT systems. Based on a large sample of IT systems, Brousseau and Quélin (1992) identified three types of services, which they categorized as enhanced communications services (e.g. email, generic electronic data interchange – EDI); information services (e.g. Reuters, Telerate); and dedicated services (e.g. transaction processing, home banking, interbank systems). We accept that our focus falls mostly on the dedicated services, which are 'especially designed to meet the needs of a particular industry, . . . often assembled by alliances dominated by users. Most of these services are industry specific applications' (*ibid.*, p. 237).

The IMP approach: atmosphere

This information-flow view of marketing has a number of implications. First, it must affect the whole atmosphere of the interaction relationship. The original IMP work recognized this aspect as an integral part of their model, arguing that 'this atmosphere can be described in terms of the power-dependence relationships which exist between companies' (Håkansson, 1982, p. 21). What we are seeing is that information flows dramatically alter the nature of these power-dependence relationships. As we argue in the case studies below, the very particular nature of the information flows emerging alongside the trend towards single sourcing (Spekman, 1988) has resulted in it being far more complex to isolate where the power or the dependence lies within a relationship. Rather, the advent of these new information chains has resulted in mutual dependency becoming far more important. We see these changes having a dramatic influence on transaction costs between companies (Williamson, 1975). A number of different elements of the economic dimension have been identified such as distribution, negotiation, administration and production costs (Håkansson, 1982). It is our contention that these various cost elements are now being handled in a different way. Typically, there may be very large investments made in negotiation costs between different possible partners in a supply chain. However, if the outcome of this investment is a structured information flow that effectively excludes other competitors from entering the supply chain, then there are radically reduced costs involved in distribution, administration and production costs. The trend towards single sourcing and JIT delivery systems is a clear indication of this trend.

A crucial component of the atmosphere surrounding a relationship is the control dimension. This has traditionally manifested itself in the extent to which partner A in the relationship is more dependent on the relationship for their long-term survival than partner B. In such instances, it is B that has the control, and may use it advantageously. As will become clearer in the case vignettes below, we see this changing. The trend towards single sourcing and close EDI links has seen the emergence of what can be called 'vertical integration without ownership' (Holland, Lockett and Blackman, 1992), where neither member in the relationship has ultimate control. Rather, the level of mutual dependency is so high as to be crucial for the longer-term survival of both companies.

The IMP approach: networks

Apart from relationships and the atmosphere surrounding them, a third cornerstone of the IMP framework has been developing an understanding of networks and how they operate. The IMP work has stressed the importance of the study of networks as a way of understanding the complex relationships that exist within and between industries. Our contention is more fundamental: that changes in IT are facilitating fundamental changes in what is possible in the construction of and delivery within networks. This fundamental change, in turn, means that new forms of networks are now emerging that were not possible before.

What this means is that we are seeing a fundamental shift in the nature of information exchange within networks. Previously, when information was exchanged principally through person-to-person contacts, it might have been appropriate to argue that 'information exchange processes between the customer and the supplier, as indicated by the number of persons having contacts and the frequency of their meetings, is an attribute of the relationship between the companies' (Hallén, Johanson and Seyed-Mohamed, 1987, p. 23). We believe that this has changed to the extent that the strength of a relationship can no longer be judged by the depth or frequency of person-to-person contact. Rather, it is now the type of data that are being exchanged through information networks that is determining the strength of the relationship. For example, an EDI network that is used to transmit information on simple orders and deliveries, as is the case in many of the international freight companies (Batchelor, 1995), we would regard as a very simplistic network, evidence of a less-than-mature relationship between the parties. On the other hand, EDI networks such as those that exist between Navistar International and Goodyear, where full and detailed strategic information covering all aspects of production planning and inventory holdings are processed, are evidence of a stable, mature relationship, irrespective of the degree of personal contact between the organizations concerned (Hammer and Champy, 1994). It is indeed the case that these information-based relationships become so strong that they 'reach such a level that they act as effective "barriers to entry" of newcomers and thus acquire the capacity for self-perpetuation' (Wilson and Mummalaneni, 1986, p. 45).

There is another emerging trend in these information-based networks that needs to be stressed. Market analysis, whether using the IMP framework or the more traditional view, has largely been dominated by an examination of the network that exists between buyer and supplier. Increasingly, however, this must be seen as too restrictive a perspective. A flyer with British Airways is offered discounts if he or she stays at a Hilton Hotel, or hires a Hertz car. Any surfer of the Internet who decides to go shopping in Barclays Bank's BarclaySquare finds that there is instant access to retailers such as Sainsbury's, Toys-R-Us or Blackwells. These examples are indicative of the new emerging networks where the information flows are between companies that have traditionally been regarded as separate entities but which, when they start to share information on customers, develop new forms of synergy between them. This is an emerging trend within networks: the original perspective was to see them as linkages between firms within the same supply chain. This was later expanded to co-operation between firms, typically in R&D-intensive industries (e.g. Esposito, Faffa and Zollo, 1994). This is no longer the case: we are increasingly finding that firms with no obvious links are coming together to their mutual benefit because of the information-based networks between them.

Case studies

Case 1: The automotive industry: the cases of Ford and Daewoo

In the late 1980s Ford faced an easily identified and obvious problem: based on its earlier worldwide organizational redesign, Ford had ended up with completely independent automotive units designing and selling their own vehicles on both sides of the Atlantic. For the benefit of organizational independence, Ford was having to pay the price of duplicated effort and waste, and the resultant high costs both in terms of the financial implications and bureaucracy. Basically, they were spending too much time and money designing new cars, and ending up with an overlap of effort. The solution, however, was less obvious, and Ford is now going through a process of radically restructuring its worldwide production facilities to the degree that they will have single manufacturing 'platforms', with particular cars being built on single sites only (see, for example, Treece, Kerwin and Dawley, 1995).

As a result of these changes, the USA and Europe are now forming a unified company, thereby creating a truly global company. There will be global product teams and single-site manufacturing. There are obvious risks: slowing the decision-making process, and the ultimate threat of designing an 'average' car that suits no specific markets. But whether or not Ford's global strategy is appropriate, *it is only feasible by designing the organization around IT systems*. All aspects of the marketing process are now managed and co-ordinated through information systems. For example, the 'Mondeo' car is credited with being the world's first mass-produced global car. Central to the co-ordination of its design, manufacture and after-sales support was the use of a single worldwide engineering database which can be accessed by almost any manager

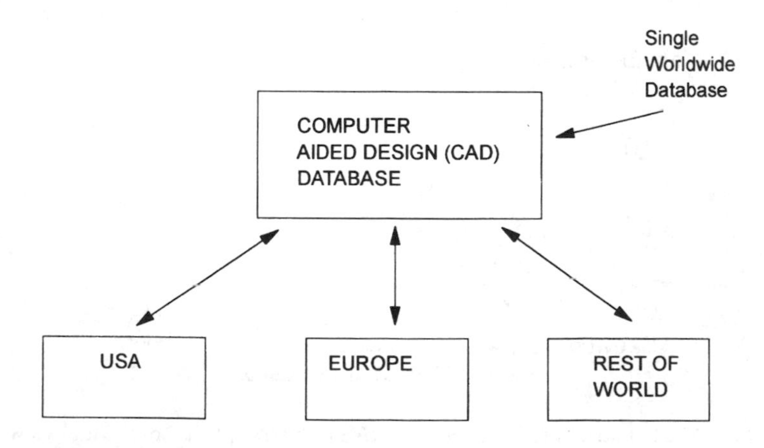

Figure 4.1 Ford's worldwide database system

worldwide from any terminal, regardless of location (see Figure 4.1). Ford are implementing a global marketing strategy to address increased homogenization across national markets and also to realize significant cost savings through internal rationalization. This global marketing strategy is synonymous with its IT strategy: internal reorganization is centred on shared worldwide databases; similarly, external relationships with customers and suppliers are organized around formal information exchanges. In summary the marketing strategy can be described and modelled in information terms. It is based on novel methods of handling information using IT, whereby geographic and organization constraints are annulled.

In the case of Daewoo the problem was very different. While Ford's problem was basically an internally focused one, indicating how IT influenced the organization design and global marketing strategy, Daewoo's was how to break into the relatively mature UK market in order to become a meaningful player in a short period of time. The results so far have been an outstanding success, with Daewoo reputedly selling 1,500 units in the first week of their summer 1995 launch (Hewson, 1995a). As shown in Figure 4.2, the usual model of the automotive industry is for a manufacturer to sell cars to the dealer, who in turn sells them to the public. For subsequent service, the customer may then either return to the original dealer or go elsewhere. This has resulted in a cut-throat market, where dealers are keen to get sales and are prepared to enter into bargaining and discounts to move units. At the same time, they cannot forgo

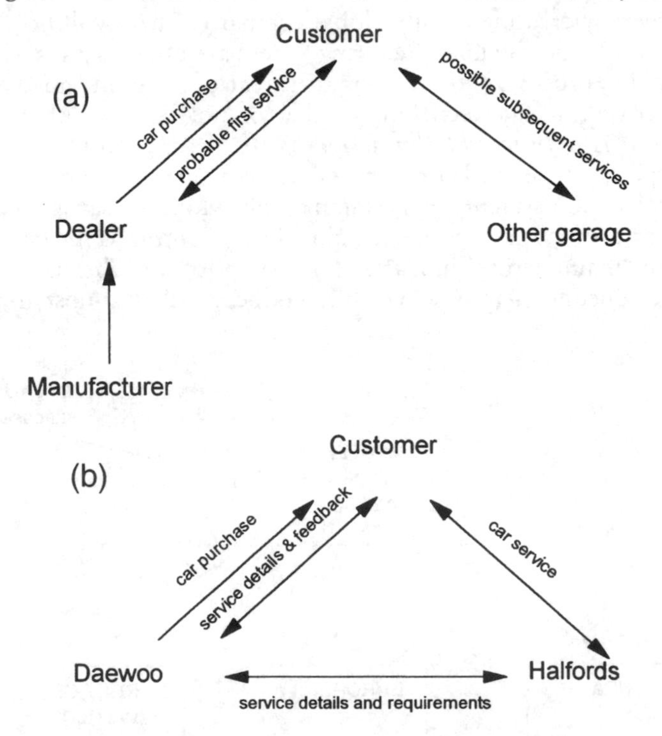

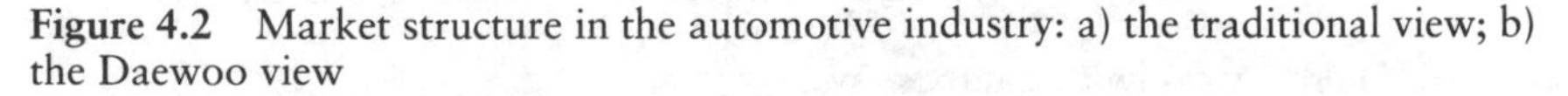

Figure 4.2 Market structure in the automotive industry: a) the traditional view; b) the Daewoo view

too much of the potential profit, since they cannot necessarily depend on the subsequent service for their profit stream.

Based on one of the largest samples of consumer research undertaken in the industry, Daewoo have changed the rules of the game. Cars are sold by salespeople operating on a fixed salary, with no commission. Customers can use IT touch-screens to view details about cars and the finance deals available, with salespeople on hand to offer advice when required. Even more innovatively, Daewoo has set up a link with Halfords to handle the servicing of cars: a customer phones a central Daewoo number to book the car in for a service. A few days before the service, the Daewoo staff phone the customer back to discuss the details of any particular requirements. Daewoo then pass these details on to Halfords, who collect the car, carry out the work and drop it off again at the customer's site. Halfords then let Daewoo know that the work has been completed, and within 72 hours the customer is contacted by Daewoo to check that he or she is satisfied.

The truly innovative element of Daewoo's sales and service strategy has been based on a radically different market structure, whose success depends on the information flow upon which it is built. The backbone of this new and innovative market network is the IT link between the two organizations. Not only is information kept on each customer, his or her service requirements and the status of his or her car in the repair/maintenance cycle but this information also passes freely and seamlessly between the two organizations. Modifications ensured that 'the two companies' computer networks . . . talk to each other so that each [Halfords] outlet can maintain a constant stock of commonly held parts and can order any unusual ones within 24 hours from a central Daewoo warehouse' (Hewson, 1995a, p. 3). As argued before, the real change that has taken place, in terms of the marketing implications, is that a long-term, formalized relationship was entered into, and a new market structure forged, that was not based on the formalization of any previous business contact between the two organizations. Rather, the relationship was the result of careful planning and merging of a customer and service-orientated IT system.

Case 2: EDS

EDS was founded by Ross Perot and is now part of General Motors. It is one of the leading companies in the market of IT outsourcing and is expanding into Europe with some large contracts to manage customers' IT systems (e.g. in the UK they have recently won a contract to manage the data processing for the Department of Inland Revenue). While such outsourcing of IT requirements is becoming increasingly common, with a growth in the supply of computer services to companies and government departments, EDS' strategy is particularly interesting. Its marketing strategy is based on three changes which it believes to be crucial to understanding the emerging trends in industry (Jackson, 1995). The first of these is that the growing application of IT worldwide has led to a dramatic rise in the data available, but not necessarily to an increase in the information available. Data are being generated because it is ever more easy to do so (e.g. by barcodes). However, increasingly innovative software is required to add value to the raw data, resulting in many companies being data rich but remaining information poor. It is the new technology from the IT industry that will allow companies not just to automate but to 'informate' (Zuboff, 1988). Having better information, in turn, is seen to be more of a strategic asset than before.

Secondly, there is increasing emphasis on supply-chain competition rather than on the more simplistic competition between traditional retail outlets. With many retailers having significant bargaining power, this has led to manufacturers being under increasing pressure, a natural outcome of which is to start to deal direct with their final customers, who are themselves increasingly demanding personal attention. The management of customer data is a key element of this emerging relationship (which is a good example of disintermediation – see below), a relationship that fundamentally alters channels of distribution. Although the adoption levels of IT by marketing are still fairly low, research has highlighted both the use that online databases will play in the future use of IT to enhance customer service (Domegan and Donaldson, 1992), and also the role of computerized marketing databases in merging data from numerous sources (Cameron and Targett, 1992). As an example, Levi Strauss & Co., the American jeans company, now sells personally tailored jeans direct to customers, based on a new IT system (Hewson, 1995b). Retail outlets consist of trained fitters who enter the details on to the company's database, and the customer has a barcode in his or her 'perfect' pair of jeans. Reordering a new pair direct from the company thus becomes a simple matter.

The third element underlying EDS' strategy is the belief that links between various elements on the (usually still separate) multimedia will greatly facilitate this exchange between supplier and customer. It has been argued that 'much current advertising and promotional activity is generally aimed at specific geodemographic or psychographic groups rather than individual households. This relatively unfocused marketing effort is the result of a lack of hard data at the household level and can cause resentment (as with junk mail) when poorly targeted' (Flowers, 1992, p. 263). However, changes in IT allow new developments. For example, if the analysis of a customer's personal credit card at a particular retail outlet reveals that he or she is a particularly heavy user of a particular product, it is already easy for them to be sent direct mail featuring related advertisements or offers of special deals. In the near future, this information will come directly to their TV, or some other form of personalized electronic mail. It is accepted that specialized IT equipment is required to reach this stage of information integration, but it will dramatically alter channels of distribution to the extent where they are determined by new information flows and not by traditional product flows. We are increasingly seeing the extent to which product flow is determined by, and does not determine, information flow.

This implies a change in the role of advertising. This has traditionally been based on a one-way flow of information, requiring the use of increasingly eye- or ear-catching information bites to capture the attention of the target market. However, the rise of information-based channels of distribution changes this, since the information flow is now two way. The distinction between advertisements and market research will become blurred. The new media will allow dialogue between customer and manufacturer, allowing the originator to give information on the range of products available, and the consumer to send back information on the detailed requirements that he or she has. Thus we are seeing the combination of IT technology and database management that permits the building of databases of best customers, and 'establishing one-to-one relationships with lifetime valued customers rather than adopting a mass-marketing approach' (Rees, 1995, p. 22).

Case 3: Electronic banking

Our third example concerns electronic banking. Already the technology exists for individuals to link in to their current account and to complete their banking requirements electronically (Lloyd, 1995) and, although only 300,000 people (0.12% of the American population) currently bank via their PC, this is expected to rise to 4.6 million by 1997 (Ellis, 1995). However, the real innovation is not electronic banking, but the emergence of electronic cash ('E-cash'). This is a system that is already being tested in England, whereby customers in Swindon carry their cash in the form of a credit card, with a micro-chip deducting the appropriate amount every time a phone or bus is used, or a supermarket transaction is completed (see Chapter 8 for more detail).

When combined with the ability to sell products or services internationally via the Internet, the full implications of E-cash become apparent. Since the Internet has no geographically constrained boundaries, the cash can move between countries with complete freedom. Already some are seeing this as signalling the end of retail banking, and the emergence of more global competition (Holland and Cortese, 1995). The implications are unclear: for example, if

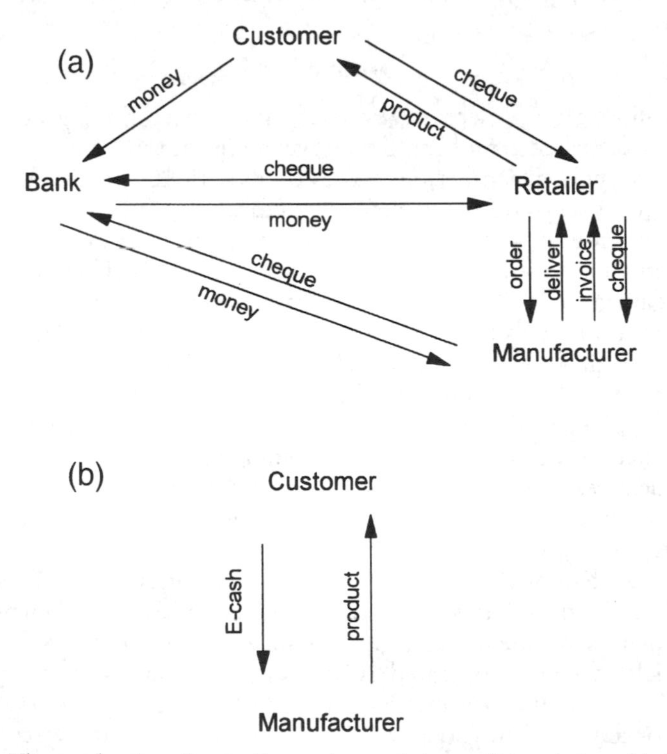

Figure 4.3 The mechanics of a credit purchase: a) the traditional view; b) the E-cash information/money flow

a supplier is in the UK, and buyer in Greece, and the software executed in the USA, in which country is the sales tax payable? But the real innovation here is not the emergence of a new form of banking that the banks themselves are launching. At stake is the very existence of the banks themselves: the emergence of E-cash means that corporations can transport money electronically between themselves, 'more cheaply, conveniently, and quickly than through the banking system' (*ibid.*, p. 36). With this exchange taking place outside the traditional banking system, there will increasingly be no need for paper currency or cheques, and hence no need for banks. This much simplified information flow is shown in Figure 4.3.

At the heart of these issues is the one of who 'creates' currency. At present most countries have a central authority which has the sole power to issue money, and which regulates how it is used (e.g. how cheques are cleared). The system is perpetuated by the banking industry, which is the only economic sector permitted to operate on a fractional service basis whereby it can lend more money than it actually has. E-cash, on the other hand, can move through multiple networks, not just the current banking system. Moreover, it can come in different forms, created by different individual organizations. The really radical change will occur therefore when (unregulated) organizations other than banks start to support the E-cash they are putting on to the market with less than 100% backing by traditional funds. In short, the amount of money in the system could potentially increase in a dramatic and unregulated way.

Discussion

The cases illustrate the pervasive impact of IT on marketing activities. The innovations described are all based on novel methods for handling information which support new structures and modes of operation. Ford and Daewoo have designed new organization and market structures respectively which are implemented through information paths defined by their IT systems – information management dictates how the companies operate. EDS is effectively transforming the organization and management of its customer organizations by applying information models to its businesses – the derivation of decision-support information from raw data, the development of shared information systems along the supply chain to improve the co-ordination of marketing from raw-materials suppliers to the final customer and the promotion of interactive one-to-one marketing with both business and retail customers (see also Chapter 2). All these ideas require an understanding of how improvements and changes to the information-handling capability of organizations can be used to support new marketing strategies. The banking case points to a revolution in the way that the whole banking industry will operate once it is viewed as a relatively simple information-exchange problem. The emergence of totally new solutions to areas such as payments, foreign exchange and monetary policy by companies which have never operated as banks before demonstrates that in banking an ability to handle information within global market networks is perhaps more important than historical banking experience. Market research, new product design, distribution and support are all defined in information terms and can be managed with very simple low-cost IT systems. Banking has always been an information-handling problem and the reductions in the cost of technology mean that a revolution will now take place in which IT knowledge and information-based marketing strategies will be the keys to success rather than historical importance, level of assets or geographic coverage.

The marketing process has traditionally been to research the market, segment and then to target a particular group of customers, positioning a carefully designed product/service at that group. It has been argued that this is changing and that organizations 'are looking to IT for increased accuracy, sophistication and cost effectiveness of marketing initiatives. More importantly they are looking to IT for radical changes in the scope of their marketing: better segmentation, customer targeting and service enhancements' (Cameron and Targett, 1992, p. 223). But increasingly the influence of IT is extending beyond these traditional boundaries. Now the trend is towards one-to-one, interactive marketing: asking individuals what they want, and delivering personalized products. This is based upon two innovations: 1) interactive media permitting the gathering and analysis of the data; and 2) computerized manufacturing techniques that permit far smaller production runs than before. There is no longer a choice between mass markets and customized markets – there is increasingly mass customization (Mitchell, 1995a). An example of this dialogue can be found for example with the Insurance Club (Pratt, 1995) operating over the Internet. Using this information-base channel, customers fill in details concerning their insurance requirements on line. The quotation is sent back in the same way and, if the customer likes the price, enters his or her credit-card number in return.

We believe that there appear to be two logical outcomes of such emerging information-based markets. These are an increase in both the number and nature of information brokers and also in disintermediation, defined here as 'the process of seizing ownership of your customer from third party intermediaries' (Mitchell, 1995b, p. 33). Considering the first, let us take the example of the Internet-based BarclaySquare described above. If the bank starts to build up a database of what an individual's purchase patterns, and hence his or her likes and dislikes are, it makes sense for the bank to act as a link, passing forward to individuals information on products that they are most likely to buy, and passing the same information back to the suppliers when products are demanded. We believe that it is the people who control these information flows who will start to act as information brokers, putting suppliers and customers in touch. Not only will they charge for such information but, more importantly, they will also be defining new channels of distribution whose structure is based on information flow and not product flow.

Disintermediation, or a reduction in the role of the middle man, will also increasingly become a reality as more and more companies that have traditionally seen themselves as manufacturers start to interact directly with their own customers, removing the need for retailers. This will not only relate to information-based products such as the insurance example mentioned above; already it is possible to buy products as diverse as books and bread on the Internet. Again, this is a clear case of a new channel of distribution emerging, based purely on the information system that underpins it.

In order to assess the overall impact that changes in IT are having, Table 4.1 shows how a range of management issues, all of which affect the marketing

Table 4.1 The factors affected by IT in the three cases

	Case 1		Case 2	Case 3
	Ford	Daewoo	EDS	E-cash
Disintermediation		Y	Y	Y
Improved customer service		Y		
Globalization	Y			Y
Generating new channels	Y	Y		Y
Better market information			Y	
Market research			Y	
Customer databases		Y	Y	Y
Business process re-engineering	Y	Y	Y	Y
Outsourcing	Y			
Segmentation			Y	
Lifetime value		Y	Y	

manager and how he or she manages relationships within the supply chain, are affected by the role of IT. It is clear that the type of relationship that IT facilitates is dependent upon other criteria. For example, Brousseau and Quélin (1992, p. 233) have pointed out that 'when a firm owns assets that are more specific than others, it can become the node of a network of subcontractors. Otherwise, the firm has to negotiate a strategic alliance with other partners in order to collectively be the joint owners of highly specific assets'. From the examples given above, it is clear that BarclaySquare operates as a node, while Daewoo/Halfords have a strategic alliance. We believe that these dramatic changes herald a new era in marketing – one that is information based not product or service based. These changes between the traditional view of marketing and an information-based view are outlined in Table 4.2.

Conclusion

Marketing practice in all industries is being revolutionized by the application of IT to support new structures, strategies and relationships. To reflect the impact of IT on marketing, marketing problems such as customer management, globalization of market networks, new product design and cash management should be transformed into the information domain and treated as information-handling problems. This method has been demonstrated in the

Table 4.2 How the marketing task is changing

Marketing activity	Traditional view	Information-based view
Exchange	Goods and services	Information
Structure	People based	Information based
Market research	Project driven	Ongoing
Segmentation	Personal attributes	Database marketing
The manager's tools	Four Ps	Information alliances
Advertising	Mass → direct	Interactive
Distribution	Channels of distribution	Disintermediation

case studies and Table 4.2 summarizes the relationship between a traditional view of a marketing activity and an information-based model. It can be seen that the design of novel methods for sharing and processing information both within and between organizations determines the marketing processes.

The dramatic and concomitant changes occurring in both management philosophies (for example, down-sizing, delayering, outsourcing, business process re-engineering – BPR) and contemporary IT applications (for example, computer networks, EDI, document image processing (DIP), electronic point of sale (EPOS)) mean that we need to redefine our understanding of what constitutes the marketing manager's role within the organization. It has been argued that 'managers perceive that IT is having a significant impact on business, government and organizational life now. They increasingly agree that IT has become a strategic resource as it brings about or facilitates major changes in industry sectors, in competitive behavior and in organizations' own strategy, structure and functioning' (Earl, 1989). But we argue that it goes further than Earl suggests – not only is IT a strategic resource at the disposal of marketing managers but it is also in fact heralding fundamental changes in the way that marketing strategies are implemented. The combination of IT capability coupled with novel information-based marketing strategies is redefining how firms organize their activities, interact with trading partners and influence the formation and development of relationships.

On the basis of the arguments and discussion of the case studies it is clear that the marketing manager of the future will have to realize and accept these changes as lasting and pervasive, and that the primary marketing issues are concerned with the setting up of the appropriate social, organization *and* IT networks and the exchange of information within these networks. To reflect and model the effects of IT on marketing, a more appropriate paradigm for the future is to treat marketing as an information-handling problem.

References

Batchelor, C. (1995) Regions leave plenty to pay for, *The Financial Times Survey into the Courier and Express Services Market*, 18 May, p. 1.

Brousseau, E. and Quélin, B. (1992) Users' knowledge as a specific asset: the case of the value added services, *Journal of Information Technology* (theme issue information technology and marketing), Vol. 7, pp. 233–43.

Cameron, R. and Targett, D. (1992) Computerized marketing databases: their role now and in the future, *Journal of Information Technology* (theme issue: information technology and marketing), Vol. 7, pp. 223–32.

Campbell, N.G.C. (1985) Buyer/seller relationships in Japan and Germany: an interaction approach, *European Journal of Marketing*, Vol. 19, pp. 57–66.

Cunningham, M.T. and Homse, E. (1986) Controlling the marketing–purchasing interface: resource development and organizational implications, *Industrial Marketing and Purchasing*, Vol. 1, pp. 3–27.

Domegan, C.T. and Donaldson, B. (1992) Customer service and information technology, *Journal of Information Technology* (theme issue: information technology and marketing), Vol. 7, pp. 203–12.

Earl, M.J. (1989) *Management Strategies for Information Technology*, Prentice-Hall, New York.

Ellis, S. (1995) Banks switch on to home computers, *The Sunday Times*, 23 July, Vol. 4, p. 5.

Esposito, E., Faffa, M. and Zollo, G. (1994) International networks in high technology industries. In W.G. Biemans and P.N. Ghauri (eds) *Meeting the Challenges of New Frontiers (Proceedings of the 10th IMP Conference)*, University of Groningen, Groningen.

Ford, D. (1980) The development of buyer–seller relationships in industrial markets, *European Journal of Marketing*, Vol. 14, pp. 339–53.

Flowers, S. (1992) A vision of the future? An innovative database micromarketing system, *Journal of Information Technology* (theme issue: information technology and marketing), Vol. 7, pp. 261–6.

Håkansson, H. (ed.) (1982) *International Marketing and Purchasing of Industrial Goods: An Interaction Approach* (a Study by the IMP Group), Wiley, Chichester.

Håkansson, H. and Snehota, I. (1989) No business is an island: the network concept of business strategy, *Scandinavian Journal of Management*, Vol. 4, pp. 187–200.

Hallén, L., Johanson, J. and Seyed-Mohamed, N. (1987) Relationship strength and stability in international and domestic industrial marketing, *Industrial Marketing and Purchasing*, Vol. 2, pp. 22–37.

Hammer, M. and Champy, J. (1994) *Reengineering the Corporation*, HarperCollins, New York.

Hewson, D. (1995a) Full of eastern promise, *The Sunday Times Supplement on Customer Care*, 11 June, p. 3.

Hewson, D. (1995b) Jean genius, *The Sunday Times Supplement on Customer Care*, 11 June, p. 6.

Holland, K. and Cortese, A. (1995) The future of money, *Business Week*, 12 June, pp. 36–46.

Holland, C.P., Lockett, A.G. and Blackman, I.D. (1992) Planning for electronic data interchange, *Strategic Management Journal*, Vol. 13, pp. 539–50.

Jackson, T. (1995) EDS is getting to know all about you, *The Financial Times*, 18 April, p. 21.

Lloyd, C. (1995) Electronic banking booms, *The Sunday Times*, 23 July, Vol. 4, p. 5.

Mitchell, A. (1995a) Cuddle up with a customer and get rich, *The Times*, 24 May, p. 30.

Mitchell, A. (1995b) The biggest thing to hit marketing since New! Improved!, *The Times*, 28 June, p. 33.

Pratt, K. (1995) Cover yourself with the net, *The Sunday Times*, 2 July, p. 3.

Rees, R. (1995) Take it from the top, *The Sunday Times*, 11 June, p. 22.

Robinson, P.J., Faris, C.W. and Wind, Y. (1967) *Industrial Buying and Creative Marketing*, Allyn & Bacon, Boston, Mass.

Sheth, J.N. (1973) A model of industrial buyer behaviour, *Journal of Marketing*, Vol. 37, pp. 50–6.

Spekman, R.E. (1988) Strategic supplier selection: understanding long-term buyer relationships, *Business Horizons*, Vol. 31, pp. 75–81.

Thorelli, H.B. (1986) Networks: between markets and hierarchies, *Strategic Management Journal*, Vol. 7, pp. 37–51.

Treece, J.B., Kerwin, K. and Dawley, H. (1995) Ford: Alex Trotman's daring global strategy, *Business Week*, 3 April, pp. 36–44.

Webster, F.E. and Wind, Y. (1972) A general model for understanding organizational buying behaviour, *Journal of Marketing*, Vol. 36, pp. 12–19.

Williamson, O.E. (1975) *Markets and Hierarchies, Analysis and Antitrust Implications*, Free Press, New York.

Wilson, D. and Mummalaneni, V. (1986) Bonding and commitment in buyer–seller relationships: a preliminary conceptualization, *Industrial Marketing and Purchasing*, Vol. 1, pp. 44–58.

Zuboff, S. (1988) *In the Age of the Smart Machine*, Heinemann, London.

5

Internal relationships

Javier F. Reynoso and Brian Moores

Introduction

Service quality is a relatively young academic discipline boasting only some two decades of research. As a consequence of the marketing background of many of those working in the area, a substantial body of the research has been focused on the *customer's perspective* of service. In associating customer service affairs with organizational matters, however, some contributions relate to that Gummesson (1993) labels the 'genesis of a service'. While some researchers are working on aspects related to service development and service design (e.g. Edvardsson, 1991; Kingman-Brundage, 1989; 1991), other authors, for example, Shostack (1984; 1987; 1992), have emphasized the importance of the production system that supports the encounters with the customer, while others have proposed conceptual models in which the internal interactions of the service provider's organization are clearly illustrated (e.g. Eiglier and Langeard, 1987; Grönroos, 1990).

Owing to the interactions which inevitably occur between departments in any company, internal organizational dynamics are of particular relevance for both the service production and its delivery in service organizations.

The more significant conclusions of those various researchers, particularly as they relate to internal customer–supplier relationships, are reviewed in this chapter. Such relationships are indeed an essential part of this RM framework, as has been explained in Chapter 1. The importance of internal service quality to successful RM is followed by the description of a research project conducted to study the nature and characteristics of such interdepartmental relationships in relation to customer service in a hospital context.

An indication of the findings which emerged from the research is then presented. These show that it is indeed possible to capture the characteristics of internal customer service as a set of readily understood dimensions. The concluding remarks of the chapter present the managerial implications of such findings.

The internal marketing concept

The concept of internal marketing in services evolved originally through the idea of 'selling' jobs in the service sector with the purpose of making the job more attractive for the employee (Sasser and Arbeit, 1976). This concept has been addressed subsequently in wider terms by a number of authors (e.g. Berry, 1981; Grönroos, 1990; Gummesson, 1990). Their belief is that, if management wants its employees to deliver an outstanding level of service to customers, then it must be prepared to do a great job with its employees. Of particular relevance in this regard is the contribution to the debate by Stershic (1990, p. 45). She claims that:

> As obvious as it may seem to recognize employees as the critical link in delivering service quality and customer satisfaction, rarely are they the focus of such research. Obtaining and understanding the employee perspective is a critical tool in managing customer satisfaction. It enables managers to exercise 'internal-marketing' – meeting the needs of the employees so they can meet the needs of the customer.

Berry and Parasuraman (1992, p. 25) define the core objectives of internal marketing as 'attracting, developing, motivating and retaining qualified employees'. An intriguing approach is that proposed by Heskett *et al.* (1994) who argue that a one-to-one correspondence exists between those issues which need to be addressed on the customer service front with those which are deserving of attention in the domain of employment practice.

Internal dynamics

Researchers in organizational behaviour have confirmed the importance of the internal marketing concept introduced by marketers. Some scholars have provided data on the ways in which staff and organizational issues are reflected in customer satisfaction and behaviour (Parkington and Schneider, 1979; Schneider, Parkington and Buxton, 1980; Schneider and Bowen, 1985). These papers have demonstrated that staff and customer perceptions, attitudes and intentions share a common basis and are related to each other.

Service organizations can be described as open systems with highly permeable boundaries in which the perceptive of organizational practices is visible both to employees and customers. In their definitive contributions to 'internal service climate', Schneider and Bowen (1985) found that when employees describe the human resource practices of a company as being service orientated, customers also hold favourable views of the quality of service they receive. This suggests that a service-orientated organization should treat front-line employees as 'partial customers', i.e. as individuals deserving the same treatment that management wants the customers to receive (Bowen and Schneider, 1988). Based on these findings, these same authors suggest that this idea of treating the employee as a customer could also be considered in the internal dynamics of the organization. In their 1985 paper, they argue that it is important to realize that organizational members not only service external customers but they also have internal customers. In other words, in any organization, staff are both receivers and providers of some services. This particular piece of research, which constituted the first major validation of the relationship between employee attitudes and customer satisfaction, marks the beginning of internal customer research.

Common concerns are emerging from organizational behaviour and marketing researchers regarding the organizational dynamics surrounding the production and consumption of services. Bowen (1990), for example, identifies those issues where the literature of both academic fields converges in its thinking and points to aspects of service operations demanding of interdisciplinary research. One of the issues he addresses is the need for additional research on the aforementioned relationship between employee behaviour and customer satisfaction. He claims that this offers a natural intersection of interests in organizational behaviour and marketing.

In the service sector today, both marketers and organizational behaviourists emphasize the importance of the internal dynamics of the organization in terms of a network of customers and suppliers interacting together to satisfy customers.

Internal customer–supplier relationships

Perspectives on service delivery

In attempting to provide an integrated discussion of the service production and delivery process, Gummesson (1993) presents what he labels a 'multiperspective approach'. This consists of four service models each associated with four groups of actors, namely, customers, contact staff, support staff and management. He argues that all these perspectives along with that of the owners need to be taken into account before one could claim to possess a comprehensive appreciation of the service delivery process. All five groups hold different perspectives, each of which is relevant to the whole service experience. Although the relevance of internal customers within the context of the service delivery process is frequently referred to in the literature by marketers and organizational behaviourists, there is something of a paucity of published research relating to the support staff's perspective. The research report on bank employees by Lewis and Entwistle (1990) is a notable exception, as are those of Gremler, Bitner and Evans (1994) and Vandermerwe and Gilbert (1989; 1991), which are referred to later.

Internal support activities

A number of writers have addressed the importance of the internal support activities and operations as the key link to external customer satisfaction (e.g. Adamson, 1988; Sanfilippo, 1990; Davis, 1991; Milite, 1991; Jablonski, 1992). In this same vein, the quality of internal service operations has been identified as one of the essential elements of an overall service quality strategy (e.g. Nagel and Cilliers, 1990; Feldman, 1991) yielding to long-term cost savings and increasing financial gains (e.g. Davis, 1991; Rowen, 1992). It has also been associated with the quality culture of organizations (e.g. Albert, 1989; McDermott and Emerson, 1991).

In further pursuit of these arguments, some scholars have contributed to the establishment of a theoretical framework within which the internal customer concept could be explored and debated. This concept has been addressed in the light of the internal processes involved throughout the service production system. Shostack (1984; 1987; 1992), for example, considers service as a system formed by interdependent and interactive systems. Similarly, Grönroos (1990) describes the service production process as a network of systems built up by inter-relations and interdependence between a number of subprocesses. He argues that every service operation comprises internal service functions which support one another and that, if poor internal service exists, the final service to the customer will be damaged. George (1990) also supports this proposition, claiming that a large number of support persons who do not come into contact with customers do themselves none the less indirectly influence the service ultimately provided to customers. He argues that these supporting personnel should recognize the contact employees as their internal customers.

Research on service quality has demonstrated the aforementioned importance of the internal customer–supplier relationship in relation to the achievement of customer expectations. The findings from an extensive research project conducted in different service companies by the research team led by Berry (Parasuraman, Zeithaml and Berry, 1985; 1988; Zeithaml, Berry and Parasuraman, 1988; Zeithaml, Parasuraman and Berry, 1990) has revealed that internal customer–supplier relationships play a particularly important role in the discrepancy or gap which can exist between service quality specifications and the actual service delivered, when employees are unable or unwilling to perform the service at the specified level. The authors found that one of the key factors that contributes to this discrepancy is a lack of teamwork.

Implementation of an internal customer approach

Another set of authors claim that to be aware of the existence of internal customers is not, of itself, sufficient. They argue that it is necessary to determine internal customers' needs and expectations (e.g. Plymire, 1990; Koska, 1992; Ludeman, 1992; Chung, 1993). Other contributors have gone beyond this initial proposition and have focused on planning the implementation process for an internal customer initiative throughout the organization (e.g. Cirasuolo and Scheuing, 1991; Davis, 1991; Vandermerwe and Gilbert, 1989; 1991). Although the approaches differ slightly, some common sequential steps can be identified. These are as follows:

- The creation of internal awareness.
- The identification of internal customers and suppliers.
- The identification of the expectations of internal customers.
- The communication of these expectations to internal suppliers in order to discuss their own capabilities and/or obstacles to meeting these requirements.
- As a result of the previous point, internal suppliers should work to make the necessary changes so as to be able to deliver the level of service required.
- And finally, obtain a measure for internal customer satisfaction. Feedback should be given to internal suppliers if services are to be improved.

One of the areas that is attracting particular attention within such a framework is that of measuring the quality of the internal service being provided in terms of needs and expectations (e.g. Davis, 1992; Garrett and Turman, 1992; Thornberry and Hennessey, 1992), as when satisfaction (Gulledge, 1991) and internal service performance are measured against service standards documented in internal contracts (Koehler, 1992).

The importance of internal service quality to successful relationship marketing

As defined by Gummesson (1995, p. 245), RM is seen as relationships, networks and interactions. He claims 'Relationships require at least parties who are in contact with each other. Networks emerge when relationships become many and complex and when it becomes difficult to obtain an overview of them. The parties enter into interaction with each other. The core interaction consists of values and supporting joint activities'.

In making RM tangible and structured, Gummesson has identified 30 different relationships, one of those being that between internal customers and internal provides. He stresses the importance of these internal relationships, arguing that 'they constitute the support to the externally directed relationships and the antecedent for them to be effective' (*ibid.*, p. 253). Clearly, the quality of such internal interactions is essential to successful RM. Thus, it is necessary to determine how internal customers perceive the quality of the service they receive from their internal providers.

Internal service quality dimensions

Various researchers have contributed to the identification of service quality dimensions which could be used to operationalize the concept of *internal* service quality. What are the criteria used by customers in assessing the quality of the service they receive? Attempts to answer this question in different settings studied from different perspectives have, perhaps not surprisingly, produced various sets of quality dimensions which are useful in measuring *external service quality*. Perhaps the most publicized is that developed by Berry and his co-workers, who originally identified ten criteria from research with customers in different types of services (Parasuraman, Zeithaml and Berry, 1985; 1988; Zeithaml, Berry and Parasuraman, 1988; Zeithaml, Parasuraman and Berry, 1990). They subsequently consolidated seven of the ten original dimensions into two broader categories resulting in five general criteria. It should be pointed out that a number of writers, including, for example, Babakus and Boller (1992), Vandamme and Leunis (1993) and Buttle (1996), have criticized the SERVQUAL approach mainly on the grounds of the transferability of these generic criteria across sectors. Other observers have argued, with some justification, that the scores secured from the expectation element of their twin-scale approach is illusory in so far as 'excellent' would appear to be a logical response to a prompt as to what is expected from a service experience (see, for example, Carman, 1990). Other authors have also identified different quality dimensions (e.g. Baker, 1987; Garvin, 1987; Norman, 1988). In a first attempt to summarize research contributions on this topic, Gummesson (1992) provides a comparison of general quality dimensions as well as examples of specific criteria for a number of service activities.

Just as the quality perceptions of customers can be captured in the form of sets of dimensions or criteria, so too is it felt that the quality of internal services that units receive from those departments which support their activities can be meaningfully categorized. That being the case, the ensuing groupings could be referred to as internal service quality dimensions.

Unfortunately, in spite of the prevalence of articles which refer to the importance of identifying such internal service dimensions, only the papers by Vandermerwe and Gilbert (1989; 1991) and the more recent one by Gremler, Bitner and Evans (1994) could be considered as being methodologically useful. Some see the measurement of the quality of internal services as being conceptually no more complex than adopting or adapting the existing findings from customer-based research. Zeithaml, Parasuraman and Berry (1990, p. 180), for example, claim that 'SERVQUAL, with appropriate adaptation, can be used by departments and divisions within a company to ascertain the quality of service they provide to employees in other departments and divisions'. This simplistic proposition has obvious appeal but, in reality, research is called for before such a sweeping generalization can be justified. If there is a justified concern about the transferability of the SERVQUAL criteria across sectors, then there is every reason to believe that this same reservation would hold when one focuses on internal as distinct from external customers. As will be seen, the results reported here will be seen to support this basic concern.

Having stressed the importance of internal service quality to develop and implement RM successfully, a research project aiming at conceptualizing and operationalizing this concern is now described.

Research background

Exploring the service perspective of interdepartmental relationships

Qualitative research on the internal network of activities that support the service delivery process was first undertaken to explore interdepartmental relationships from a service perspective. Various questions need to be answered. Do employees in one department actually recognize other units as their customers? Do they see the products of their jobs as the provision of internal services to other units? Do they really harbour expectations about the services they receive from their support units and, if so, what kind of expectations do they have? Do these expectations refer solely to the 'outcome' of the service they receive? Would it be possible to identify any kind of pattern or criteria?

This project was conducted in the health service sector based on the findings of a previous study in the hotel industry (Moores and Reynoso, 1993). Hospitals were chosen as the environment in which to conduct this research as it is difficult to envisage an organization which boasts a wider variety of interdepartmental relationships. The objective was to obtain a deeper understanding of those factors which determine how organizational units perceive the quality of the support they receive from other units. The research was conducted in two hospitals located in the north of England. One is a part of the NHS while the other operates in the private sector. Both hospitals offer a wide range of inpatient and outpatient clinical services across a range of specialities. For each hospital, two specific customer episodes, one surgical and one medical, were identified and these were used to provide a focus for the discussions.

The selection of two pairs of contrasting cases was made in order to obtain observations relating to a representative sample of units providing different types of relationships and contexts during the delivery process of healthcare to the patient.

All the activities involved during the service delivery process for each episode were identified and the networks of internal customer–supplier relationships were then depicted using Shostack's (1984; 1987) blueprinting technique. A total of 33 interviews with staff from the departments or groups involved were then conducted within the NHS hospital and 26 in the private one. In both hospitals, respondents included staff from clinical units (e.g. operating theatre, consultants, senior house officers, junior doctors, secretaries); paramedical departments (e.g. physiotherapy, speech therapy); wards (e.g. senior sisters); clinical support units (e.g. X-ray, pathology, pharmacy); non-clinical support units (e.g. porters, domestics, maintenance, stores, catering); and administrative departments (e.g. personnel, medical records, admissions, accounts, finance).

Interviewees were asked to identify all those departments from which their units require any kind of internal support during the specific clinical episode. They were also asked to describe their own expectations of these requirements. In the second part of the interview, respondents were asked to identify all the departments they support in the same episode. They were then asked to describe their understanding of the expectations that each of the departments they support has of these internal services. For those departments involved in both types of episode, managers were asked first to answer the questions in relation to the one in which they felt the participation of their department was most relevant. At the end of each question, they were asked to consider the second case and to complement their initial answers, if necessary.

Identification of departmental expectations

The discussions around the two contrasting clinical cases in the two different hospital environments yielded details of a great variety of departmental relationships. The 59 interviews generated in excess of 750 statements about internal service expectations in the NHS hospital and nearly 400 in the private hospital. The information was detailed, being illustrative of several particular situations and associated sets of expectations. This material was subjected to a rigorous examination aimed at identifying the core themes being addressed by respondents in each of the many hundreds of recorded statements. In order to categorize them properly, the underlying root cause of each statement was identified. Gradually, different groups containing common accounts emerged. Owing to the great variety of interactions explored in the complexity of a hospital environment, various items were included within each of the service categories identified. All in all, this content analysis of the information provided by interviewees resulted in the identification of ten internal service quality dimensions, each of which incorporated a limited number of themes of the same nature.

In Table 5.1 is set out a summary of the generic statements grouped by the identified service dimensions and their relative frequencies for the two hospitals.

Table 5.1 Departmental expectations of the internal service received from other units (results from content analysis)

Hospitals	Frequency of statements							
	Public				Private			
Conceptual service dimension/expectations	Frt-line	Suprt	Total	%	Frt-line	Suprt	Total	%
Reliability. To			271	36			136	36
perform the internal service right the first time	34	42	76		31	30	61	
provide the internal service at the required/promised time	20	26	46		9	4	13	
provide correct/accurate information	10	16	26		20	7	27	
provide the necessary information	23	22	45		8	2	10	
perform the internal service required/promised	34	23	57		10	7	17	
show sincere interest/effort in solving a problem	2	3	5		1	1	2	
do something by a certain time	5	3	8		3	1	4	
provide the internal service at the frequency required	7	1	8		1	1	2	
Responsiveness. To			164	22			69	19
give prompt/immediate internal service	24	22	46		25	12	37	
be willing to co-operate/help/support	30	40	70		16	8	24	
provide advice/guidance	17	28	45		2	4	6	
be flexible	2	1	3		0	2	2	
Competence. To			83	11			38	10
have the knowledge/skills/experience/training/to perform the internal service	24	9	33		18	9	27	
perform efficiently	9	6	15		6	0	6	
have the necessary/adequate resources	2	3	5		0	2	2	
provide the service require to patients	26	4	30		3	0	3	
Communication. To			118	16			53	14
complaints/progress/problems/changes/needs	69	31	100		30	15	45	
provide feedback	2	4	6		2	3	5	
consult decisions	4	1	5		0	1	1	
listen	3	1	4		1	0	1	
ask for support	2	1	3		0	1	1	

Table 5.1 *Continued*

	Frequency of statements							
Hospitals	Public				Private			
Conceptual service dimension/expectations	Frt-line	Suprt	Total	%	Frt-line	Suprt	Total	%
Understanding. To			40	5			19	5
inform/request with enough anticipation	10	4	14		1	2	3	
put attention/consideration to others' needs/problems/limitations	7	4	11		6	3	9	
understand others' specific needs/problems/limitations	2	4	6		4	2	6	
have realistic requests/expectations	5	4	9		0	1	1	
Courtesy			38	5			32	9
courteous/polite/friendly/pleasant/decent/respect attitude, relationships	25	13	38		26	6	32	
Credibility. To			15	2			9	2
be honest	2	2	4		1	3	4	
trust others' capacity	2	3	5		1	3	4	
accept others' decisions	1	0	1		0	0	0	
recognize others' role	3	0	3		1	0	1	
be consistent	0	2	2		0	0	0	
Access. To			11	1			6	2
be available	7	4	11		6	0	6	
Tangibles. To			14	2			8	2
have a good appearance/condition of physical facilities/equipment/ materials/products/information/neat appearance of staff	10	4	14		8	0	8	
Confidentiality. To			3	–			5	1
handle confidential information properly	1	1	2		2	1	3	
display discretion when dealing with delicate situations	1	0	1		1	1	2	
Total			757	100			375	100

Operationalizing internal service quality

Development of a perceived internal service quality scale

Items were developed in order to measure how organizational units perceive the quality of the support they receive from other units. Statements were included for each of the ten main themes obtained from the content analysis. Illustrative examples of the items featured in the final, edited questionnaire along with the accompanying set of instructions are set out in Table 5.2. Based on the concerns that researchers have expressed about measuring customers' expectations and perceptions in two separate lists (e.g. Carman, 1990; Babakus and Boller, 1992; Vandamme and Leunis, 1993), the scale was designed so as to incorporate both parts into its wording. In the original version of the questionnaire, each item was measured on a six-point scale ranging from 'falls far short of my expectations' to 'exceeds my expectations'.

Table 5.2 Internal customers questionnaire (summary of results)

Instructions

For the following statements there is a six-point answer scale with brief descriptions of what the numbers on the scale represent. This is printed on the top of the page.

The specific units listed below have been selected as a representative sample of those units which provide support to your ward.

For each of the statements you are asked to provide an answer *for each* of those units. Therefore, please choose one number that most accurately reflects your answer to each statement for each of the units listed below and write them in the appropriate columns.

Scale

1. Completely fails to meet our expectations	2. Fails to meet our expectations in many ways	3. Fails to meet our expectations in some way or other	4. Almost always meets our expectations	5. Completely meets our expectations	6. Exceeds our expectations

	Units				
Examples	1	2	3	4	5
The way this unit keeps us informed about progress, problems or changes which may impact upon our activities:					
The ability of this unit to perform the service we need right the first time:					
The understanding this unit has of our needs, problems and any constraints we might be experiencing:					
The courtesy members of this unit display towards us:					
The speed of this unit in responding to our service requests:					
The condition and appearance of the materials and products this unit provides us with:					
The way this unit is organized so as to be able to perform the service we require:					

The instrument was remotely tested in a pilot study conducted in a third large district hospital where the internal customer–supplier chain was modelled. Three wards with clinical diversity were selected as exemplars of units which are continuously receiving support from other departments in delivering healthcare to patients. These units were identified as internal customers. At the same time, ten departments which provide support to those wards were identified (e.g. medical records, porters, supplies, pharmacy, haematology). Respondents answered each item in relation to each of the support units identified in the questionnaire. Based on the results of the pilot test, the questionnaire was carefully reviewed. Modifications were made to the wording of some items and others were deleted. The six-point scale was also modified as to include improved options for discrimination.

Empirical test of the instrument

The revised version of the questionnaire was empirically tested in a large NHS teaching hospital and the original private institution.

NHS hospital

Nine wards were selected as a sample of internal customers. These represented a diversity of clinical areas such as trauma and orthopaedics, general surgery, ENT, dermatology, general medicine and gynaecology. Ten support units were identified as the sample of internal suppliers. Interviews with each of the nursing managers responsible for the selected wards confirmed the assumed relationship between each ward and those ten support units. The correct match between each internal customer–supplier relationship was, of course, essential if appropriate responses from nursing staff were to be obtained. For each ward, all members of staff were scheduled into one of 84 designated one-hour sessions extending over a three-week period. At each session they were provided with an overview of the research and a brief explanation as to what was required of them. Any questions were raised and answered at the beginning of each session after which the respondents completed the questionnaires. Of the 176 persons programmed to appear, only 11 failed to attend owing to sickness or annual leave, producing a 94% response rate.

The questionnaire consisted of 45 items relating to the ten internal service dimensions which had emerged from the earlier stages, one item that asked internal customers to provide an overall satisfaction rating of each of the ten support units involved, and other summary items. All the items were worded positively and each of them was to be answered using an integrated six-point scale ranging from ‘completely fails to meet our expectations’ to ‘exceeds our expectations’. The overall satisfaction item was answered with a five-point scale (‘very dissatisfied/satisfied’), and for the summary items, a five-point scale (‘strongly disagree/agree’) was adopted.

Each item was answered in relation to each of the selected support units producing a total of 1,650 responses per item. The names of the units were listed on top of each of the five pages of the questionnaire indicating, whenever necessary, the specific unit or service involved in the assessment (i.e. catering only for patients; admissions in medical records).

Private hospital

With one exception, the collection of data followed the same pattern and criteria as at the NHS hospital. Seven wards were selected in the survey. These represent a variety of clinical areas covering cardiology, general medicine, ENT, intensive care, gynaecology, urology, orthopaedics, paediatrics and ophthalmology. Internal customer questionnaires were distributed to the senior sister in each ward. The number of nursing and clerical staff totalled 144 and the response rate was 41%. This was lower than that obtained in the NHS facility primarily on account of the fact that, in this case, the survey was conducted remotely. Questionnaires were returned by respondents using a self-addressed envelope over a period of three weeks.

Data analysis: dimensionality

Responses from both hospitals were analysed using pooled data (i.e. for each item raw data about all ten support units were considered together). This procedure was chosen because the basic objective at this stage was to determine whether or not internal service dimensions, which would be meaningful in assessing the quality of a variety of internal services in hospitals, could be identified.

From the qualitative stage, it will be recalled that ten conceptual dimensions had been identified and labelled using content analysis (see Table 5.1). Thus, the 45-item scale was factor analysed using principal component analysis constrained to ten factors. An initial factor pattern emerged using Varimax orthogonal rotation for the ten-factor solution. However, many items exhibited high loadings on more than one factor. This was not completely unexpected owing to the dependent nature of the hypothesized dimensions during which had become apparent the qualitative stage. The ten-factor solution was, therefore, subjected to oblique rotation using the Oblimin procedure in SPSS-Windows 6.0 to facilitate interpretation of the factors. A purification process followed as it was crucial to obtain clear, distinctive factors, both in the statistical and in the intuitive sense. Thus, items were relocated or excluded from the content of the factors initially obtained. They included those items with a loading less than 0.30, those with low face validity and those with loadings > .30 in more than one factor which did not make any sense in the solution. Eventually, it was felt that a nine-factor solution comprising 32 items provided the best interpretation of the data. A summary of the results is presented in Table 5.3.

Only two of the ten hypothesized dimensions did not appear in the obtained solution, these being courtesy and access. Items related to these two constructs were confused with other factors. The other eight original criteria were in some way present in the content of nine factors obtained. Communication, confidentiality and tangibles remained unaltered in their core structure, resulting in the same three dimensions. The content of the original reliability, responsiveness and competence dimensions was regrouped resulting in five modified dimensions. Finally, the two criteria hypothesized as understanding and credibility were merged into one modified service dimension. The above criteria are defined in Table 5.4.

Table 5.3 Internal service dimensions in hospitals

Dimension	Items	Factor loading*	Alpha coefficient
Helpfulness	Helpfulness of unit when we need it	0.46	0.92
	Willingness of unit to co-operate with us	0.42	
Timeliness	Ability of unit to deliver service within certain time	0.85	0.89
	Ability of unit to deliver service at required frequency	0.79	
	Speed of unit in responding to our service requests	0.72	
	Ability of unit to deal with patients promptly	0.49	
Communication	Unit consults with us on those decisions which impact upon our activities	0.90	0.94
	The feedback we get from this unit	0.88	
	Unit keeps us informed about progress, problems or changes	0.74	
	Willingness of unit to ask us for support	0.73	
	Unit keeps patients informed	0.64	
	Willingness of unit to listen to us	0.57	
Tangibles	Condition and appearance of facilities and equipment of unit	0.87	0.86
	Condition and appearance of materials and products provided by unit	0.83	
	Condition and appearance of written information provided by unit	0.44	
Reliability	Ability of unit to provide necessary information	0.85	0.90
	Ability of unit to provide accurate information	0.85	
	Ability of unit to provide actual service required	0.57	
	Ability of unit to provide service right the first time	0.51	
	Extent to which unit tries to sort problems out	0.45	
Professionalism	Skills unit members appear to possess to perform service	0.84	0.92
	Experience unit members appear to possess to perform service	0.81	
	Knowledge unit members appear to possess to perform service	0.77	
	The advice unit provides us with	0.49	
Confidentiality	Unit's handling of confidential information	0.92	0.83
	The discretion unit displays in dealing with delicate situations	0.62	
Preparedness	Suitability of resources in unit to perform the service	0.63	0.82
	The way unit is organized so as to be able to perform the service	0.42	
Consideration	Trust unit appears to have in us	0.86	0.89
	Extent to which unit appears to value our ward's contribution	0.80	
	Understanding unit has of our needs, problems and constraints	0.56	
	Extent to which we can rely on unit's honesty	0.47	

Note:
* Numbers are absolute values rounded to two decimals.

Table 5.4 Internal service quality dimensions

Helpfulness
The willingness of the supplier unit to help and co-operate with customer units. This is one of the two groups of items from responsiveness which was split in the analysis.

Promptness
The ability to provide the service promptly responding rapidly to service requests. The second group of items from responsiveness was clearly related to this time-related factor.

Communication
To keep the internal customer and the patient informed and consulted with regard to progress, problems or changes which may impact upon its activities.

Tangibles
The condition and physical appearance of facilities, equipment, materials and written information of the supplier unit.

Reliability
The ability of the unit to provde the internal service required correctly, including the provision of accurate information. The time-related items of this factor were split and associated with timeliness.

Professionalism
The skills, knowledge and experience that members of the supplier unit require to provide the service and to give advice. These items were associated with the technical side of the competence factor.

Confidentiality
The supplier unit's handling of confidential information and delicate situations.

Preparedness
The internal organization and resources required by the supplier unit to be able to provide the service. These items were clearly indicating the structural competence of the unit.

Consideration
The understanding, recognition, trust and honesty of the supplier unit towards the internal customer. Understanding and credibility were merged into this new dimension.

Reliability and validity of the scale

Content validity

The reliability of each of the nine dimensions was high. As can be seen from Table 5.3, Cronbach-alpha coefficients using the total sample ranged from 0.83 to 0.94 and the total scale reliability obtained was 0.98. These results indicate good internal consistency among items within each dimension. The percentage of variance extracted by the nine factors was 80.4%.

Reliabilities were also high for the subsamples of both the NHS and private hospital. Table 5.5 shows alpha scores, total scale reliability and percentage of variance explained for the two independent samples. These results provides further evidence of the content validity of the dimensions.

Discriminant validity

Factor analyses of the data obtained at each of the two hospitals were conducted to ascertain the extent to which the factor structure obtained with

Table 5.5 Alpha scores

Service dimension	NHS hospital	Private hospital
Helpfulness	0.93	0.88
Promptness	0.89	0.88
Communication	0.94	0.94
Tangibles	0.87	0.83
Reliability	0.91	0.87
Professionalism	0.92	0.92
Confidentiality	0.83	0.83
Preparedness	0.84	0.76
Consideration	0.90	0.88
Total scale reliability	0.98	0.97
% of variance explained	80.90	79.50

Note:
Numbers are mean values of internal service dimensions.

pooled data was consistent using data from each of the two independent subsamples. Consistency of the factor structures secured from the two hospitals would provide further evidence about the discriminant validity of the identified dimensions. Thus, the 32 items included in the general solution were factor analysed using oblique rotation. All in all, the nine-factor solution which emerged was almost identical. Data from the NHS hospital produced exactly the same nine factors originally obtained from the pooled analysis. Very few items exhibited loading above 0.30 on more than one factor.

In the case of the private hospital, eight of the nine service dimensions emerged again with few items loading in more than one factor. The two items referring to confidentiality were confused with those of empathy. A possible explanation for this could be the fact that confidentiality in the private hospital was more likely to be associated with patient matters and not with departmental activities, as they operate an open-door policy.

Convergent validity

The explanatory power of the scale was also assessed. To do so, the association between internal service dimensions scores and responses to the question concerned with overall internal service satisfaction was evaluated. The scale used to answer this question contained five ascending categories ranging from very dissatisfied to very satisfied. The internal service dimensions scores were the average of the items' values included in each of the obtained factors. The correspondence between the overall satisfaction score and the internal service dimensions measures was analysed using one-way ANOVA.

For each of the two hospitals, separate ANOVA tests were conducted for each of the nine dimensions and for the combined score of them, named ISQ. For those significant results, Duncan's multiple-range test was used to identify significant differences across the five levels of satisfaction. A summary of the results is shown in Table 5.6. In this table, numbers in each service dimension and in the combined ISQ score with no asterisk are mean values significantly different at the 5% level across different categories of internal service satisfaction.

Table 5.6 Satisfaction against ISQ dimension

	Internal service-satisfaction categories				
ISQ dimension	1	2	3	4	5
NHS hospital					
Helpfulness	2.02	3.14	3.71	4.38	4.99
Promptness	2.33	3.03	3.50	4.05	4.54
Communication	2.11	2.98	3.40	3.98	4.62
Tangibles	2.71	3.46	3.82	4.34	4.75
Reliability	2.33	3.11	3.64	4.27	4.76
Professionalism	2.52	3.45	3.90	4.51	4.98
Confidentiality	3.37	3.72	4.10	4.54	4.99
Preparedness	2.43	3.17	3.64	4.20	4.68
Consideration	2.34	3.27	3.68	4.26	4.81
Combined ISQ score[1]	2.46	3.26	3.71	4.28	4.79
Private hospital					
Helpfulness	2.50	3.38	3.84	4.37	4.85
Promptness	2.17	3.22	3.79	4.10	4.58
Communication	1.83	2.90	3.52	4.12	4.60
Tangibles	2.56	3.77	4.31	4.52	4.80
Reliability	2.67*	3.27*	3.87	4.22	4.69
Professionalism	1.92	3.55	4.00	4.43	4.90
Confidentiality	2.33	3.79	4.34	4.55	4.86
Preparedness	2.17	3.50	4.13	4.33	4.76
Consideration	2.08	3.01	3.84	4.31	4.73
Combined ISQ score[1]	2.25	3.38	3.96	4.33	4.75

Notes:
1. Combined ISQ score is the average of the nine dimensions.
* Means *not* significantly different at the 5% level.

As can be seen, results from both hospitals indicate a clear relationship between each of the service dimensions values and internal service-satisfaction categories. Only reliability values for categories 1 and 2 appeared not to be significant. The results are consistent with those of the combined ISQ score. This evidence suggests good validity of the ISQ dimensions in predicting with cost-related measures.

Summary

This chapter has stressed the importance of extending the framework of RM into the internal environment of the organization. Indeed, what the research project has revealed is that employees, like customers, are prepared and able to produce scaled assessments of the service they themselves receive from other parts of the organization. The statistical analysis of those assessments indicates that they can be captured as a limited number of dimensions which are intuitively reasonable.

Some obvious similarities and differences between the factors which have emerged from this project and those identified by Berry's team are apparent.

To that extent, therefore, the earlier caveat relating to Zeithaml's observation of straightforward transferability of the SERVQUAL dimensions from the external to the internal environment of the organization would appear to be justified.

Managerial implications

The ISQ criteria could also be of considerable potential for those managers intent on bringing about improvements. These dimensions give managers the opportunity to explore in greater detail the different facets of the service on which their employees are basing their expectations when dealing with different support units. It is felt that these nine dimensions provide a useful framework to managers analysing and improving RM.

The differences and similarities between internal and external service dimensions suggest that what managers should perhaps be considering, if RM is to succeed, is a set of criteria, some of which are generic whereas others are peculiar to a specific situation. If true, then this proposal could be germane in the external as well as the internal environment of customer service. The implication for those interested in RM is that concepts developed in the context of external customers might also be of relevance to relationships between different parts of an organization. The work reported here, while admittedly exploratory in nature, could well constitute the basis for a whole series of projects conducted in other service environments. Not only would such a body of research provide further insights into the concept of the internal customer but it is also entirely possibly that these would, in turn, augment the more long-standing discussion relating to external customers.

References

Adamson, J.D. (1988) Becoming 'bilingual' can help solve those internal clashes, *Bank Marketing*, Vol. 20, pp. 4, 104.

Albert, M. (1989) Developing a service-oriented health care culture, *Hospital and Health Services Administration*, Vol. 34, pp. 167–83.

Babakus, E. and Boller, G.W. (1992) An empirical assessment of the SERVQUAL scale, *Journal of Business Research*, Vol. 24, pp. 253–68.

Baker, J. (1987) The role of the environment in marketing services. In J. Czepiel, C. Congram and J. Shananhan (eds) *The Service Challenge: Integrating for Competitive Advantage*, American Marketing Association, Chicago, Ill.

Berry, L.L. (1981) The employee as a customer, *Journal of Retail Banking*, Vol. 3, pp. 33–40.

Berry, L.L. and Parasuraman, A. (1992) Services marketing starts from within, *Marketing Management*, Winter, pp. 25–34.

Bowen, D. (1990) Interdisciplinary study of service: some progress, some prospects, *Journal of Business Research*, Vol. 20, pp. 71–9.

Bowen, D. and Schneider, B. (1988) Services marketing and management: implications for organizational behavior. In B. Shaw and L.L. Cummings (eds) *Research in Organizational Behavior*, Vol. 20, pp. 5–22. JAI Press, Greenwich, Conn.

Buttle, F.A. (1996) SERVQUAL: review critique research agenda, *European Journal of Marketing*, Vol. 30, pp. 8–32.

Carman, J. (1990) Consumer perceptions of service quality: an assessment of the SERVQUAL dimensions, *Journal of Retailing*, Vol. 66, pp. 33–55.

Chung, R.K. (1993) TQM: internal client satisfaction, *Business Credit*, Vol. 95, pp. 26–39.

Cirasuolo, G. and Scheuing, E. (1991) Using internal marketing to enlighten co-workers, *Risk Management*, Vol. 38, pp. 42–4.
Davis, T.R.V. (1991) Internal service operations: strategies for increasing their effectiveness and controlling their cost, *Organizational Dynamics*, Vol. 20, pp. 5–22.
Davis, T.R.V. (1992) Satisfying internal customers: the link to external customer satisfaction, *Planning Review*, Vol. 20, pp. 34–7.
Edvardsson, B. (1991) Service design: a powerful tool in quality improvement. Unpublished working paper, Service Research Centre, University of Karlstad, Karlstad.
Eiglier, P. and Langeard, E. (1987) *Servuction*, McGraw-Hill, Paris.
Feldman, S. (1991) Keeping the customer satisfied – inside and out, *Management Review*, Vol. 80, pp. 58–60.
Garrett, M. and Turman, K.G. (1992) TQM in a health care environment, *Internal Auditing*, Vol. 8, pp. 78–83.
Garvin, D.A. (1987) Competing on the eight dimensions of quality, *Harvard Business Review*, Vol. 65, pp. 101–9.
George, W. (1990) Internal marketing and organizational behaviour: a partnership in developing customer-conscious employees at every level, *Journal of Business Research*, Vol. 20, pp. 63–70.
Gremler, D.D., Bitner, M.J. and Evans, K.R. (1994) The internal service encounter, *International Journal of Service Industry Management*, Vol. 5, pp. 34–56.
Grönroos, C. (1990) *Service Management and Marketing: Managing the Moments of Truth in Service Competition*, Lexington Books, Lexington, Mass.
Gulledge, L.G. (1991) Satisfying the internal customer, *Bank Marketing*, Vol. 23, pp. 46–8.
Gummesson, E. (1990) *The Part-Time Marketer*. Research report, Service Research Centre, University of Karlstad, Karlstad.
Gummesson, E. (1992) Quality dimensions: what to measure in service organizations. In T. Swartz, D.E. Bowen and S.W. Brown (eds) *Advances in Services Marketing and Management*, JAI Press, Greenwich, Conn.
Gummesson, E. (1993) *Quality Management in Service Organizations*, International Service Quality Association, New York, NY.
Gummesson, E. (1995) Relationship marketing: its role in the service economy. In W. Glynn and J.G. Barnes (eds.) *Understanding Services Management*, John Wiley, Chichester.
Heskett, J.L., Jones, T.O., Loveman, G.W., Sasser, W.E. and Schlesinger, L.A. (1994) Putting the service-profit chain to work, *Harvard Business Review*, March–April, pp. 164–74.
Horovitz, J. and Jurgens-Panak, M. (1992) *Total Customer Satisfaction: Lessons from 50 European Companies with Top Quality Service*, Pitman, London.
Jablonski, R. (1992) Customer focus: the cornerstone of quality management, *Healthcare Financial Management*, Vol. 46, pp. 17–18.
Kingman-Brundage, J. (1989) The ABCs of service system blue printing. In M.J. Bitner and L.A. Crosby (eds.) *Designing A Winning Service Strategy, Proceedings of the 7th Annual Services Marketing Conference*, American Marketing Association, Chicago, (pp. 30–3).
Kingman-Brundage, J. (1991) Technology, design and service quality, *International Journal of Service Industry Management*, Vol. 2, pp. 47–59.
Koehler, K.G. (1992) Measuring service performance, *CMA Magazine*, Vol. 66, p. 15.
Koska, M.T. (1992) Surveying customer needs, not satisfaction, is crucial to CQI, *Hospitals*, Vol. 66, pp. 50–4.
Lewis, B.R. (1989) *Customer Care in Service Organisations: The Employees' Perspective*. Research report, Financial Services Research Centre, Manchester School of Management, UMIST, Manchester.
Lewis, B.R. and Entwistle, T.W. (1990) Managing the service encounter: a focus on the employee, *International Journal of Service Industry Management*, Vol. 1, pp. 41–52.
Ludeman, K. (1992) Using employee surveys to revitalize TQM, *Training*, Vol. 29, pp. 51–7.

McDermott, L.C. and Emerson, M. (1991) Quality and service for internal customers, *Training and Development Journal*, Vol. 45, pp. 61–4.
Milite, G. (1991) Don't take internal customers for granted, *Supervisory Management*, Vol. 36, p. 9.
Moores, B. and Reynoso, J.F. (1993) Exploring interdepartmental relationships in the service delivery process: a case study in the hospitality industry. In *Proceedings of Workshop on Quality Management in Services III*, Helsinki School of Economics, Helsinki.
Nagel, P. and Cilliers, W. (1990) Customer satisfaction: a comprehensive approach, *International Journal of Physical Distribution and Logistics Management*, Vol. 20, pp. 2–46.
Norman, D.A. (1988) *The Psychology of Everyday Things*, Basic Books, New York.
Parasuraman, A., Zeithaml, V. and Berry, L. (1985) A conceptual model of service quality and its implications for future research, *Journal of Marketing*, Vol. 49, pp. 41–50.
Parasuraman, A., Zeithaml, V. and Berry, L. (1988) SERVQUAL: a multiple-item scale for measuring consumer perceptions of service quality, *Journal of Retailing*, Vol. 64, pp. 12–40.
Parkington, J. and Schneider, B. (1979) Some correlates of experienced job stress: a boundary role study, *Academy of Management Journal*, Vol. 22, pp. 270–81.
Plymire, J. (1990) Internal service: solving problems, *Supervisory Management*, Vol. 35, p. 5.
Rowen, R. (1992) Financial implications of TQM, *Health Systems Review*, Vol. 25, pp. 44–8.
Sanfilippo, B. (1990) 8 ideas to stimulate internal service, *Bank Marketing*, Vol. 22, pp. 26–9.
Sasser, W. and Arbeit, S. (1976) Selling jobs in the service sector, *Business Horizons*, June, pp. 61–5.
Schneider, B. and Bowen, D. (1985) Employee and customer perceptions of service in banks: replication and extension, *Journal of Applied Psychology*, Vol. 70, pp. 423–33.
Schneider, B., Parkington, J.J. and Buxton, V.M. (1980) Employee and customer perceptions of service in banks, *Administrative Science Quarterly*, Vol. 25, pp. 252–67.
Shostack, G.L. (1984) Designing services that deliver, *Harvard Business Review*, January–February, pp. 133–9.
Shostack, G.L. (1987) Service positioning through structural change, *Journal of Marketing*, Vol. 51, pp. 34–43.
Shostack, G.L. (1992) Understanding services through blueprinting. In F.A. Swartz, D.E. Bowen and S.W. Brown (eds) *Advances in Services Marketing and Management*, JAI Press, Conn.
Stershic, S.F. (1990) The flip side of customer satisfaction research, *Marketing Research*, December, pp. 45–50.
Thornberry, N. and Hennessey, H. (1992) Customer care, much more than a smile: developing a customer service infrastructure, *European Management Journal*, Vol. 10, pp. 460–4.
Vandamme, R. and Leunis, J. (1993) Development of a multiple-item scale for measuring hospital service quality, *International Journal of Service Industry Management*, Vol. 4, pp. 30–49.
Vandermerwe, S. and Gilbert, D. (1989) Making internal services market driven, *Business Horizons*, Vol. 32, pp. 83–9.
Vandermerwe, S. and Gilbert, D. (1991) Internal services: gaps in needs/performance and prescriptions for effectiveness, *International Journal of Service Industry Management*, Vol. 2, pp. 50–60.
Zeithaml, V., Berry, L. and Parasuraman, A. (1988) Communication and control processes in the delivery of service quality, *Journal of Marketing*, Vol. 52, pp. 35–48.
Zeithaml, V., Parasuraman, A. and Berry, L. (1990) *Delivering Quality Service: Balancing Customer Perceptions and Expectations*, Macmillan, New York.

6

Retail banking

John A. Murphy

Introduction

The financial services sector has experienced many upheavals in the past decade, resulting in an environment which is characterized by deregulation, a relatively mature market for retail banking, little growth in primary demand beyond that generated by population growth, depressed demand for many financial services, and intense competition from new and innovative companies such as First Direct. For consumers, this type of market profile has, by and large, positive effects, including increased choice, electronic banking (ATMs) and improved product and service offerings. Conventional financial service providers, on the other hand, are now facing vigorous competition from many sources in attracting and retaining a shrinking customer base which is sophisticated, knowledgeable and increasingly asserting its 'right' to high levels of service quality.

Traditionally, few people changed their bank unless serious problems occurred. In the past there was, to a certain extent, a committed, often inherited, relationship between a customer and his or her bank. The philosophy, culture and organization of financial institutions were grounded in this assumption and reflected in their marketing policies which were product and transaction orientated, reactionary, focused on discrete rather than continuous activities, and based on perceptions of a captive 'mass' market for their services. Today, financial institutions can no longer rely on these committed relationships or established marketing techniques to attract and retain customers. As markets break down into heterogeneous segments a more precisely targeted marketing technique is required which creates a dialogue with smaller groups of customers and identifies individual needs. This situation, coupled with the pressures of competitive and dynamic markets, has contributed to the growth of RM as a new marketing model for the financial services sector.

The benefits of relationship marketing to the retail banking sector

It is now accepted by progressive companies in all sectors that in a highly competitive market it is more profitable to retain customers through developing relationships than to devote high levels of marketing effort to acquiring new customers or stemming customer turnover. The evidence in support of RM as a profitable strategy for retail banking is impressive. The Council on Financial Competition's report, *Perfecting Customer Retention and Recovery – Overview of Economics and Proven Strategies* (1995), shows that

- increasing customer retention by 5% adds more than three years to the average customer lifetime;
- defection rates decline markedly across customer tenure with a financial institution; and
- account usage per relationship increases over time.

Likewise, Cumberland Bank's (USA) analysis of the top 5% of their branch customer base reveals that

- these top customers generate 40% of total deposits;
- a 5% increase in retention among top customers yields a 24% increase in profitability; and
- the minimum balance of the top 20% of customers is $20,000.

These statistics confirm the value of developing long-term relationships with customers. Short-term relationships are expensive, while long-term relationships bring long-term benefits. Cram (1994, p. 44) illustrates the profitability of long-term customer relationships and customer retention with reference to financial institutions:

> In financial services, most new cheque accounts are unprofitable for the first three years. In the UK, to attract 150,000 new student/youth accounts could cost £3,000,000 in advertising, and another £20 per head in incentives, mailings literature, computer costs and administration. In early years, with high transaction levels and low balances, the business will be unprofitable. Profit comes with customer maturity, through higher income, higher balances, lending services, deposit products and insurance commissions. The proposition is only viable where the customer is retained.

This example clearly illustrates the benefits which accrue to financial institutions from pursuing an RM strategy. A retail bank customer is effectively unprofitable for the first three years, taking up to six years to break even and become a net profit contributor to the bank. Customers become profitable over time for a number of reasons:

- Over time, retail bank customers tend to increase their holding of other products from across the range of financial products/services available.
- Long-term customers are more likely to become a referral source.
- The longer a relationship continues, the better a bank can understand the customer and his or her needs and preferences and so the greater the opportunity to tailor products and services and cross-sell the product/service range.
- Customers in long-term relationships are more comfortable with the service, the organization, methods and procedures. This helps to reduce operating costs and costs arising from customer error.

The costs of not developing a relationship with customers are also well documented. Not only must the costs of winning a new customer be considered (customer research, advertising and promotion, sales staff, time, incentive, etc.) but also the costs of handling that new customer account (credit checks, account-opening systems, administration costs, etc.). These costs may never be recouped unless a long-term relationship, in the case of a retail bank a relationship lasting at least six years, is established and maintained.

The nature of relationship marketing in retail banking

In examining the role and nature of RM in the financial services sector, it is important to determine what exactly constitutes a 'relationship' for a retail bank. Successful relationships, whether social or professional, are characterized by mutual trust and loyalty, interaction and dialogue, commitment, and the satisfactory performance of respective roles. These are also the key elements in an RM strategy and it is these components which contribute to the effectiveness of RM and distinguish it from general marketing. The roots of a successful RM programme lie in the ability of retail banks to understand their customers and their individual preferences, expectations and changing needs, thereby enabling them to target their customers more effectively and efficiently. The myopic view of customers as mere users rather than as people with many interests, needs and attitudes must be eradicated if RM is to succeed. This can only be achieved by financial institutions who are willing to undergo major changes in organizational culture and capabilities. Retail banks in particular will have to focus on achieving a greater integration of all those activities which impact on customers' experience and perceptions of them as a service provider. Customer-related issues such as reliability, responsiveness, empathy, service and communication should all be vital concerns when developing future strategies and plans.

A recent survey conducted by Abram, Hawkes (1995) which investigated RM in the financial services industry seems to suggest that progress in developing a relationship approach to markets is slow and sporadic among financial institutions in the UK. While there was a high awareness and a reasonable understanding of the term 'relationship marketing' among the 40 retail financial services companies who participated in the research (see Figure 6.1), few organizations were actively pursuing the major concepts associated with an RM strategy and there was no common understanding of how RM is applied in practice.

This study also investigated financial institutions' position *vis-à-vis* their understanding and practice of three critical concepts underlying RM, namely, that

- customers are assigned a lifetime value;
- communication with customers is two way; and
- interaction with customers is truly personalized to their particular situation (treating customers as individuals through a detailed understanding of their needs and preferences and personalized, differentiated messages).

The results of the study in these three areas illustrate the poor state of play with regard to RM in the financial services sector and 'suggest that the theory is much better understood than the practice' (Abram, Hawkes, 1995).

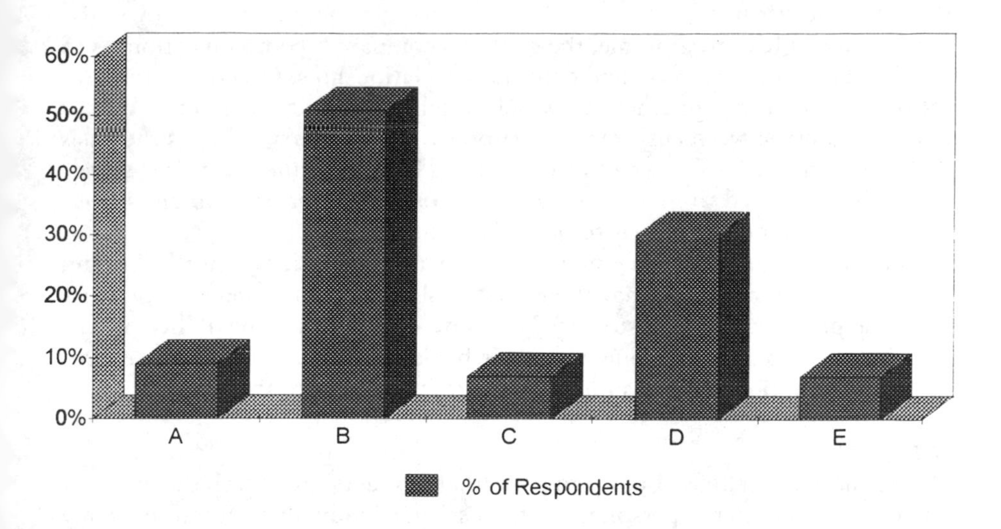

Figure 6.1 What is understood by the term RM

Key

A The new model that will replace the old outdated concept of marketing.
B Developing a continuous relationship with customers across a family of related services.
C A marriage, with asymmetrical responsibilities between the supplier and customer.
D An integrated effort to identify, maintain and build up a network of individual customers and continually to strengthen the network to the mutual benefit of both sides, through interactive and individualized value-added contacts.
E A combination of general advertising, sales promotion, public relations and direct marketing to create more effective and efficient ways of reaching customers.

Source: Abram, Hawkes (1995)

Customer lifetime value

Considering customers from an RM viewpoint implies that companies no longer focus on the costs of a single transaction; rather, they see each customer as a stream of potential income over time. When a customer account is closed, a lifetime's income stream is lost. The customer lifetime-value concept illustrates a customer's potential income stream over the length of the relationship.

Only 20% of respondents to the Abram, Hawkes survey were able to define the lifetime value of a customer, based on his or her likely needs and product holdings, while 70% were working towards this goal. However, as the authors point out, given that this subject area is quite complex, 20% is encouragingly high and it may indicate a gradual move towards the treatment of customers as individuals. More worrying is the fact that over 50% of respondents had no customer retention objectives in place and only 50% had developed programmes to combat attrition. Relatively few organizations had fully addressed the measurement of customer profitability, and a high proportion were unaware of the duration of their existing relationships.

Communication

In pursuing an RM programme, the goal of a company's communications is to build and develop long-term and continuous relationships. Effective communication is based on interaction which establishes and maintains mutual understanding between customer and supplier. This understanding is the basis of RM. As the 1995 Unisys report entitled *The Age of the Customer* states, 'Organizations need to make it easy for customers to not only obtain service but also to communicate their service requirements' p. 26.

Unfortunately, many of the financial companies interviewed in the Abram, Hawkes (1995) study felt that their relationship with customers is one way, from the provider to the customer. This obviously restricts the ability of customers to engage in a dialogue with their bank and also constrains the degree of personalization in any communication from the bank to them.

Interaction

One of the goals of an RM programme is that interaction between the provider and customers becomes personalized to customers' individual situations. Only 20% of respondents to the Abram, Hawkes (1995) survey regularly deliver personalized, differentiated messages to their customers based on the preference and behaviour of those customers. It appears from this survey that inadequate information, particularly regarding customers' needs and preferences, and poor knowledge of a customer's lifetime value have contributed to the development and persistence of this problem.

Customer databases, incorporating up-to-date, accurate information that is both accessible and relevant, are seen as one of the building blocks of RM. Cram (1994, p. 15) gives the example of the benefits of regional databases such as TSB Bank's 'Customer Information Database' which allows TSB Bank to 'know what has been communicated to individual customers and how they have responded'. Information systems, and databases in particular, are vital in the adoption of RM. They allow companies to share pertinent information with their customers and to hold information on customers' needs and preferences thereby accommodating a closer understanding of customers and enhanced service based on a two-way dialogue.

The Abram, Hawkes (1995, pp. 16–17) study explored the degree to which customer databases were being used within respondents' organizations. Of the organizations, 80% claimed that they held information on

- source of business;
- product holdings; and
- duration of relationship.

More significantly, less than 30% held information on customer needs and preferences and only 20% held information on customer lifetime value. These statistics seem to suggest that respondents' databases are more product orientated than customer orientated and are therefore of limited use in developing the level of interaction necessary for effective RM. This observation is underscored by the fact that 30% of respondents viewed database marketing as being 'used alongside other activities such as advertising'.

Relationship marketing and segmentation practices in the retail banking sector

Developing a relationship with customers necessitates an understanding of those customers. To understand customers better, many financial institutions are depending, to a large extent, on segmentation studies. Segmentation is the division of a total market into homogeneous subsets, each of which displays differing requirements. Theoretically, a company which segments a market down into these cohesive, homogeneous groups should then select the group or groups which are most 'attractive', i.e. those whose different needs, requirements, preferences and expectations can be met with superior value.

Therefore, to be effective, segmentation must recognize and clearly identify 'attractive' customer groups so that retail banks can target them to achieve cost-effective acquisition, cross-selling and develop customer loyalty. The question for retail banks is how to implement the segmentation process effectively from an RM viewpoint.

Kotler (1994) identifies four basic segmentation bases:

- Geographic (nation, region, county size, density, climate).
- Demographic (age, sex, family life cycle, family size, income, religion, race, social class, occupation, education).
- Psychographic (lifestyle, personality).
- Behaviouristic (purchase occasion, benefits sought, needs, preferences, usage rate, loyalty).

In effect, each of these bases should be used in varying combinations to achieve the best results. However, with regard to RM, variables such as customer needs and preferences, loyalty and the age of the relationship are particularly important in highlighting attractive and profitable customer groups. Not all groups represent the same level of profitability for a company. In developing an RM strategy companies are concerned with identifying customers who will remain loyal in the long term. The segmentation process employed should reflect this goal. For this reason the variables associated with behaviouristic segmentation are particularly relevant to RM.

Segmentation policies among UK retail financial services companies were also investigated by the Abram, Hawkes (1995) study referred to earlier. Many of the financial services companies interviewed saw segmentation as the basis for building long-term relationships. This suggests that they initially choose to interpret RM at a group rather than at an individual level. While this is an important first step towards recognizing the necessity of catering for differing customer needs, preferences and expectations, it should be noted that the ultimate goal of RM is the development of close, personal, one-to-one, mutually beneficial relationships with *individual* customers.

Although segmentation provides a basis for identifying and attracting a preferred customer base, it is difficult to develop a range of services that will appeal to all customers within a group and that will be distinct in the customer's mind from those offered by competing financial institutions targeting the same segment.

Table 6.1 Use of segmentation and targeting methods

Method	Institutions using the approach No.	%
Customer file	74	95
Acorn	26	33
Mosaic	18	23
Socioeconomic	15	19
Pinpoint	7	9
Superprofiles	6	8

Note: Some institutions use a variety of methods.

Source: Thwaites and Lee (1994).

The Abram, Hawkes (*ibid.*) study also explored usage of segmentation bases among their respondents. The majority of businesses interviewed were still dependent on traditional measures such as geography, demography and product behaviour. Those segmentation variables which are particularly important in RM are less well used (see Figure 6.2).

With regard to the methods available for segmentation, a study conducted by Thwaites and Lee (1994) indicated that the majority of financial services institutions surveyed were heavily reliant on customer files, with fewer organizations using more sophisticated proprietary techniques (see Table 6.1).

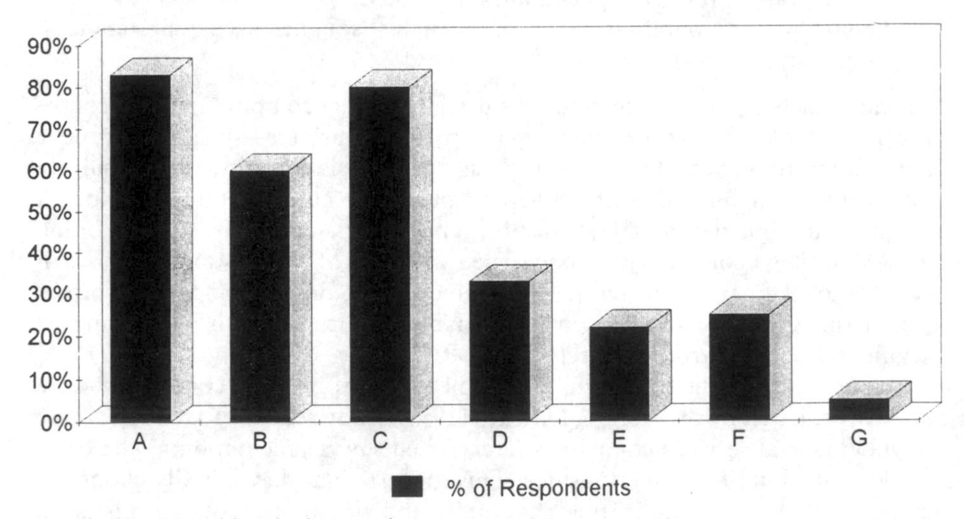

Figure 6.2 Variables used in market segmentation

Key

A Physical factors – e.g. geography
B General indicators – e.g. demography
C Product behaviour – e.g. product usage
D Customer needs
E Origin of business
F Age of relationship
G Other

Source: Abram, Hawkes (1995)

The role of service quality and customer service

Financial service providers implementing segmentation and targeting policies have realized the benefits of building lasting relationships with profitable customers and of providing further products and services, tailored to individual needs where possible. They have recognized the importance of three key requirements in pursuing this approach:

- Up-to-date, accurate information on customers' individual requirements, needs and preferences usually contained on a database.
- Interactive, two-way communications.
- High, consistent and increasingly personalized levels of service.

The first two requirements, the role of databases and interactive communications, have been discussed in the previous section. Service quality and high levels of customer service have taken on increasing significance as competing financial institutions become more alike in terms of their product and service offerings. Lacking meaningful ways (such as price, range, value, etc.) to distinguish between competing financial services companies, customers are using service as a key differentiator. Customers are demanding not just satisfactory but superior customer service:

> Competing financial institutions are much alike in the services they offer – checking accounts, credit cards, individual retirement accounts, automobile loans. Their prices are comparative, and – with branch banking and automatic teller machines (ATMs) – they often offer comparable convenience of location. They may even look alike. Where they differ is in service. Competing institutions may offer the same services, but they do not offer the same service . . . Quality of service is the great differentiator; quality of service gets – and keeps – the customer's attention.
>
> (Berry, Bennett and Brown, 1989, pp. 4–5)

Service quality and high levels of customer service are vital in achieving an offering that is distinct from that of competitors and in winning customer loyalty. Berry, Bennett and Brown (*ibid.*) refer to the results of a 1987 *American Banker* consumer survey in this regard. The results of the survey showed that of the 10% of those interviewed who had changed their principal financial business to a new institution in the prior year, 21% did so because of issues related to service or errors. The Forum Corporation (Unisys, 1995, p. 50) reports that 65% of customers switch suppliers for service quality-related issues such as lack of personal attention, while only 35% switch for product-related reasons such as price or range. Service quality, or lack of it, appears to be the main reason for customer defection.

High levels of service quality and customer service are inseparable from the concept of RM. Service excellence has a major role to play in attracting, maintaining and enhancing customer relationships. Berry, Bennett and Brown (1989) suggest that the following approach should be used to enhance the role of service excellence in developing customer relationships. This approach distinguishes between 'client' and 'customer':

- Customers may be nameless to the institution; clients cannot be nameless.
- Customers are served as part of the mass; clients are served on an individual basis and handled with tender loving care.

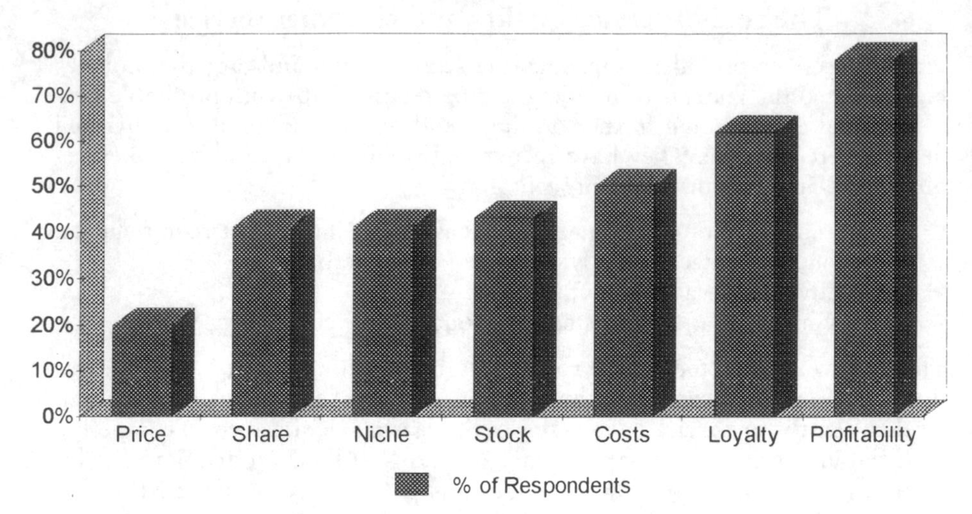

Figure 6.3 Future benefits of quality

Key

Price	Premium price
Share	Overall market share
Niche	Niche market share
Stock	Price of stock
Costs	Cost reduction
Loyalty	Loyalty/repeat business

Source: Ernst and Young (1992)

- Customers are statistics. Their needs are reflected in computer printout summaries. Clients are entities in and of themselves, and specifics about them – a demographic profile, a listing of services used, special requirements – are captured on a data base and then used to heighten their satisfaction levels.
- Customers are served by anyone who happens to be available; clients are served for their nonroutine needs by skilled professionals assigned to them – their personal banker, their personal problem solver.
- Customers have no particular reason to feel an allegience to a given financial institution; clients perceive they have a personal relationship with the institution.
- Customers probably have a good reason to look for the best price or the best deal; clients have no reason to be 'looking'.

An international quality study on the banking industry conducted by Ernst and Young (1992) suggests that retail banks are optimistic about the benefits of quality. Respondents to the survey believe that improved quality will bring significant benefits and that these benefits will grow in importance in the future. Figure 6.3 illustrates the major benefits that banks believe will occur from higher levels of quality. In addition, quality is expected to become the single most important component of a bank's reputation.

According to Ernst and Young's *Banking Industry Report* (*ibid.*), banks believe that quality can contribute to most strategic goals and are placing increased emphasis on five key parameters which have been identified as vital

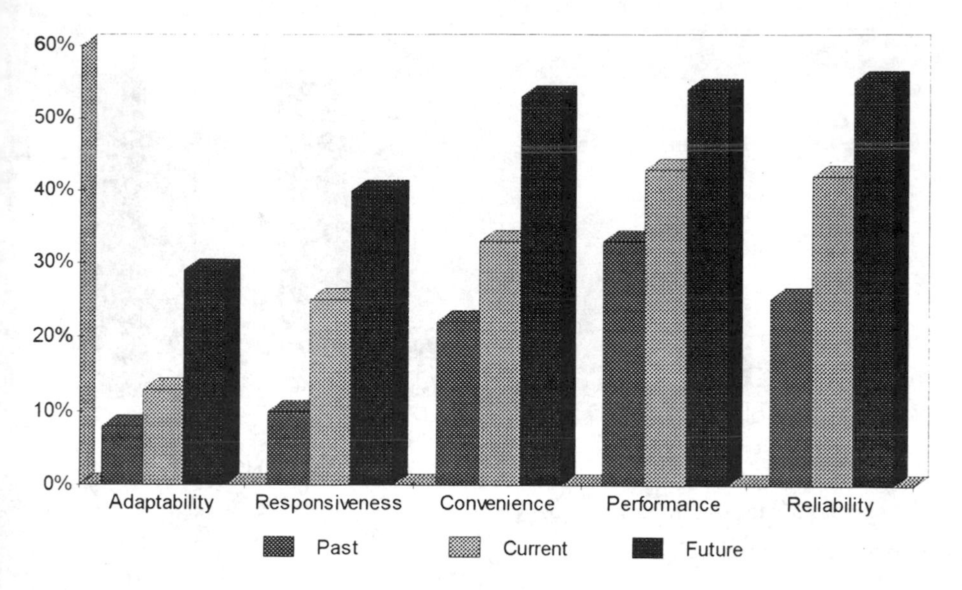

Figure 6.4 Overall quality strategy for basic products

Source: Ernst and Young (1992)

to the success of quality improvement policies (see Figure 6.4). All these parameters play a key role in retail banking:

- *Reliability*: in terms of the integrity of retail products.
- *Performance*: by adding more capability, features and functions to the product.
- *Convenience*: in making transactions or in obtaining customer service.
- *Responsiveness*: to the needs of customers regarding product features/functions.
- *Adaptability*: in terms of individual tailoring of products and services.

Banks worldwide are focusing their efforts on these five issues. Reliability in terms of the integrity of retail products and customer confidence in these products has become the most important attribute, while performance (the functions and features of a product), which was emphasized in the past, has taken on a lesser role. Adaptability, which was the least prevalent of the five parameters, has shown significant growth.

The banks surveyed as part of this international quality study are approaching the issue of service quality in various ways. The main focus is on 'doing things right the first time' and respondents intend to rely on four primary means of establishing quality in their institutions (see Figure 6.5).

Companies have differing views of customer service. Christopher, Payne and Ballantyne (1993, p. 5) believe that customer service is concerned with 'the building of bonds with customers and other markets or groups to ensure long-term relationships of mutual advantage'. Considered as such, customer service is obviously a vital component in ensuring customer satisfaction and in developing a relationship approach to marketing. Delivering high levels of

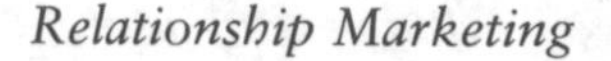

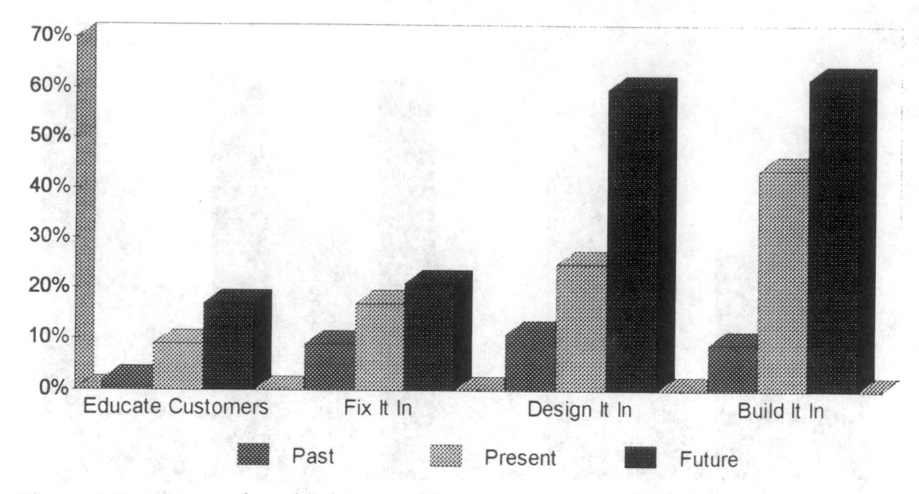

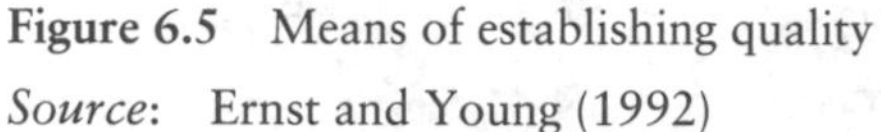
Figure 6.5 Means of establishing quality
Source: Ernst and Young (1992)

customer service necessitates a close understanding of customer needs and the provision of added value based on this understanding. There are a number of factors which contribute to the effectiveness of customer service. Design of the environment, work processes and job organization, for example, support or inhibit the ability of retail banks to deliver high levels of customer service. Therefore, the role of people and processes in the provision of service quality and customer service must be examined.

People

The contribution which employees make to the acquisition and retention of customers cannot be overemphasized. Ultimately, it is people who develop and achieve an RM strategy. For this reason, the creation of a genuine customer focus among all employees which motivates them to deliver consistent, reliable, responsive and flexible service is vital. In the context of retail banking, front-line employees *are* the company as far as the customer is concerned. To ensure that they perform to customer expectations they must be trained, prepared and motivated to serve customers on a day-to-day basis in a responsive manner. Recruitment, evaluation and reward policies should be based on responsiveness to customer needs. First Direct, for example, select banking representatives on the basis of telephone manner and empathy and ensure that all front-line personnel receive a minimum of six weeks' intensive training in product and systems, communications, telephone techniques, voice projection and listening skills before serving customers.

However, the focus should not only be on front-line employees: all staff have a role to play in the provision of customer service. Support staff should be sensitive to the fact that internal customers as well as external customers have expectations which must be satisfied. They need to understand the company's overall marketing strategy and how their functions contribute to the quality of service delivered to the customer.

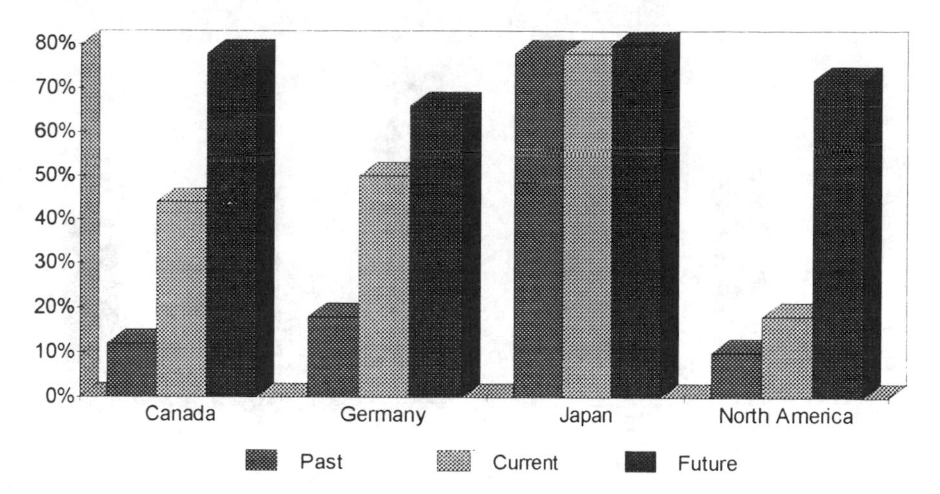

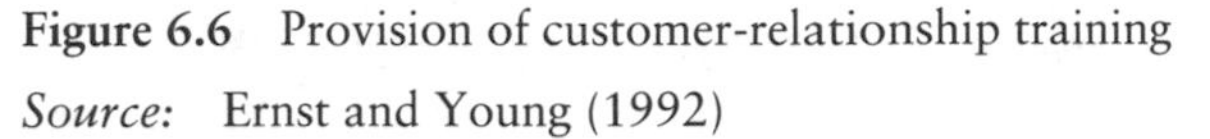

Figure 6.6 Provision of customer-relationship training

Source: Ernst and Young (1992)

Improving customer service, especially at the critical customer interface, has been an area of interest and progress for most financial service providers over the past ten years. 'Customer care' programmes are now commonplace if not always successful. The 1992 Ernst and Young report indicates that banks are increasing their emphasis on proactively providing customer-relationship training to employees with up to 60% of respondents stating that they continuously provide this type of training. However, significant differences between countries were found (see Figure 6.6). Three-quarters of all Japanese banks continually provide customer-relationship training. In contrast, German and North American banks have historically made little use of this practice but plan to increase their usage dramatically. To improve service at the customer interface further, the percentage of employees, at the point of contact with customers, empowered to make decisions (within their realm of activity and according to guidelines), is expected to grow from 35% in the past to 90% in the future.

Results from the Abram, Hawkes (1995) survey are surprising in this regard. Only 6% of respondents indicated that skilled and trained staff was a critical success factor in implementing RM. This would seem to indicate that retail banks in the UK still have some way to go in marshalling their human resources towards establishing a customer focus across all those areas of the business which impact on a customer's experience.

Process

Process management involves the procedures, task schedules, mechanisms, activities and routines by which a product or service is delivered to the customer. Traditionally, banks have had a strong process orientation in handling transactions. However, as the range of retail banking products and delivery channels has grown, the use of modern technology and process re-engineering to improve and simplify processes both for banks themselves and for

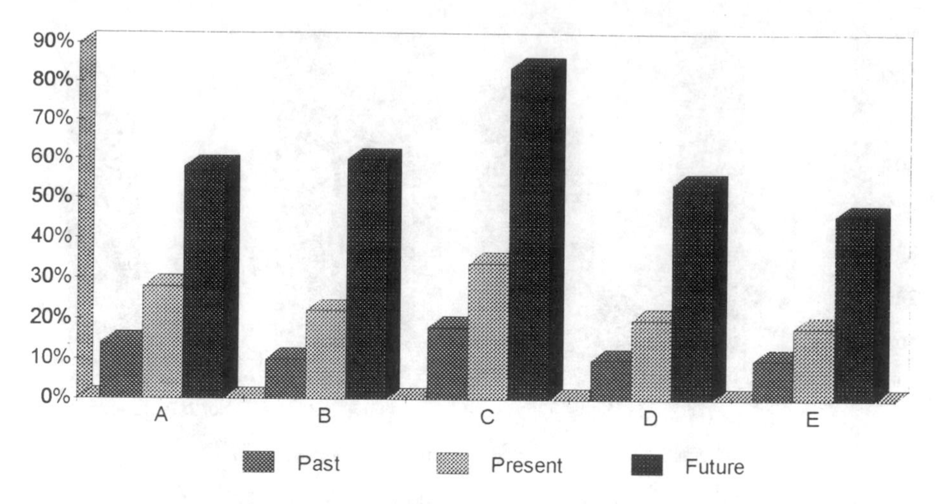

Figure 6.7 Usage of process improvement techniques

Key
A Process capability studies
B Process value analysis
C Process simplification
D Process cycle time analysis
E Statistical process control

Source: Ernst and Young (1992)

customers has become of paramount importance. For example, by reconfiguring the way in which they deliver service through the introduction of ATMs, banks have been able to free staff to handle more complex customer needs by diverting cash-only customers to the ATMs. Process simplification is essential and must be implemented in conjunction with and aided by new technologies which provide the opportunity to displace much of the paper, create automatic work-flow control and reduce banks' heavy cost of data entry. Figure 6.7 illustrates the process improvement tools which have been and are in use among respondents to the Ernst and Young (1992) *International Quality Study – Banking Industry Report*. Clearly the application of process improvement techniques is at a very early stage. On the other hand, the use of these tools has already grown and is projected to grow at an even greater rate in the future.

Best practice in the retail banking sector

Progressive companies are constantly seeking out information on and learning from customers, competitors and successful practitioners in the marketplace. New practices, methods and techniques implemented by 'best practice' companies in any sector can be utilized by retail banks to provide the basis for improvements in effectiveness and efficiency. Likewise, there are lessons to be learnt from identifying the characteristics of successful and unsuccessful RM practitioners. To elicit possible role models among RM practitioners, the

Abram, Hawkes survey sought respondents' evaluations of 'best practice' companies in the industry.

Of the respondents, 60% felt that, at present, there were no organizations undertaking RM as they perceived it. The majority of these respondents did however believe that several organizations were making progress towards implementing RM, albeit not fully. First Direct and American Express were by far the most commonly quoted. It is worth while noting that the majority of those financial services companies perceived as being at the 'leading edge' with regard to RM practice (First Direct and Direct Line in addition to American Express and Coutts) are recent entrants to or 'high profile' within the financial services market.

First Direct was launched in October 1989 as a direct banking and financial services organization providing a full person-to-person banking service by telephone, 24 hours a day, 365 days a year. First Direct's strategy has focused on attracting and retaining upscale customers who are frustrated with conventional banking systems. Moving away from traditional retail banking models towards providing personal, 24-hour, full banking services by telephone has allowed First Direct, and its parent company, Midland Bank, to offer an attractive alternative to this market segment. First Direct's success in meeting the needs and expectations of this segment is reflected in the growth of its account base (10,000 to 12,000 new cheque accounts opened every month), significant levels of referrals from existing customers (25% of customer acquisition is by word of mouth; 93% of customers whose main account is with First Direct profess to have recommended First Direct to someone else) and high levels of conversion and retention (an estimated 74% of customers change their main account to First Direct within three months of opening an account with the company).

First Direct believe that their success rests in their ability to sustain competitive advantage through service quality. In practice, First Direct have achieved superior service quality by

- creating a delivery mechanism which provides higher quality, more conveniently and at a lower cost;
- creating a corporate culture designed to support high-quality service and enable rapid response to changing needs; and
- developing systems and technology which enable the company to provide service quality and deliver the information necessary to manage the business better than the competition.

The future of relationship marketing in the retail banking sector

RM in the retail banking sector in the UK is at a crossroads. Most retail banks have adopted at least some of the principles of RM (see Figure 6.8). For example, 25% of banks surveyed in the Abram, Hawkes (1995) study claimed to have made a high level of progress in customer retention planning, 65% a medium level of progress, while 10% reported a low level of progress. However, it is unclear whether this is the result of genuine strategic intent (in which case the future seems bright) or of a series of *ad hoc*, reactive tactics (in which case the future of RM is in some doubt).

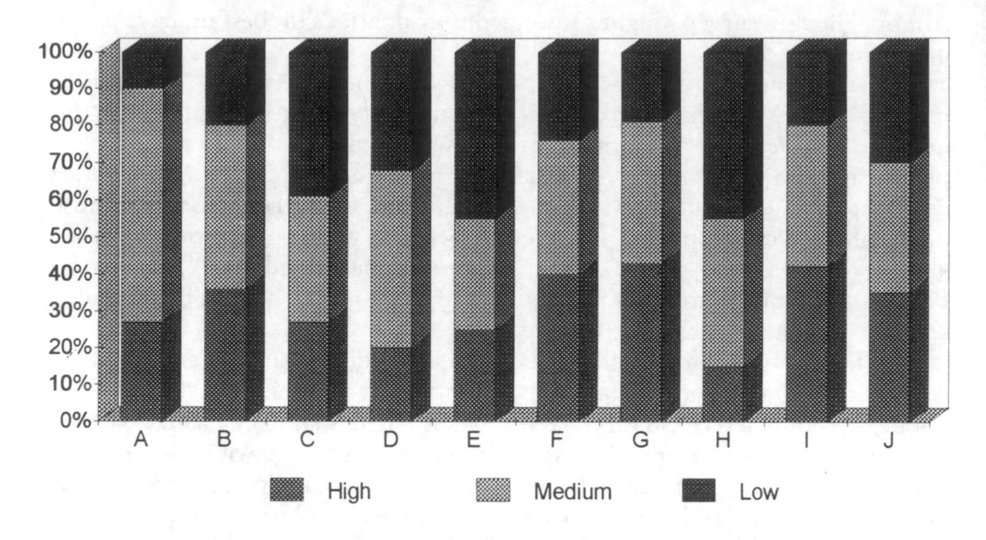

Figure 6.8 Progress in implementing components of RM

Key
A Customer retention planning
B Appointment of relationship managers
C Cross-selling
D A customer-based information system
E Use of the database for direct marketing
F Two-way customer dialogue
G Relationship rather than a transaction orientation
H Segmented approach to customers
I Measures of customer profitability
J Delivering personalized and/or differentiated communication

Source: Abram, Hawkes (1995)

To date, according to the Abram, Hawkes survey, retail banks feel that they have made progress in the following areas:

- Ability to segment customers (41%)
- Use of database for direct marketing (41%)
- Development of a customer-based information system (38%)
- Cross-selling (38%)

More problematic areas or areas of low progress were judged to be the following:

- Measuring customer profitability (42%)
- Establishing a relationship rather than a transaction orientation (42%)
- Developing two-way customer dialogue (42%)
- Delivering personalized communication (38%)

The latter areas will have to be the focus of strategic planning and development in the future if retail banks in the UK are serious about introducing a relationship orientation into their marketing practice.

According to the Abram, Hawkes survey, retail banks are willing to take up the challenge that RM represents. Of respondents, 55% believed that focusing on individual's needs was key in building long-term relationships in the future, while 40% indicated that service quality was of greater importance. Respondents felt that the two most important factors in implementing RM were as follows:

- Commitment of senior management (77%)
- Modern information systems (54%)

RM is concerned with changing business practices and it is therefore vital that senior management commit the time, resources and energy to its successful implementation. Technology too has a role to play in the areas of communications, information and business processes. The Abram, Hawkes study states that priority areas for retail banks will include the following:

- Understanding the role and importance of information: determining what is needed, how it will be used, and how it will be maintained and accessed.
- Developing appropriate information systems.
- Establishing genuine customer focus across all parts of the business.
- Potentially, establishing process rather than function-based organization structures, removing the traditionally isolated, and often badly informed, marketing department.
- Setting measurable objectives by which to assess the organization's progress in building lasting customer relationships.

Information, and customer feedback in particular, will be of critical importance in determining those business practices which must be changed in order to achieve a relationship orientation among retail banks. Smith (1994) outlines the value that Abbey National has realized from utilizing customer feedback in developing customer relationship and customer loyalty programmes. While the ultimate objective of both quality and RM programmes should be 'zero defections' and zero complaints, Abbey National has found that data obtained from customer complaints are important in providing detailed information on key customer concerns relating to retail banking. The group has also discovered that effective and efficient complaint management can actually help to cement a relationship.

A survey conducted by Abbey National indicated that complaining customers' main concerns were

- prompt acknowledgement;
- confidence that the matter will be resolved;
- professionalism of staff;
- courtesy of staff;
- helpfulness and friendliness of staff; and
- knowledge of the overall time for resolution of the complaint.

Based on the results of this survey, Abbey National have implemented a complaints management process which has had a significant impact on customer retention and provided the group with valuable information on the reasons for customer dissatisfaction and account closure.

Customer information in all its forms has to be the basis for the implementation of relationship-building programmes by retail banks. It is only with a complete and thorough knowledge of customer needs, wants and expectations that effective RM can be achieved.

References

Abram, Hawkes (1995) *Relationship Marketing in the Financial Services Industry*, Abram, Hawkes, London.

Berry, L.L., Bennett, D.R. and Brown, C.W. (1989) *Service Quality – A Profit Strategy for Financial Institutions*, Dow Jones-Irwin, Homewood, Ill.

Buzzell, R.D. and Gale, B.T. (1987) *The PIMS Principles*, Free Press, New York.

Christopher, M., Payne, A. and Ballantyne, D. (1993) *Relationship Marketing – Bringing Quality, Customer Service and Marketing Together*, Butterworth-Heinemann, Oxford.

Council on Financial Competition (1995) *Perfecting Customer Retention and Recovery – Overview of Economics and Proven Strategies*, Advisory Board Company, Washington, DC.

Cram, T. (1994) *The Power of Relationship Marketing – Keeping Customers for Life*, Pitman, London.

Ernst and Young (1992) *International Quality Study – Banking Industry Report*, Ernst and Young, Cleveland, OH.

Kotler, P. (1994) *Marketing Management – Analysis, Planning and Control*, Prentice-Hall, Englewood Cliffs, NJ.

Smith, J. (1994) Successfully handling customer complaints, *Customer Service Management*, Issue 2, pp. 41–2.

Thwaites, D. and Lee, S.C.I. (1994) Direct marketing in the financial services industry, *Journal of Marketing Management*, Vol. 10, pp. 377–90.

Unisys Corporation (1995) *The Age of the Customer*, Unysis Corporation, Washington, DC.

7

Corporate banking

Charles Schell

The combined pressures of disintermediation, deregulation and industry restructuring have helped to redefine the nature and importance of bank–client relationships. The financial services sector has lost its clearly defined roles of providers and users of services, and now even moderately sophisticated corporate customers are able to develop in-house skills once the province of bankers. In some cases customers even compete with banks, selling their specialist treasury skills to suppliers and customers. This combination of environmental and competitive pressures has reopened the concept of RM for redefinition.

Extending the marriage metaphor proposed by Levitt (1983) and Dwyer, Schurr and Oh (1987), it is difficult to determine if partners to corporate banking relationships are casual, monogamist, polygamist or even serial monogamist. Bank relationships have been traditionally characterized as monogamous, with customer relationships often spanning generations. More recently corporate relationships, in particular those of larger firms, would be characterized as polygamous, with concurrent relationships developed with more than one main relationship bank and secondary relationships with regionally or functionally specialized banks. A subset of monogamous customers, perhaps as large as 8% according to Wood *et al.* (1995a), can be described as monogamous but prone to itchy feet, switching relationships frequently, often expressing an equal lack of fulfilment in their new relationship. The casual, or transactional relationship model may be more relevant for an increasing proportion of businesses, as credit relationships are perhaps becoming less significant than service (fee-based) relationships. Certainly, many relationships which would have once been considered stable and monogamist are now characterized as short term and informal, with a number of financial suppliers providing specialist services in niches which represent functional or regional strengths. Uncertainty about the nature of bank–client relationships leads to interesting problems of valuing relationships and measuring the cost of or returns to relationship building.

The concept of a stable and monogamistic bank–client relationship is predicated on the social contract which obliges the client to channel a majority share of banking transactions through its main relationship bank in exchange

Table 7.1 Recent performance of the UK clearing banks (£ billion)

	1989	1990	1991	1992	1993
Income:					
Interest income	42.0	45.4	40.3	36.4	30.3
Interest expense	(31.1)	(34.4)	(34.4)	(24.8)	(18.8)
Margin	10.9	11.0	11.4	11.6	11.5
Commission	4.6	5.0	6.0	6.5	7.1
Other income	2.2	2.3	2.5	2.8	3.4
	6.8	7.3	8.5	9.3	10.5
	17.7	18.3	19.9	20.9	22.0
Operation expenses:					
Staff costs	(6.9)	(7.2)	(7.5)	(7.7)	(7.9)
Other	(4.9)	(5.3)	(5.9)	(5.9)	(6.1)
	(11.8)	(12.5)	(13.4)	(13.6)	(14.0)
Bad debts	(3.7)	(3.9)	(5.2)	(5.9)	(4.4)
Exceptional items	(2.4)	(0.1)	(0.1)	(0.4)	(0.2)
Associated companies	0.3	0.1	0.1	0.1	0.1
Profit before tax	0.1	1.9	1.3	1.1	3.5

for future support in case of difficulties. Obviously, this intertemporal contract requires trust on the part of the client, since the bank's side of the contract is not exercised until long after the client has done its part. Similarly, the bank needs a greater than average return from its established relationships in order to fund the relationship commitments it is undertaking within the contract. If trust on the part of the client, or the returns to the bank from the relationship do not exist, the relationship is clearly devalued.

Traditional banking relationships could be understood and valued as a mixed deposit–credit relationship, with longer-term deposits providing a stability to the relationship which could be expected to extend beyond the term of the lending relationship. Wood (1975) suggested that bank relationships have tended to reflect the increased importance of the credit relationship, whereby banks and their customers established a relationship over repeated or serial loan transactions. Credit-based corporate banking relationships are discussed below. Table 7.1 illustrates the relative decline in the credit revenues as a contributor to UK bank performance over the last few years, a condition which suggests that the relative growth in fee income (commissions and other income) in corporate banking has made credit-driven relationships less important than transaction income. This may be short-sighted for, as will be shown below, returns to transaction business are highly correlated with longer-term bank–customer relationships.

The trend towards lower returns from lending activity have been compounded by increased bad debt provisions and lending restrictions required by the Basle guidelines. At the same time, increased competitive pressure in the financial services industry and restructuring within banks have put new pressures on conventional relationship development.

Arguably, the cement which has held together bank–customer relationships may be weaker than in recent history and the tendency towards multiple bank relations suggests a move from traditional bank relationships towards a transactional model. In this chapter the basis of the traditional credit-based corporate banking relationship is examined alongside alternative models which have been proposed. We will also look at impediments to relationship development, examples of practice among UK lenders and some prescriptions for the future development of RM.

Credit-based relationships

The value of a corporate banking relationship has been described as a function of the higher returns available to established relationship bankers and the reduced risk which results from improved information about the client. Greenbaum, Kanatas and Venezia (1989) examined the value to a bank of a repeat lending relationship with a corporate customer. They suggested that lending rates tended to be higher for established relationship customers than new customers, since competitor banks will often offer rates lower than their cost of funds in order to attract new business, with the hope of charging higher rates on repeat business. Repeat lending to existing credit customers will also result in lower risk of default, since an existing relationship provides customer information which is not available for new customers nor, for that matter, available to competitors. They also suggested that the higher cost of borrowing from the established relationship bank would lead to an increased probability of customer defections, and hence the longer the duration of a relationship, the shorter the expected remaining duration of the relationship. This suggests that the bank–customer relationship has an option-like nature, with banks accepting lower returns and higher expected rates of default from new clients in order to benefit in subsequent years from higher loan rates and lower default rates. Based on the above, it would be expected that banks would tend to regard a credit-based relationship as a wasting asset with a strictly finite duration. The credit-based relationship may be contrasted with debt-security markets where the bank–customer relationship is purely transactional, with debt priced exogenously.

Sharpe (1990) further develops the idea that customer relationships arise in corporate banking because repeated lending allows a bank to learn more about its customers than is possible for competitor banks. The creation of this information advantage produces informational asymmetries between bank competitors, allowing the client to be 'informationally captured'. This effectively produces a monopoly return for the relationship bank, at least in the short term. Information asymmetry means that companies may recognize that other banks offer lower-cost loans, but they are unable to signal their firm's superior quality to the alternative providers. Competitor banks may thus only skim off better-quality customers from each other at the cost of attracting an equal share of less desirable ones.

Many of the widely reported problems in relationship banking stem from the poor understanding of the nature of the credit–customer relationship. To a large extent, customer dissatisfaction with 'value for money' in its banking relationship can be attributed to high expectations of a poorly defined contract, expectations often fuelled by the banks' own advertising campaigns. A credit relationship may be described as a combination of a limited group of formal contracts and a much broader set of informal understandings. Principal among these informal understandings is an implicit obligation of the firm to provide the bank with a large proportion of transaction business in exchange for future support when the company faces difficulties. In a survey of UK bank relationships, Wood *et al.* (1995b) found that 25% of over 1,500 respondent companies did not feel that their main relationship bank would provide dependable support in a crisis, 18% did not feel that their bank would stick to the spirit of its commitments and only 25% of respondents agreed that a relationship meant paying over the odds for some products.

These problems are largely anticipated by Morgan and Hunt's (1994) commitment-trust theory. Of the precursors to a relationship commitment and trust they identified three which seem to be particularly important in the case of commercial banking:

1. *Relationship termination costs* influence commitment to a relationship. These are probably better understood as switching costs, or the combined costs of ending a relationship and of establishing an alternative relationship. High switching costs have been used to explain customer loyalty, particularly when allegorical proof (Forum of Private Business, 1994; Wood *et al.*, 1992a; 1995a) suggests customers remain loyal to a main relationship bank despite relatively high levels of dissatisfaction. Wood *et al.* (1995a) suggest that nearly three times as many firms plan to change main relationship within the two years than actually do. For the bank, the unamortized value of early-stage investment in the relationship will make switching particularly unattractive. Logically, commitment would be expected to be greatest for the bank in the early stages of the relationship where the cost of termination is greater, while the customer would become more committed over time, as the promise of relationship benefit accrues. This assumes that customer trust matches bank commitment.
2. *Shared values* are considered to be a precursor to both commitment and trust. Banking tends to have clearly established internal 'norms' which are most recently manifest as credit culture. Customers are less likely to have a clear and homogeneous set of beliefs, and the common or shared set of beliefs about behaviours and goals which banks and customers would both ascribe to are limited. Clearly, banks and their customers do not share a culture, common underlying assumptions or even a strong desire for affiliation. Shared values, when they do exist, are likely to be manifest as behaviours which result from a requirement for compliance.
3. *Communication.* Trust requires formal and informal sharing of information between firms, and in a banking relationship the timing and control of information is probably more important than in any other industry. The bank–customer relationship requires imperfect balance of information, since the terms of exchange of information are important in defining the relationship. The banking relationship is founded upon asymmetry of information between bank and customer. The bank has superior information

about products, capital market conditions, alternative financial products, foreign exchange and increasingly complex financial products, while company finance directors and treasurers have a better understanding of company conditions, markets and future prospects. The bank's ability to understand and 'price' the inherent risk in a customer's business is the principal differentiation factor between banks in a credit relationship.

An additional condition, opportunistic behaviour, mitigates this trust. Opportunistic behaviour, defined by Williamson (1975) as 'self-interest seeking with guile', leads to decreased trust and ultimately a lack of commitment. In banking, opportunistic behaviour may be exemplified by customers' perception that banks are slow to pass along interest-rate cuts or the benefits of efficiencies which result from technology, such as shorter cheque-clearing periods. Recent controversy regarding European payment systems has provided another good example of this. Morgan and Hunt (1994) suggest that opportunistic behaviour resulted in decreased commitment because of loss of trust.

In theory, the credit relationship can be valued in roughly the same way as any other long-lived asset by both the bank and its customer. Essentially, each party to the relationship would seek to assess the net present value of incremental cash flows which result from the investment in a close relationship. The use of a discounted cash-flow approach to most long-term relationships encourages banks to use commitment and arrangement fees and cross-selling of related bank products like insurance and risk management products in order to load more revenue into the early stages of the credit relationship, providing a significantly greater net present value.

Unfortunately, the intentions of partners in the relationship are difficult to observe and even more difficult to measure because of the asymmetry of information discussed above. As bank business shifts from credit relationships to a larger proportion of largely transactional fee-based service business the cost and returns to a relationship need to be more carefully considered.

Contingent commitment banking

The traditional credit relationship has in many cases been radically changed by the increased practice of contingent commitment banking. These transactions involve banks selling promises to supply specific financial services in the event of certain events occurring. For example, the bank may provide loan commitments, interest-rate swaps and forward exchange contracts, products which may be off-balance sheet for the bank because of their probabilistic nature. This type of bank activity is most significantly different from traditional credit relationship banking because individual transaction contracts make explicit the implicit promises of credit relationship banking.

Holland (1994) suggests that banks which have existing credit relationships are able to exploit any information advantage which arises from a close relationship, allowing the bank to sell promises at a lower price than possible for competitor transaction-orientated banks and exchange-based markets for futures and securities. This would suggest that main relationship banks would be expected to provide explicit contracts according to the contingent commitment model discussed above, as well as traditional, implicitly guaranteed support in a more traditional credit relationship.

In a banking industry where multiple bank relationships are seen as a norm, even for most medium-sized corporate clients, a change from credit-driven relationships to fee-income-driven relationships does not automatically rule out positive returns from relationship development. For the bank, a relationship offers an implicit right of first refusal for fee business, an opportunity to develop new derivative products to meet a specialized requirement and development of informational superiority in loan pricing.

Impediments to forming a relationship

Disintermediation

For the largest firms, the information asymmetry upon which the relationship may be dependent may be lost as increasingly sophisticated company treasury teams are able to develop in-house skills which rival those of the best banks. In addition, the information asymmetry which provides the relationship bank with better data than competitor financial service providers may be lost owing to the improved quality of information about the firm which results from increased capital market and public scrutiny.

Deregulation

Changes in the banking industry itself have encouraged company financial directors to consider alternative sources of financial services, including insurance companies, investment and merchant banks and even (in the case of KPMG in New York) financial intermediaries like accounting firms.

Changes in bank culture

Recent changes in commercial banking have also thrown up a number of impediments to forming and sustaining relationships. Perrien, Filiatrault and Ricard (1992) identified eight specific areas which create problems in bank relationships, of which credit culture and norms, the organization and management of bank lending officers and the restructuring of credit controls are particularly relevant.

Relationship development is often at odds with bank credit norms, particularly the need to balance a portfolio, and to monitor and manage aggregate exposure across sectoral and geographic divisions. Bank customers usually do not understand the bank's credit standards, nor do they easily accept the logic of the bank's portfolio approach to risk management when it affects their particular case.

The individual relationships between bank managers and company directors seems to have been a major casualty of restructuring within banks. The loss of many experienced relationship managers during successive rounds of 'downsizing' and turnover among account managers has led to a loss of relationships. Directors of most firms surveyed by Wood *et al.* (1995a) agreed that their relationship was with the bank manager rather than the bank, and where the relationship was with the manager, the respondents were significantly more

Table 7.2 Bank managers have a recognized role in relationship building

Relationship with	Understand business		Quality of advice	
	Hardly	Very well	Poor	Excellent
Manager	17.1	46.3	17.1	42.1
Bank	27.1	33.8	22.8	35.8

likely to agree that the bank understood the company's business, and that the quality of advice provided by the bank was of reasonable quality.

At the same time, it is generally recognized that relationship managers within banks have a reduced role in evaluating risk and approving credit. Where the customer recognizes that the manager does not have a significant role in approving credit, the value of the relationship may be reduced (Table 7.2).

Credit-driven bank cultures and the increasing centralization of credit functions within banks are probably the most important impediments to relationship development. Credit policies tend to emphasize short-term profitability, while customers see relationship building as a long-term process. As pointed out above, front-loading a credit relationship with fees will improve short-term returns and reduce exposure, although this will be clearly recognized as opportunistic behaviour by customers. It would be simplistic to suggest that credit culture should be abandoned, although it seems reasonable to propose a balanced application of this approach, one which accounts for both short-term exigency and longer-term relationships.

Customer propensity to change banks

While the banks seem less capable of supporting stable customer relationships, corporate customers are both less reliant on their relationship banks and more prone to multiple or casual relationships. In spite of a devaluation of relationships, businesses are less faithful to their main relationship bank. If half of the businesses who claim that they will change bank actually do change, banks will have to replace their customers completely about once every seven years.

Wood *et al.* (1995a) asked respondents whether they planned to change their main relationship bank in the next two years, and 38% of the sample said that they would definitely or possibly change bank. Experience suggests that a significant proportion of this group will not change, although about 22% did report that they had changed bank in the last five years.

Industry sources suggest that this figure is still higher than actual experience. Perhaps a more significant, albeit more subtle source of defection is the movement to multiple banking arrangements. About 18% of respondents said that they were dealing with more banks than previously and 10% said that they were reducing the share of business which they gave to their relationship bank. The dissatisfaction which leads to planned defection seems to be more related to dissatisfaction with a bank manager or lack of understanding of the business rather than levels of existing or new service charges or credit rationing. The scale on the left in Figure 7.1 represents the strength of satisfaction, with 5 high and 1 very low.

In reality, many will not change, because they do not find a better replacement, and among those who do change, a significant proportion will change

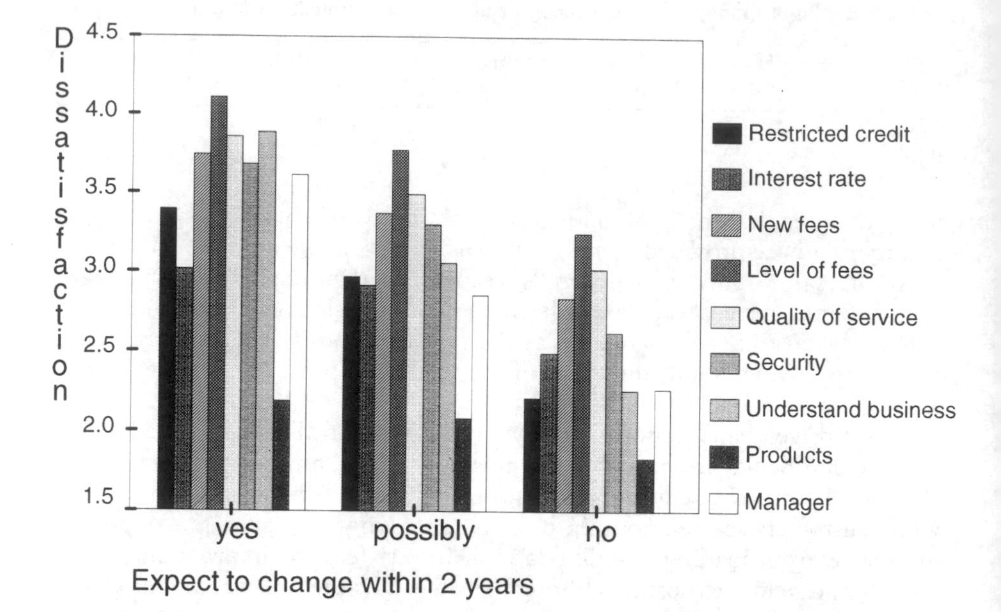

Figure 7.1 While customers who say they will definitely change are generally more dissatisfied, manager and understanding of business seem to be deciding factors

more than once. Wood *et al.* (1995a) called these frequent changers serial monogamists, since they tend to have high expectations of their relationships, and despite a poor track record in previous relationships, continue to look for a stable relationship. In Figure 7.2, these changers are represented as the intersection set of dissatisfied bank customers who plan to change in the next couple of years, and bank customers who have already changed in the past couple of years yet are still dissatisfied.

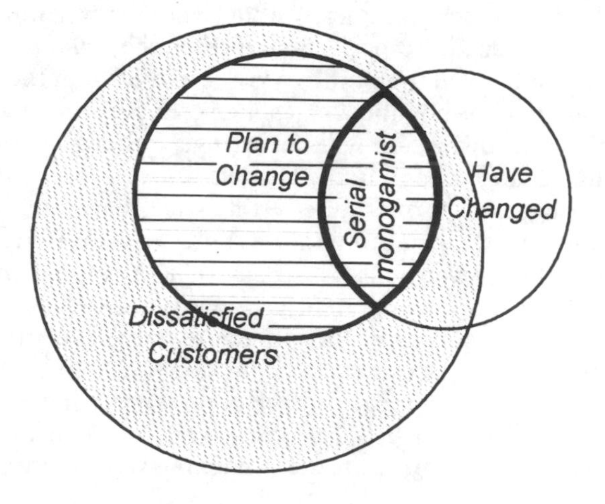

Figure 7.2 Segmentation by switching intention

Table 7.3 Switching banks improved satisfaction with understanding of business and relationship with manager – but only for those who don't plan to switch again

Per cent who agree with the following statements	Total %	Serial monogamists	Customers who changed, are now loyal
Service was a problem, is still a problem	37.7	45.1	32.6
(Service less of a problem with new bank)	(11.7)	(7.8)	(15.6)
Problem with old manager, problem with new manager	28.5	36.0	24.2
(Happier with new manager)	(18.9)	(14.0)	(22.0)
Level of fees were too high, still too high with new bank	40.3	49.1	34.8
(Fees less of a problem)	(9.9)	(9.4)	(11.1)
Bank didn't understand business, new bank doesn't either	23.7	29.2	23.9
(New bank understands business)	(17.1)	(10.4)	(21.6)

The research suggested that these serial monogamists might represent as much as 8.5% of bank customers and up to 13% of small business customers (classified by turnover less than £2 million). Again, the ability to build relationships with the bank manager and to establish understanding and trust differentiated the serial monogamists and those who settled in their new relationship.

In this case, there is a clear indication that the serial monogamists remain significantly more dissatisfied with the quality of service that they receive from their new bank, the relationship that they have with their new manager, the level of fees and the new bank's understanding of their business. These factors

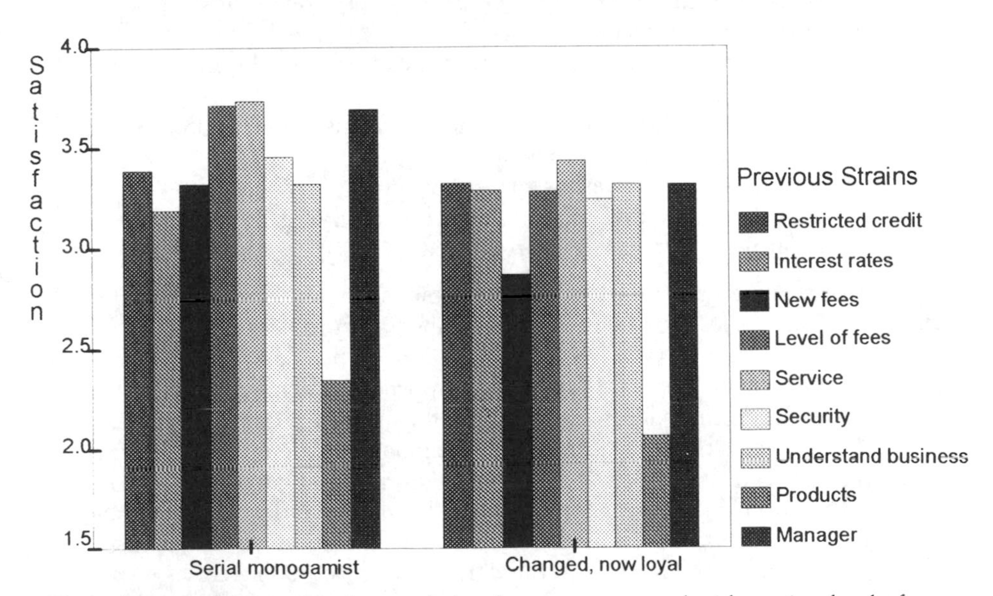

Figure 7.3 Serial monogamists tended to be more concerned with service, level of fees and the manager in their previous relationship

distinguish serial monogamists from the group who have changed and do not plan to change with relatively high statistical significance (Table 7.3). This relationship is also illustrated by looking at the mean levels of satisfaction in Figure 7.3.

Clearly, there is limited scope for the banks to compete on the supply and cost of credit, or even the cost of fees. The support for relationships seems to be the area in which banks can make a difference, although it seems that the match of strategic demands and performance has been less than perfect.

Relationship management in practice

The underestimation of the importance of the client–manager relationship seems to be highlighted by allegorical proof. Customers report that managers from different parts of the same bank will make separate calls on the company, often only days apart and make contradictory claims. A customer will make an inquiry to head office, but head office cannot react because it has no access to non-financial records of the relationship, nor can it identify the individual relationship manager responsible for the customer's account. Cross-selling opportunities are lost because information available to a single manager is not shared for fear of jeopardizing the relationship, and profitable relationships are not identified because performance is measured by transaction rather than relationship.

Perrien, Filiatrault and Ricard (1993) asked a sample of 57 corporate account managers from six banks to identify and rank barriers to relationship development between banks and their corporate customers. Of the 29 factors identified, the top ten were

1. staff turnover is too high;
2. focus on short-term profitability versus long-term relationships;
3. the workload of the account manager;
4. inadequate decentralized authority to match responsibility;
5. lack of training of personnel;
6. assessment of the account manager's job on transactional criteria;
7. inadequate training for relationship managers;
8. lack of an effective long-term strategy/vision;
9. the size of the account manager's portfolio is too large; and
10. the organization is transaction orientated.

By category, human resource management, manager job deficiencies and bank culture and strategies ranked as the most important problems.

Corporate markets may be segmented by size of business, product requirements of the firm (a clearly transactional approach), demands of the bank's delivery system (branch dependence), as well as industry characteristics. Holland (1994) reports that the large UK clearing banks have up to 1,000 regular long-established relationships with UK or multinational corporate customers. A typical relationship banking structure might involve industry segmentation, with up to 100 firms in each industrial segment and seven to ten relationship managers per industrial team or about 10–15 firms per manager.

Service delivery systems need to accommodate the complex problem of meeting the demands of diverse corporate business which vary by size as well as product demands. The role and future of branch banking in corporate lending remains an open question, with the development of corporate branches in the last few years moving control, decisions, contracts and business away from the small branch to the corporate branch. While this centralization of corporate staff encourages the development of specialized skills and focus on corporate business, it requires rebuilding a relationship which has been disrupted. Most of the UK clearers have moved to corporate branches for mid-corporate and larger clients, with each centralizing business in 60–100 corporate branches. The smaller business sector will probably continue to be managed through local branches or, in exceptional cases, through specialist small business centres in corporate branches.

Information technology strategy continues to be a key factor in banks' ability to provide a differentiable service. The accessibility and content of client records are particularly important as marketing tools, especially when a relationship can be characterized as a series of discrete transactions linked by a common understanding of customer needs. Where a relationship manager is a primary point of contact with the bank, it would seem obvious that the manager's name is somehow attached to the client records so that direct inquiries can be referred back to the individual manager, or cross-selling can be co-ordinated with the manager. There seems to be little evidence that any of the UK clearing banks have this capability.

The future of relationship banking

Relationships management in banking is clearly an asymmetrical process, with customers following the initiatives of their bankers. Criticisms of the bank's lack of effectiveness in generating effective relationships typically arise from recognition that relationships are seen as a tactical measure used to generate incremental sales rather than a real strategic initiative. The lack of real commitment to relationship banking stems from the short-term profit requirements of management and shareholders and the lack of trust which this approach engenders.

Banks' relationships may be segmented into three classes as defined by Holland (1994): the top-tier relationship banks which take the largest share of client banking business; the second tier which consists of a mixture of specialist banks dominant in one world region, financial centre or specialist service (also characterized as first-tier in waiting); and the third tier, transaction-orientated banks. The first-tier banks attract the most stable, least price-sensitive business, but also the highest costs and longest-term commitments. The second-tier banks pursue a relationship strategy which is typically a lower-cost, more focused (or niche) strategy, and the third-tier banks follow a strategy which seeks lowest costs and possibly higher volumes. Banks will need to make a strategic decision as to which level of relationship they aspire.

For banks which adopt RM as a strategic imperative, implementation issues are likely to include the following:

- Careful selection of targeted market segments, since not all customers seek relationship benefits. Perrien, Filiatrault and Ricard (1993) use the example

of motor dealers, who are particularly transaction orientated, as poor targets for relationship development. It is necessary to identify customers who are best served by the option-like contract implicit in relationship banking.
- Bank policy needs to reflect the demands of RM. In some cases this means refocusing profit centres so that customers are seen as profit drivers rather than products or transactions.
- The bank credit culture needs to be adjusted to accommodate the longer gestation periods which relationship building requires and this needs to be communicated to bank staff through cultural adjustment and training. Rewards need to be based on relationship indicators as well as profit indicators, with factors such as customer retention rates and cross-selling included.
- Authority within banks needs to be reallocated to the level at which relationships are formed. Credit decisions, in particular, should be at least monitored by relationship managers, so that portfolio considerations and credit management objectives are more fairly balanced against long-term relationship support. This is a significant and fundamental change in policy for most banks, but it can be justified by the higher returns and lower risk inherent in a longer-term relationship.
- Since relationships are typically formed between people rather than institutions, manager–client relationships need to be supported. This may mean reducing the turnover of account managers or at least improving the continuity of relationships.
- BDO Binder Hamlyn (1994) also suggest recruiting bankers who are also business people. The trust-commitment basis for a relationship requires shared values, and the difference in cultures may prove an important barrier to relationship forming. The way that bankers are recruited and trained would obviously need to be reconsidered.

Considering the scope and nature of the strategic demands above, it is unlikely that many banks will commit to full-scale adoption of corporate relationship banking. By the same token, it seems unlikely that businesses will commit themselves to relationships which may be characterized as totally monogamistic. It is probably better that they do not, since companies, like individuals, prefer a certain amount of variety. Unfortunately, this search for variety represents high real and opportunity costs for banks, particularly when relationship development costs are not recovered during the life of the relationship.

References

BDO Binder Hamlyn (1994) *Special Briefing* No. 89, BDO Binder Hamlyn, London.

Dwyer, F.R., Schurr, P.H. and Oh, S. (1987) Developing buyer–seller relationships, *Journal of Marketing*, Vol. 51, pp. 11–27.

Forum of Private Business (1994) *Small Businesses and their Banks 1994 – Report One*, Forum of Private Business, Knutsford, Cheshire.

Greenbaum, S.I., Kanatas, G. and Venezia, I. (1989) Loan pricing under the bank–client relationship, *Journal of Banking and Finance*, Vol. 13, pp. 221–35.

Holland, J. (1988) *Bank/Corporate Relationships. ACCA Research Report* 12, Certified Accountant Publications, London.

Holland, J. (1994) Bank lending relationships and the complex nature of bank–corporate relations, *Journal of Business Finance and Accounting*, Vol. 21, pp. 367–93.
Levitt, T. (1983) After the sale is over . . . *Harvard Business Review*, September–October, pp. 87–93.
Morgan, R.M. and Hunt, S.D. (1994) The commitment-trust theory of relationship marketing, *Journal of Marketing*, Vol. 58, pp. 20–38.
Perrien, J., Filiatrault, P. and Ricard, L. (1992) Relationship marketing and commercial banking: a critical analysis, *International Journal of Bank Marketing*, Vol. 10, pp. 25–35.
Perrien, J., Filiatrault, P. and Ricard, L. (1993) The implementation of relationship marketing in commercial banking, *Industrial Marketing Management*, Vol. 22, pp. 141–9.
Sharpe, S.A. (1990) Asymmetrical information, bank lending and implicit contracts: a stylized model of customer relationships, *Journal of Finance*, Vol. XLV, pp. 1069–87.
Smith, A.M. (1989) Service quality: relationships between banks and their small business clients, *International Journal of Bank Marketing*, Vol. 7, pp. 28–35.
Williamson, O.E. (1975) *Markets and Hierarchies, Analysis and Antitrust Implications*, Free Press, New York.
Wood, D., Collett, N., Erturk, I. and Schell, C. (1992a) *Bank Relationship Survey 1992*, Manchester Business School, Manchester.
Wood, D., Collett, N., Erturk, I. and Schell, C. (1992b) Relationship banking and the FD, *Financial Director*, November, pp. 20–5.
Wood, D., Collett, N., Erturk, I. and Schell, C. (1995a) *Bank Relationship Survey 1995*, Manchester Business School, Manchester.
Wood, D., Collett, N., Erturk, I. and Schell, C. (1995b) Customers call the banks to account, *Financial Director*, November, pp. 20–5.
Wood, J.H. (1975) *Commercial Bank Loan and Investment Behavior*, Wiley, New York.

8

Credit cards

Steve Worthington

The worldwide market for plastic payment cards continues to grow rapidly and their possession and usage provide a good example of a mutually beneficial relationship between supplier and customer. The supplier in this instance is a financial institution who issues a plastic payment card to a customer, for use either as a payment mechanism with merchants who accept such payment, or to access cash through an automatic teller machine (ATM), which belongs to a network which accepts such cards.

The major networks in the credit-card market are MasterCard and Visa, also called card associations. Their members and owners are the financial institutions who issue plastic payment cards under the MasterCard or Visa marque. The card association marques guarantee the acceptance of the plastic card in a payment or cash-access situation and the card associations themselves facilitate the movement of these transactions back to the card issuer and hence on the card holder for settlement.

At the end of 1994, the worldwide number of merchants who accepted MasterCard and Visa payments was 12 million and the number of credit and debit cards in circulation throughout the world was 277 million MasterCards and 391 million Visa. Besides credit and debit cards, the card associations are also developing the so-called stored value cards, where money is preloaded on to a plastic card, usually through an integrated chip embedded into the card. That value is then decremented as the card is used, until the card is reloaded with further value. When such 'smart cards' are fully accepted by consumers and merchants, it will be possible to have all three time-related payment functions on the one card. The three (pay-later credit, pay-now debit and pay-before stored value) could then all be accessed through the one piece of plastic. Under this scenario, whoever issues the multipurpose plastic card that the consumer holds and uses will potentially have the key to the entire payment relationship with that consumer. Card issuers are therefore keen to increase their share of the customer's wallet or purse, and this chapter now goes on to examine how, in the UK, card issuers have sought to use the principles espoused by RM to build mutual loyalty between themselves and their customers.

The UK credit-card market

There are approximately 27 million credit cards on issue in the UK, under the MasterCard and Visa marques. Traditionally the Access marque was the sub-brand used in the UK by those banks affiliated to MasterCard, but increasingly the Access brand is being subsumed by the more internationally recognized MasterCard brand. In addition to these bank – and building society – issued cards, there are also approximately 10 million 'store cards' issued by retailers for the use by their customers as credit cards in their stores. The development of retailer credit cards and the use of direct marketing to build privileged customer relationships is dealt with by Worthington (1986; 1990).

According to figures released by the British Bankers Association (BBA) in May 1995, UK banks accounted for 91% of all credit cards issued under the MasterCard and Visa marques, the remaining 9% being issued by UK building societies. The BBA figures also reveal the number of charge cards on issue in the UK from card issuers such as American Express (1.1 million) and Diners Club (300,000).

These charge cards, although akin to credit cards in many ways, are in fact fundamentally different in that any spending carried out on such cards must be paid off in full at the end of the account period. This differs from credit cards, where the holder has the option of taking revolving credit, i.e. not paying off the full balance of the account but revolving the debt into future account periods, thus incurring an interest payment on the debt outstanding. Charge cards are marketed to the high-spending business person and are often used as an expense account, to be settled directly by the card holder's employer. The number of charge cards on issue has been static for a number of years and in a recognition of the growth potential of the credit card, American Express in 1995 launched a stand-alone credit card, marketed to the individual consumer.

The potential of the credit card as a payment mechanism and as a key element in the building of a relationship between the supplier and the consumer is illustrated by information released in May 1995 from the Credit Card Research Group (CCRG). This group represents all the major UK issuers of credit cards and those banks who 'acquire' transactions from merchants made by consumers using credit cards. The CCRG figures reveal that the percentage of high-street spending that is attributed to credit cards is growing strongly. Retail sales grew by 6% between January 1993 and January 1995, according to the Central Statistical Office. Over the same two years, credit-card spending on the high street increased by 31.8%. The reasons behind this are varied: consumers are becoming more familiar with using plastic cards to purchase goods and services with either credit or debit cards; more merchant outlets now accept payment by credit cards; and there have been new credit-card issuers entering the UK market, e.g. HFC Bank, Maryland Bank of North America (MBNA) and American Express – some of whom have usage-incentive schemes which reward their credit-card holders in direct proportion to the amount spent on their credit card. These usage-incentive schemes have provoked existing card issuers into developing their own retaliatory schemes and, in consequence, many credit-card holders are now actively encouraged to use their cards as often as possible to take advantage of these schemes.

Table 8.1 The credit-card loyalty league table (a comparison of UK credit cards, July 1995)

Card issuer	Monthly interest (%)	Annual fee	Purchase apr (%)	Interest-free days	Usage incentives
Bank of Scotland	1.570	£10	21.7	50	Every £150 charged to the card earns £10 mortgage bonus points, to a maximum of £600 rebate against mortgage costs
Barclaycard	1.650	£10	22.9	56	Every £100 charged to the card equals 10 Profiles points which can be redeemed against Profiles catalogue goods; 4,500 Profile points allows £1,500 worth of cash-back on a new Barclays mortgage
GM card	1.600	Nil	20.9	52	Every £100 charged to the card earns £5 towards the cost of a new Vauxhall. Savings up to £500 a year (£2,500 over 5 years). Partner programme and company car scheme also attached to the card
MBNA Burberry card	1.450	Nil	18.9	56	Every £100 charged to the card earns a £2 Burberry bond, redeemable against purchases in Burberry stores
Midland Bank	1.595	£12	22.3	56	Every £100 charged to the card earns 10 points, redeemable against motoring, leisure, travel or financial services, e.g. 220 points pay off the annual fee
Nat West Bank	1.670	£12	23.4	56	Every £100 charged to the card earns five Air Miles
Texaco Global	1.570	£10	21.7	50	Every £100 charged to the card earns 10 stars redeemable against the Texaco Star Collection

Table 8.1, the credit-card loyalty league table, shows the UK credit cards that have usage-incentive schemes, as of July 1995. Once a credit-card holder has a rebate value built up on his or her card as a result of a usage-incentive scheme, he or she is less likely to 'switch' cards and indeed it is more likely that the card holder will close his or her other credit-card accounts in order to concentrate spending on the preferred credit card so as to maximize his or her potential rebate or loyalty reward.

Table 8.2 The credit card 'no annual fee' league table (a comparison of UK credit-cards, July 1995)

Card issuer	Monthly interest (%)	Purchase APR (%)	Cash advances APR (%)	Qualifications
The Co-operative Bank Robert Owen Card	1.70	22.40	24.90	
GM card	1.60	20.90	20.90	
Leeds Permanent	1.67	21.99	23.84	Existing customers only
National and Provincial	1.63	21.40	23.20	
Royal Bank of Scotland Master Card	1.14	14.50	14.50	No interest-free period
TSB	1.67	21.90	22.50	
Yorkshire Bank	1.75	23.10	23.80	

The rewards associated with these usage-incentive schemes are financed out of the various income streams associated with the holding and usage of credit cards. The first of these is any annual fee that the card issuer levies on card holders. Not all card issuers charge an annual fee and Table 8.2 shows those UK card issuers with no annual fee, again as of July 1995. The second income stream is any interest charged on the debt outstanding on the line of credit attached to the credit card and this is expressed as an annualized percentage rate (APR), which can differ between purchases and cash advances made with the credit card. The May 1995 figures from the BBA reveal that for their constituency of card issuers, 73% of all accounts incurred interest. Their figure was taken as of December 1994, when traditionally Christmas spending on credit cards is at its highest and repayment in full therefore most difficult. Barclaycard, the largest UK credit-card issuer, with around one-third of the market, claims that in an average month over 50% of their card holders are 'full payers', in that they pay off their account in full at the end of that account period. This is a figure confirmed by a number of other UK card issuers.

Where the card issuer has no annual fee and where a large percentage of their card holders are full payers, other income streams must be relied upon to fund the activities of the card issuer. These can be related to the merchant service charge (MSC) imposed on merchants who accept payment by credit card and which can be between 1.7% and 4.0% of the value of the transaction. These MSCs are collected by the 'acquirer' of these transactions, who will then refund the merchant the value of the transaction minus the MSC before processing the transactions into batches to be then passed to each card issuer as appropriate. A fixed percentage of the MSC is also passed by the acquirer to the issuer, to compensate the latter for the expenses involving in operating the credit-card account. This is called the interchange fee, which is approximately 1% of the MSC. If a card issuer can incentivize its card holders to spend more on their credit cards, then that card issuer will receive a proportionately larger income stream from the interchange fee. This has been part of the rationale of those card issuers who have introduced usage-incentive schemes.

The final substantial income stream available to card issuers comes from the card-protection insurance policies that they endeavour to cross-sell to their card-holder base. These offer insurance in case of the card being lost, the card holder becoming unemployed or ill, and repayments then being difficult to maintain. These card-protection policies can be a very useful income stream, as they are designed to be profitable. Obviously the more card holders that a card issuer has, the more such policies can be cross-sold to the entire card base and the larger the income stream received as a result.

With such a variety of income streams, plus the surge of spending on credit cards and the worldwide acceptance of the major card association brands, the credit card has been a very profitable element of any financial institution's portfolio of products. Returns on equity for the credit-card divisions of these financial institutions have in recent years been well over 20%, although historically credit-card profitability has been cyclical, with periods of profitability being followed by unprofitability. The profits earned by the credit-card divisions of banks and building societies have been used to help offset losses incurred elsewhere in their operations. In particular the current account, with its cheque and/or passbook, has, in an era of free banking for those whose accounts are in credit, had to be cross-subsidized from other areas of activity. Historically the current account was believed to be the key account in the relationship between the financial institution who supplied financial services and the customer who used those services. This was because the account and its physical manifestation, the cheque or passbook, were thought to be the reason that the customer came to the branch, where he or she would interact with employees of the financial institution who would then build a wider and deeper relationship with the customer.

Changes in customer lifestyles and developments in technologies have, however, undermined the role of the branch and its staff in the formation and development of relationships between financial service providers and customers. Many customers now expect 24-hour, seven days a week, 365 days a year accessibility to their accounts. Technology provides ATMs, telephone banking and remote access to banking facilities that have transformed the basis of the relationship such that the branch is an increasingly obsolete distribution channel for financial services. What will replace the branch and the paper cheque is the electronic delivery of financial services via the telephone, the screen or at the point of sale. It is here that the plastic card will hold the key to the access and delivery of those financial services. The information encoded on the plastic card will both validate the card as eligible to access various financial services and then authorize transfers and payments as appropriate.

This scenario is tantalizingly close. However, it is still in the future, and those financial institutions who wish eventually to deliver their services electronically face a challenge as they attempt to capture new customers. How can such financial services suppliers develop relationships through plastic-card products, independent of current account relationships, in the here and now? The answer is via the credit card! The reason is that a credit-card relationship can be established that is independent of other banking relationships. This differentiates it from the debit card, which must be tied to a current or savings account upon whose funds it can draw in a pay-now situation. Credit cards, as pay-later instruments, do not require an instantly accessible account to be held with the card issuer, for payment is made at a later date when the credit-card account is presented to the card holder for payment.

These accounts, presented as statements issued on a monthly basis, provide the ideal opportunity for the credit-card issuer to communicate a variety of messages to their card holders. The statement itself can be used to relay information; inserts can be enclosed with the statement (called statement stuffers) which communicate information to the card holder; and solus mailings can also be made to the credit-card database. Information from the card issuer to the card holder to help build the relationship is complemented by information from the card holder to the credit-card issuer. This information is both historical and ongoing. First, the credit-card issuer will require information from the prospective credit-card holder, as to their personal circumstances and family commitments, in order to credit score their application so that credit is not offered to those who cannot afford it. Secondly, as the card is used, an ongoing flow of information comes to the credit-card issuer about the volume and value of spending on the card, where this takes place and the repayment patterns associated with the card. This total sum of information can then be used to judge what other financial service offers to place before the individual card holder: offers that can be justifiably communicated via the monthly statement.

An example of the use of the credit-card relationship to develop other relationships with card holders is offered by Table 8.1, the credit-card loyalty league table. Here a number of credit-card issuers are using their usage-incentive scheme to market some of their other financial services to their card holders. Thus both Bank of Scotland and Barclaycard offers cash rebates on mortgages taken out with them from the usage-incentive points accumulated by their credit-card holders. Similarly the Midland Bank Choice Scheme enables card holders to exchange their rebate points for stock-broking services offered by that bank. This has become known as 'internal marketing', used in this context to refer to the situation where credit-card holders of a particular card issuer, who may not have any other financial service relationship with that financial institution, are encouraged by their credit-card issuer to take out other financial service relationships with the card issuer's parent. In doing so they not only reinforce their relationship with the card issuer and its parent but they also deny those relationships to competitor institutions.

This chapter now goes on to examine how credit-card issuers can build relationships with card holders who hold no other relationship with their parent institution. By doing so, these credit-card issuers hope to establish an ongoing relationship with their card holders and use their information flows and communication channels to develop further relationships. Two of the more successful ways of recruiting new card holders to credit-card issuers are by the offering of the so-called affinity and cobranded credit cards. These are now discussed below.

Affinity credit cards

The affinity credit-card product is a subset of the generic credit card, and of the approximately 27 million credit cards on issue in the UK, some 5% (1.35

million) are estimated to be affinity cards. These cards are issued by banks and building societies to members or supporters of various affinity groups and they are then used as regular credit cards, with interest-free periods and the ability (if so required) to take revolving credit. The essential difference between an affinity credit card and a generic credit card is that payments are made by the credit-card issuer to the affinity group, in return for access to their member or supporter base, in order to help market the credit card. These payments are usually related to how many affinity credit cards are issued to each affinity group base and how much their members or supporters spend on their affinity credit cards. The history and economics of the affinity credit-card product are described in full in Worthington and Horne (1993), and that article also looks closely at the synergies available to both charities and credit-card issuers through the affinity-card concept. In later work, Worthington (1994a) has produced a typology of affinity groups interested in credit cards, known as the four Cs. Those groups with affinity credit cards include charities, clubs (e.g. alumni associations, professional groups, football clubs), causes (e.g. political parties, pressure, environmental and heritage groups) and cobrands (e.g. car manufacturers, petrol companies, retailers). This last category is the most recent addition to the affinity-card market and is a more markedly self-interest product than the other types of affinity credit card. Cobranded cards are dealt with in the next section of this chapter. Although the economics of such cards are based on similar principles to those of the other categories of affinity cards, the key difference is that the recipient of the affinity benefit is an individual credit-card holder rather than an affinity group. Table 8.3 gives a comparison of affinity credit cards and includes examples of charities, clubs and causes.

The reason why the various card issuers have come into the affinity-card market vary and have been dealt with by Worthington and Horne (1992). However, all affinity-card issuers share the same objective in this market: to establish relationships based on the holding and usage of affinity credit cards, with card holders they would otherwise have no relationship with. The relationship is complicated by the existence of three parties to it: the card issuer, the affinity group and the affinity-card holder, who are all part of a triangular relationship. While the card issuers describe this triangular relationship as a win–win–win situation, recent research into the alumni affinity credit-card

Table 8.3 The affinity credit-card league table (a comparison of UK affinity credit cards, July 1995)

Card issuer	Affinity partner	Monthly interest (%)	Annual fee	Purchase APR (%)
Bank of Scotland	RSPCA	1.63	£7.50	22.30
Beneficial Bank	Open University	1.60	NIL	20.90
Co-operative Bank	Amnesty International	1.70	NIL	22.40
Leeds Permanent	Mencap	1.49	£12.00	20.87
MBNA	River Island	1.45	NIL	18.90
Midland Bank	National Trust	1.75	NIL	23.10
Royal Bank of Scotland	Glasgow Rangers FC	1.53	NIL	19.90

market has thrown doubt upon the equitable nature of the mutually beneficial relationship between these suppliers and their customer groups. This research is described below.

University alumni affinity credit cards

One of the most 'successful' affinity groups from the point of view of the credit-card issuers is the alumni and staff of various universities. Figures from Bank of Scotland, one of the UK's most active affinity-card issuers, show that the responses to their marketing of affinity credit cards are highest for groups of university alumni. Such a group is very attractive to a credit-card issuer for, besides the high response rates, the alumni database offers potential card holders with relatively high incomes who may eventually become high net-worth individuals as their careers unfold.

Universities themselves have become interested in the affinity card, as they can see the possibility of adding another income stream to their finances and in the belated recognition that building and nurturing ongoing relationships with their alumni can eventually result in substantial legacy income, as alumni endeavour to put back into the education system some of the wealth they have accumulated as a result of their participation in higher education. Universities in the UK have followed the example of their counterparts in North America by establishing alumni officers and development offices to build proactively the alumni base and to then pursue the donation of funds from the alumni.

The alumni affinity credit card serves a number of purposes in pursuit of this overall aim. First, it establishes an ongoing relationship between the university and the alumni affinity credit-card holder, which is reinforced every time the card holder uses the card and subsequently receives a statement. The monthly statement offers the university an opportunity to place a message on the statement itself or to send information to the alumni via a 'statement stuffer'. Furthermore, every time alumni affinity-card holders use a card, there is at least some visual identification through the credit card that reminds them that they are alumni of a particular university, and this helps further to develop and reinforce their relationship with their university.

Recent research (Worthington and Horne, 1994; Worthington, 1995b) has sought to quantify the number of UK universities with alumni affinity cards, the total number of alumni cards on issue, whom they are issued by, and on what terms and how much has been raised in total by these cards for the university sector. From this research it was found that there were four affinity credit-cards issuers with interests in the alumni affinity-card market in the UK: Bank of Scotland, Beneficial Bank, Bank of Ireland and MBNA. Further research by Worthington and Horne (1995) has explored the development of the relationship between the affinity credit-card issuer and the individual(s) in the university responsible for establishing and monitoring the alumni affinity credit card. The evolution of the relationship was modelled around five phases, developed by Dwyer, Schurr and Oh (1987) and identified as 1) awareness; 2) exploration; 3) expansion; 4) commitment; and 5) dissolution. While the research programme initially examines the relationship from the point of view of the university alumni officers, the five-phase model offers the potential further

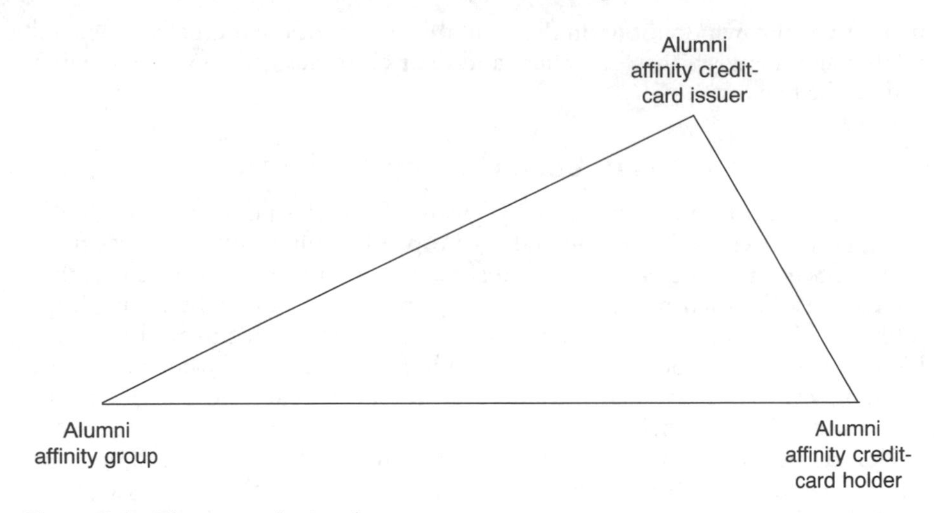

Figure 8.1 The unequal triangle

to examine the development of the relationship from the point of view of the card issuer and the card holder.

The alumni affinity credit-card product does offer an interesting example of the challenges associated with RM, for here there are three potential relationships, yet they are unequal in depth. Figure 8.1 shows the relationship and the unequal nature of the triangle of the three parties involved, the affinity credit-card issuer, the university and the alumni affinity credit-card holder.

Once the affinity credit-card issuer has established a relationship with an individual alumnus of a university, then the 'prime' relationship concerning that credit card is between the card issuer and the card holder. This is because the credit card can be issued only if the potential card holder is willing to reveal to the card issuer a number of personal details such as income, other credit commitments, family and employment circumstances. These enable the card issuer to credit score the application and thus be responsible in only offering credit to those able and willing to manage it. The relationship between the card issuer and the card holder is tight (hence the short side of the triangle), and this relationship is reinforced by the continual use of the card, the issuing of monthly statements and the transfer of payments from the card holder to card issuer. Furthermore, in recent research on alumni affinity credit cards, Worthington and Horne (1995) have revealed that the alumni officers do not necessarily know which of their alumni have taken up the offer of the alumni affinity credit card. The card issuer believes that it now has the 'prime' relationship with its card holders and that the banking code of customer confidentiality prevents it from revealing who its customers are to 'third parties', even if that 'third party' (i.e. the alumni group) had been responsible for introducing the card holder to the card issuer. The relationship between the card issuer and the university alumni group will nevertheless remain fairly strong, because they now have mutual vested interests. The card issuer is reliant on the university to allow continued access to its alumni for the purposes of recruiting more affinity card holders, while the university is regularly receiving from the card issuer income streams relating to either new cards taken out or to the value of the spending taking place on those cards.

Meanwhile, the initial relationship, which was between the university and their alumni, becomes the weakest of this triangle of relationships, represented by the largest side. Here contact is intermittent (i.e via alumni magazines, reunions, etc.) and the relationship is more distant than is the case with the other two sides of the triangle. Furthermore, the university alumni office may well be unaware of the existence of the 'prime' relationship between the card issuer and the individual alumni group members and hence 'blind' to the dilution of its original relationship with its alumni.

Despite the inequitable nature of the relationship, the affinity-card concept does offer all parties to it a mutually beneficial relationship. The affinity credit-card holder receives a credit card that has as much utility as a generic credit card, yet it also offers additional benefits to the card holder for he or she knows that in taking out the card and by its subsequent use they are financially supporting their chosen affinity group. The affinity group itself benefits from the income it receives from the credit-card issuer in return for access to the affinity partner's member or supporter database. By agreeing potentially to share their relationship with their members or supporters with an affinity credit-card issuer, they gain both an immediate reward (dependent on the number of cards issued) and an ongoing income stream related to the value of spending, plus a further opportunity to communicate with their members or supporters via the monthly statements. Indeed for the affinity partner who has been successful in persuading many of its members or supporters to take out an affinity card, there exists the possibility of 'reverse marketing', where the affinity partner uses its leverage with the credit-card issuer to mail its proposition to the entire base of the issuer. This occurs only where the affinity partner has negotiating clout, by virtue of the large number of credit cards issued under their affinity-card programme.

By and large, however, it is the credit-card issuer who stands to gain most from the establishment of an affinity credit-card relationship. Besides providing a cost-effective means of recruiting new card holders, the affinity credit-card concept encourages card holders to concentrate their spending on their affinity card, to the detriment of other credit or charge cards that they may hold and even as an alternative to debit card, cheque or cash payments. Such spending provides an income stream to the card issuer, irrespective of whether they charge an annual fee or whether the card holder pays interest on any revolving credit he or she may take. Furthermore, the lifetime value of such a customer can be substantial, as the work of Reichheld and Sasser (1990) and Reichheld (1993) with MBNA, the largest affinity credit-card issuer in the USA, has shown. Their research showed how small movements in a credit-card company's defection rate can produce very large increases in profits. For example, a reduction in defection from 20% to 10% means that the average lifespan of a relationship with a customer doubles from five years to ten, and the value of that customer more than doubles. As the defection rate drops another 5%, the average lifespan of the customer relationship doubles again and profits rise accordingly. At MBNA, a 5% increase in retention grew the company's profits by 60% in the fifth year. In addition the communication channels now exist to cross-sell other financial service products to an affinity credit-card base, with a known spending and repayment pattern. Small wonder, then, that MBNA have entered the UK credit-card market, with their affinity-card concept, and that other credit-card issuers are using affinity programmes to reach customers with whom they would otherwise not have a relationship. In addition they are developing cobranded programmes with commercial partners.

Cobranded credit cards

The cobranded credit-card product is a further subset of the generic credit card and one with approximately 2.5% of the total market (700,000 cards). Under cobranding, the card holders accumulate rebate value on their credit cards in direct proportion to their value of spending on the card. These rebates can then be used against the purchase of goods or services provided by the organization that sponsored the credit card. Worthington (1994b; 1995a) discusses the rationale and the implications of the entry by car manufacturers into the credit-card market by the means of cobranded cards.

By far the most successful cobranded credit card is the GM card, sponsored by the car manufacturer, General Motors. First launched in the USA in 1992, it has subsequently been extended to Canada, the UK, Brazil and Australia, and now has a total of 15 million card holders of whom over 500,000 are in the UK. These UK card holders can accumulate rebates, calculated as 5% of the value of all purchases made on the card up to a maximum of £500 a year or £2,500 over five years. These rebates can then be exchanged against the purchase of a new General Motors vehicle, over and above any discount the purchaser may be able to negotiate with the dealer. As of mid-1995, some 12,000 new General Motors vehicles had been sold under this basis in the UK and some 450,000 in the USA. These incremental sales are of great value to a car manufacturer with high fixed costs. The cobranded cards helped their sponsoring organizations to achieve the three Rs for survival, if not prosperity, in the late 1990s. These are retention of existing customers; recruitment of new customers wherever possible; and relationship building with all customers.

The success of the GM card has prompted other car manufacturers to enter the cobranded credit-card market. Ford, Peugeot and Fiat have already established cobranded partnerships with credit-card issuers. The cobranded concept has also been adopted by other producers of goods and services. Thus petrol companies (Texaco), building societies (Bradford and Bingley), retailers (Burberry's) and newspapers (*The Times/The Sunday Times*) have all entered the cobranded credit-card market, with usage-incentive cards issued by a partner bank.

Once again, there is a triangle of relationships involved in cobranded credit cards. The first relationship, chronologically speaking, will be between the commercial organization and the credit-card issuer. The establishment of such a relationship is the prelude to the issuance of a cobranded credit card and one where, once again, mutual benefits must be recognized and evaluated. The mutual benefits consist of the commercial partner being able, via the credit-card issuer, to establish relationships with their end-user customers, a group of people about whom they may have previously known very little. Motor car manufacturers, for example, concentrate on the development and production of vehicles and historically have left the customer relationship with their dealer networks. Car manufacturers who wish to learn more about their end-user customers and who want to have a channel of communication to the customers, that is, an alternative to their dealer network, have seen the cobranded credit card as a means of building that relationship. Worthington (1995a) discusses the synergies of metal and plastic that are exhibited here.

For the credit-card issuer, a commercial partner in a cobranded credit card offers the possibility of sharing revenues to establish an attractive usage-incentive scheme, of marketing support to help launch the card and of access to the partner's databases, where relevant, to endorse and market the card. The distribution of power in the relationship between the commercial partner and the credit-card issuer depends very much on the relevant strengths of the two parties in the cobranded relationship. The General Motors card was launched in the USA with Household Credit Services and in the UK with HFC Bank, both wholly owned subsidiaries of Household International, the US consumer finance company. Both Household Credit Services and HFC Bank have used the GM card as their main weapon in their entry strategies into both the US and UK credit-card markets. General Motors, in choosing relatively unknown credit-card issuers as partners, has been able to be the dominant partner in this cobranded relationship.

The Ford Motor Company, one of General Motor's main global rivals, has followed their initiative in cobranded credit cards by creating their own cobranded partnerships with Citibank in the USA and Barclaycard in the UK. These are the largest card issuers in their respective countries and it is a moot point where the power lies in these cobranded relationships.

The triangle of relationships is completed by the card holder. One significant question is: What is the card holder's relationship with both the credit-card issuer and the commercial cobranded partner? Both of them have the intention of building wider and deeper relations with the credit-card holder, sometimes in direct opposition to each other. For the credit-card issuer, the situation is very much akin to that of the affinity card, referred to earlier. The card issuer is using the cobranded proposition to attract new card holders and, having attracted them, to encourage them to concentrate their spending on the cobranded credit card so as to maximize their rebate and inhibit their relationships to other card issuers. Once again, besides the lifetime income streams associated with the holding and usage of such a credit card, the card issuer will also be looking to develop its relationship with its card holders, so as to cross-sell other finanical services to them.

Whereas the affinity partner in an affinity card relationship has no ambitions to cross-sell other financial services to the card base, the commercial partner in the cobranded relationship may not be so passive. Most motor car manufacturers, for example, have very large and profitable finance arms, which traditionally have been used to offer finance to prospective car purchasers. In some cases, these finance arms (e.g. General Motors Acceptance Company (GMAC) and Ford Motor Credit) have become more profitable pro rata than their manufacturing parent companies. Recently they have widened their product portfolios to respond to the financial needs of their customer bases. In a cobranded relationship these finance arms may wish to cross-sell their financial services to what they believe is the credit-card database of their parent, the motor car manufacturer. Thus in the autumn of 1994, GMAC in the USA announced that it would begin marketing home equity loans and other financial services such as car insurance to holders of the GM card. Their rationale was that the detailed customer data available through the credit card application and subsequent transactions enhanced the prospects for target marketing. Their relationship with their cobranded credit-card issuer, Household Credit Services, is obviously one where the credit-card issuer felt unable to prevent such an initiative. Other financial institutions in other cobranded partnerships might feel more reluctant to allow their cobranded partner to develop further financial services relationships with a card base that the card issuer might consider to be its 'own'.

These examples reveal why cobranded credit cards offer their own nuances for those concerned with RM. As with affinity credit cards, the basic concept does offer a mutually beneficial relationship to all the parties involved. Thus card holder, cobranded partners and credit-card issuers can all gain from a well designed cobranded credit-card scheme. However, just who gains and how much is gained can only be ascertained by a close examination of each different cobranded scheme and a thorough understanding of the power relationship between each of the parties involved.

Conclusion

This chapter set out to describe, analyse and critique RM practices in the credit-card sector. The credit card, unlike other plastic payment cards, can be a stand-alone product, in that a credit-card holder need have no other relationship with the credit-card issuer. As such it offers those financial institutions with credit-card interests an opportunity to establish relationships with customers they otherwise would have no contact with.

Besides its power as a recruitment mechanism, the credit card can be a powerful retention agent. A credit card with good 'hygiene' factors of customer service, enhanced by 'motivation' factors of affinity contributions or usage-incentive rebates, can 'lock' a card holder into a particular card issuer and allow the lifetime value to be then 'unlocked' by that card issuer. Furthermore the very nature of the credit-card product means that it is ideal for relationship building. The application process reveals information about the card holder, and this is enhanced by the subsequent usage of the card. The monthly statement offers the perfect, justified opportunity to communicate with the card holder, through a variety of messages either on the statement or as statement stuffers. These messages can either relate to recruitment (tell your friends how good your credit cards is), retention (let us remind you how valuable your credit card is) or relationship building (now you know how good your credit card is, let us offer you some other financial services). By these means, the three Rs of recruitment, retention and relationship building can be simultaneously achieved!

Not all credit-card issuers, however, have understood or adopted the principles associated with RM and there is a series of questions which could be asked to help ascertain their awareness of RM practices. These are: Is your credit-card product operated as an independent profit centre or integrated with the total portfolio of products that you offer? Do you concentrate on cross-selling your credit card to your existing personal customer base or are you cross-selling your other financial services to your credit-card base? Have you examined the affinity or the cobranded credit-card market as a means of building up your credit-card portfolio? Have you introduced usage-incentives schemes to capture more of your card holders total expenditure on to your credit cards? Do you measure your customer retention? Have you considered how to reward those of your credit-card holders whose business you have held for a number of years and whose ongoing value to you is considerable? How will you respond to the concept of the relationship card which, using the power of the integrated chip, has the potential to offer all payment facilities on the one piece of plastic? Will it be your card that the customers hold and will they therefore have their entire relationship with you or will it be the card issued by one of your competitors?

References

Dwyer, R., Schurr, P. and Oh, S. (1987) Developing buyer–seller relationships, *Journal of Marketing*, Vol. 51, pp. 11–27.

Reichheld, F. (1993) Loyalty-based management, *Harvard Business Review*, March–April, pp. 64–73.

Reichheld, F. and Sasser, E. (1990) Zero defections: quality comes to service, *Harvard Business Review*, September–October, pp. 105–11.

Worthington, S. (1986) Credit cards and direct marketing – a question of synergy, *Journal of Marketing Management*, Vol. 2, pp. 125–31.

Worthington, S. (1990) Retailer credit cards: a competitive threat, *International Journal of Bank Marketing*, Vol. 8, pp. 3–9.

Worthington, S. (1994a) The four C's of affinity credit cards, *The Scottish Banker, Financial Self Service*, May, pp. 9–10.

Worthington, S. (1994b) Metal cars and plastic cards – what is the connection? In *Proceedings of the 1994 Marketing Education Group Annual Conference*, University of Ulster, Coleraine.

Worthington, S. (1995a) Flashing the plastic and moving the metal – where the credit card meets the automobile. In *Proceedings of the Seventh World Marketing Congress*, Monash University, Melbourne.

Worthington, S. (1995b) Alumni affinity credit cards – the story continues, *Education Marketing*, November, pp. 12–13.

Worthington, S. and Horne, S. (1992) Affinity credit cards in the United Kingdom – card issuer strategies and affinity group aspirations, *International Journal of Bank Marketing*, Vol. 10, pp. 3–10.

Worthington, S. and Horne, S. (1993) Charity affinity credit cards – marketing synergy for both card issuers and charities? *Journal of Marketing Management*, Vol. 9, pp. 301–13.

Worthington, S. and Horne, S. (1994) Alumni affinity cards – the story so far, *Education Marketing*, March, pp. 13–15.

Worthington, S. and Horne, S. (1995) Alumni affinity credit cards: making the relationship work, *International Journal of Bank Marketing*, Vol. 13, pp. 24–30.

9

Financial advisers and savings and investment products

Christine Ennew and Mary Hartley

Introduction

The principles of RM outlined in the opening chapter of this book have particular relevance in the financial services sector. Previous chapters have already examined the importance of RM in the context of banking and credit cards. For service providers in these areas the growing interest in RM is largely a reflection of the maturity of the market; specifically, limited opportunities for market penetration have resulted in a growing interest in retention and an increased emphasis on the need to cross-sell in the context of product development strategies. The situation with financial advisers and with savings and investment products is perhaps somewhat different. It is clear that the relevant markets are highly competitive, but equally it is apparent that there is still considerable growth potential. However, the services concerned are complex and long term, and customers perceive them to be highly risky; thus on the demand side there is arguably a need for RM from the customers' perspective. Equally, on the supply side, the opportunities for cross-selling in the context of an established relationship have also stimulated an active interest in both customer relationships and customer retention on the part of product providers. Finally, regulatory concern about high lapse rates for many products and the potential for mis-selling mean that more and more providers and advisers are focusing attention on RM as a means of enhancing retention rates and improving customer satisfaction.

In financial services, as in many other services, it is arguably the processes of promotion and distribution which provide the key to effective marketing. The latter is of particular importance because, typically, it is through the distribution system that a service organization builds and manages relationships with customers. Furthermore, in the context of personal financial services, the distribution system (which may or not be independent of the product provider) plays a key role in advising consumers about the choice of product. Therefore, it might be argued that it is in the distribution system for financial services that we would find many of the clues towards understanding the issues of customer relationships. The ability of a particular intermediary (financial adviser) to build relationships with customers may depend on the personal characteristics of that adviser and the nature of his or her own organization's strategy. The ability of a product provider to build relationships with final consumers may be more heavily dependent on the type of distribution channel being used. In particular, we suggest that the degree of integration in the channel structure and the remuneration of channel members may have the potential to impact significantly on the opportunities for building customer relationships and improving retention rates.

In order to address these issues, this chapter proceeds by first examining the nature of the market in which financial advisers operate, paying particular attention to savings and investment products. The following section explores the nature of RM with particular emphasis on the roles played by different distribution channels. The final section presents a summary and conclusions.

Financial advisers and savings and investment products

Financial advisers have a broad role, providing guidance to consumers with respect to a large range of financial products. Probably the single most important group of products are those known collectively as savings and investments products. These services are effectively 'produced' by a range of organizations (insurance companies, unit trust companies, etc.) but are typically made available to consumers through a variety of different types of financial adviser.[1] Savings and investment products provide an interesting illustration of many of the issues and problems in RM. The nature of the basic product is such that RM is particularly appropriate for both customer and supplier and yet, for many, the recent history of this sector is one that is characterized by, at best, a failure to exploit these opportunities and, at worst, a complete reliance on short-term profit at the expense of longer-term customer relationships. In order to understand the potential for RM and the development of this approach in relation to financial advice, it is necessary to provide some brief background on some of the more salient characteristics of the marketplace.

The market for savings and investment products has experienced considerable growth in recent years both in the volume of sales and the diversity of products on offer. Rising disposable incomes have facilitated increased consumer spending on these products while deregulation, changes in fiscal policy and developments in information technology have encouraged an increasing variety of different types of savings and investment products. The majority of these products are distributed through intermediaries who traditionally worked primarily on a commission basis. The growing complexity of the marketplace is such that these intermediaries are not simply providers of the products; they have a key role to play in providing advice to consumers.

The potential vulnerability of consumers to unscrupulous marketing and selling practices has been recognized for some time (Gower, 1982) and is reflected in the existing regulatory framework (Devlin and Wright, 1995). Consumer vulnerability arises as a result of imperfect and asymmetric information and is reinforced by the complex, risky and long-term nature of many financial products. *Ex ante*, the suppliers of savings and investment products typically have more and better product information than the buyers, partly because they have specialist knowledge and partly because they have access to company-specific information. Although some of this information may be shared with potential customers, some may be withheld and even when information is provided, there is no assurance that customers will be in a position fully to utilize this information. Despite the apparently growing degree of financial sophistication among consumers (Burton, 1994), there continues to be evidence of a substantial lack of understanding of savings and investment products among consumers (Ennew, 1992; OFT, 1992). A consequence of these information problems is that the development of trust and confidence has a crucial role to play in the process of providing financial advice and making a sale (Palmer and Bejou, 1994).

The underlying problem facing consumers is the fact that most savings and investment products are highly complex. Complexity is a function of both the confusing nature of many financial products and services as well as the vast choice available. This in turn greatly increases the complexity of the consumer's decision-making process (McAlexander and Scammon, 1988). In order to make an informed choice when purchasing a savings or investment product, consumers must understand the essential differences between simple products like interest-bearing savings accounts and more complex services such as pooled investment products and direct equity purchases. In addition to the vast array of products and services available to the consumer, the problem is compounded by the many different brands of each variety to choose from. Each will have its own particular features and conditions which add to the complexity of the task.

This problem is reinforced by the risk associated with most savings or investment products. The final benefits payable are determined both by the skills of the product provider and by the future performance of the economy as a whole. Returns for similar product types may vary considerably according to the time period involved, and returns for different product types may also vary at any point in time as a consequence of chance and the differing skills of fund managers. Thus unlike many goods and services, the quality of a savings or investment product may be determined by factors which are beyond the control of the provider. This risk element is reinforced by the long-term nature of many of the products which means that the benefits from purchase are not received until some time in the future. Thus consumers rely heavily on credence qualities when making a purchase and there is also the risk that the consumer's needs and circumstances may change, making a product ultimately inappropriate for the consumer's current needs.

The structure of regulation in this market, as outlined in the Financial Services Act, attempts to deal explicitly with many of these problems (Devlin and Ennew, 1993). The introduction of polarization obliged financial advisers to declare their status (independent or tied to a single provider) and best advice was required to ensure that, irrespective of the type of intermediary being employed, consumers would not be sold products which were unsuited to their needs. Subsequently, full commission disclosure was also introduced to make customers aware of the intermediary's incentive structure. The evidence to date suggests that the regulations imposed by the FSA may have been less than successful in providing the required degree of investor protection (Ennew, MacGregor and Diacon, 1994). An increasing volume of customer complaints is indicative of a growing degree of dissatisfaction with financial advice. This evidence is reinforced by relatively high levels of early surrender or lapse of long-term insurance policies, and the preliminary results of investigations into the sale of personal pensions suggest that the degree of mis-selling has been considerable.

In summary, then, information asymmetries and product complexity make consumer choice in relation to many financial services a difficult process. Full information may not be available and even information that is available may be difficult to interpret. In such a situation, customers will look to factors such as trust and reputation to guide their choice (McKechnie, 1992) and are likely to be rather more willing to restrict their choice set and form relationships with a particular supplier rather than undergo the high search costs associated with establishing credibility every time a purchase is made. From the supplier's perspective, most savings and investment products are long term in nature and many require regular contact (payment of premiums, policy updates) between supplier and customer. Consequently, the infrastructure for building a relationship is largely in place. However, anecdotal evidence would suggest that this opportunity has yet to be fully exploited by suppliers of savings and investment products.

Customer relationships in financial services

The concept of building long-term relationships with customers has its origins in industrial marketing and specifically the work of the IMP group (see, for example, Ford, 1990). Increasingly, theorists and practitioners are recognizing that many of the features and processes of relational exchange can be transferred from organizational to final consumer markets and that such a transfer, if implemented effectively, can result in benefits to both buyers and sellers. These benefits are particularly important in the case of highly intangible services such as financial advice and the purchase of savings and investment products. From the customers' perspective, the purchase process is characterized by a heavy reliance on credence qualities and information asymmetries are significant. Accordingly, the perceived risk associated with the purchase is high and consumers are likely to experience high levels of postpurchase dissonance. From the perspective of the buyer an effective relationship with a financial adviser can help to reduce risk (Zeithaml, 1981; Berry, 1983) and mitigate the adverse effect of dissonance; such a relationship may also serve to reduce search costs and other forms of transactions costs relating to future purchases. From the perspective of the seller, it is argued that relationships influence loyalty and satisfaction and thus can have positive effects on profitability (Reichheld and Sasser, 1990; Rust and Zahorik, 1993). Furthermore, the fact that many savings and investment products are long term in nature provides a context for the development of a relationship.

The nature of the financial services marketplace is such that RM would appear to offer many benefits, particularly in the form of improved retention rates. However this approach is not without problems. In consumer markets, relationships have to be developed with a large number of small customers rather than with a small number of large customers. This is, in many senses, a much more complex exercise (Hogg *et al.*, 1993) and the success of such approaches will be heavily dependent on the effective use of information technology and customer databases to support those involved in developing relationships. Care must be taken, however, to avoid implementing a form of database marketing and disguising this as RM (Barnes, 1994). Otherwise, as Gummesson (1994) suggests, RM will not move beyond a form of customer manipulation, as sometimes witnessed in transaction marketing. In the same way that there are problems associated with transferring the relationship concept from industrial to consumer markets, there are also problems associated with transferring the retention concept from consumer markets to personal financial services. In particular, it is necessary to clarify the meaning of the term 'retention' in the context of financial services.

Retention generally refers to the decision (active or passive) of a customer to continue to purchase goods or services from a particular organization. As many financial services are long term in nature, it may be appropriate to distinguish between two different dimensions of retention. The first would refer to the continuance of a particular contract, whether in the form of the continued use of a bank account or the continued payment of premiums on a life-insurance policy. The second dimension is concerned with the retention of the customer and the ability of the organization to sell an increasing number and variety of products (cross-selling). The former can be described as contract retention while the latter we describe as client retention. Both forms of retention can be facilitated by the development of effective relationships with clients, although it seems likely that client retention will prove more difficult without contract retention. Contract retention does not, however, guarantee client retention. Simply because a contract is retained does not mean that a customer is satisfied; some retained contracts will reflect a form of spurious loyalty (Dick and Basu, 1994) owing to inertia and/or switching costs. This phenomenon is likely to be common in a number of markets. However, in financial services there is an additional problem of latent loyalty – the satisfied customer who does not repurchase, and in some segments of the market this may reflect a rational decision by the customer to spread risk through purchases from a number of different suppliers.

The development of RM in personal financial services is heavily dependent on the operation and behaviour of distribution channels. Channel structure is essentially simple; there are product providers (insurance companies, unit and investment trusts) who effectively 'manufacture' a range of financial services and there are intermediaries (sales staff, financial advisers, brokers, etc.) who make these various services available to the end user. A key feature of these intermediaries is their role in the provision of financial advice; with the exception of a small number of direct sellers (such as Virgin Direct), all other intermediaries have an advisory role. For analytical purposes, intermediaries may be part of the provider organization[2] (i.e. a direct salesforce) or organizationally separate. Those intermediaries which are organizationally separate may be further divided according to whether they are independent financial advisers (IFAs) who are required to advise on the products of all providers or authorized representatives (ARs) who are authorized to advise only on the products of a single provider. In many respects, ARs can be viewed as a franchised direct salesforce.

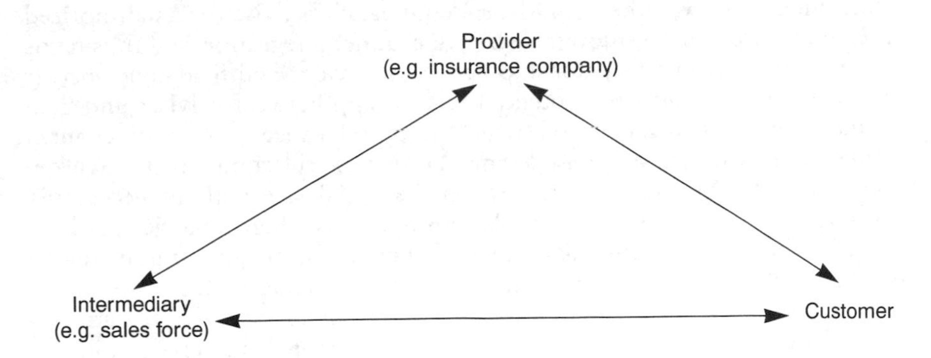

Figure 9.1 Channel relationships

As Figure 9.1 shows, within the basic channel structure, three types of relationship exist – provider–intermediary, provider–customer and intermediary–customer. Customers typically have stronger relationships with the intermediary than with the company providing the relevant financial services, a situation typified by the eponymous 'man from the Pru'. Quite simply, the personal contact between adviser and client traditionally provided a much stronger base for the development of a relationship than the formal and impersonal contact between provider and client.[3] Increasingly, however, product providers are attempting to build stronger relationships with the customer to enhance both contract and client retention. This strategy reflects both the value of retaining customers and the threats to retention which may exist because of the strength of the customer's relationship with an individual adviser. If the primary relationship exists between customer and financial adviser then the provider–customer relationship becomes vulnerable to changes in the provider–intermediary relationship. If an intermediary ends a relationship with a particular provider then that provider may risk losing the customers who have a relationship with that intermediary. In some respects the IFA presents less of a threat in this context because IFAs will have relationships with a range of providers and in principle must always advise on (and recommend from) the full range of products available. Of much greater significance to an individual provider is the loss of members of a salesforce or the decision of an AR to switch providers, since either of these occurrences could result in customers following an intermediary to a competing supplier. Clearly, then, a provider's ability to retain customers depends not only on the provider–customer relationship but also on the provider–intermediary relationship.

Analytically, there are a number of other important features of the structure of distribution channels which have important implications for the understanding of marketing relationships. Where a supplier can also act as an adviser/distributor (through its own direct salesforce or, increasingly, through bancassurance) then the distribution channel is highly integrated and the ultimate supplier is closer to the customer. This closeness to the customer should enhance the supplier's ability to build relationships with final consumers because, although these customers may have their primary relationship with a particular adviser, that adviser has a clear tie to the provider. The use of a distinct intermediary, either an independent financial adviser or an authorized representative, produces a lower degree of channel integration and thus tends to weaken the potential relationship between provider and final consumer. It may however strengthen the potential relationship between adviser and final consumer. A further dimension which is of relevance is that of channel remuneration. Commission-based remuneration is still common (though declining) and its main effect is to reward the initial sale without necessarily encouraging the development of a relationship. Thus where a particular channel relies heavily on commission-based remuneration the intermediary–customer link is likely to be more transactional than relational.

To explore more fully the implications of these dimensions of distribution, it is appropriate to consider the major distribution channels in more detail. The focus is on those channels which have an advisory role since this provides the context for the interaction which forms the basis of the relationship between adviser and customer. Direct channels which do not have an advisory role are still small but increasing in importance. RM will undoubtedly have a role to play in such channels, but it seems likely that with direct sales the relationship is likely to be with the brand, rather than with an individual.

Independent financial advisers (IFAs)

The distinguishing characteristic of IFAs is that the IFA is required to give customers 'best advice' on the full range of products available. The IFA should have no specific company preference. In principle, the requirements associated with independent status suggest that the IFA is the most desirable channel from the perspective of the consumer. Furthermore, independent status should enhance the ability of an IFA to build and maintain customer trust simply because the IFA is explicitly working on behalf of the customer rather than on behalf of a product provider. In practice, limited consumer knowledge (Ennew, 1992) tends to restrict the extent to which consumers rely on IFAs, and certain biases in commission structures (Devlin and Ennew, 1993) have meant that advice has not always been truly independent. Nevertheless, recent sales figures from the Association of British Insurers suggest that IFAs are increasing their share of new business and this may reflect greater customer awareness of this channel and greater distrust of some of the alternative channels following extensive publicity about mis-selling.

While the nature of the IFA channels is one that should facilitate RM between intermediary and customer, its implications for the relationship between provider and customer are rather different. Distributing via an IFA lengthens the distance between consumer and company in terms of communication, making it difficult to control the information that is being passed to the consumer. In principle, the higher quality of advice which might be expected from an IFA might suggest that the scope for contract retention is higher than with non-independent channels, although the opportunity for client retention may be restricted because there is no certainty that the IFA will continue to recommend the same company's products. Indeed, there are regulatory problems when an IFA displays heavy dependence on a single company's product. From a company perspective, retention via IFA channels can really only be built on by providing a quality product with appropriate support and marketing to the

IFA to encourage recommendation of that company's products. However, although such exercises can encourage the take-up of products, they may have limited impact on client retention.

Direct salesforces

The direct salesforce (DSF) channel consists of sales personnel who are retained by a particular life-insurance company or financial services supplier to sell the company's products to the public. This has been used successfully to distribute products to all segments of the financial services marketplace. The continuing publicity engendered by regulation and mis-selling tends to suggest that this channel is under some pressure, particularly in terms of remuneration structures. Many companies have withdrawn from the use of the DSF channel entirely[4] and others have altered remuneration structures to increase the salary element. In addition, bancassurers currently have a cost advantage, which some will undoubtedly turn into a price advantage.

Since the DSF is integrated with the product supplier, there are shorter communication links between customer and company. This closer relationship should in principle enhance client retention and even contract retention. However, in practice, traditional commission structures rewarded the DSF for customer acquisition but not for customer servicing. While this reliance on commission provided a logical means of reducing the agency costs associated with the selling function, it also tended to restrict the opportunities for client retention. Recent research by Morgan and Chadha (1995) suggests that customer orientation is weak in the DSF channel, that greater emphasis is given to client acquisition than to retention and that much of the business conducted through this channel is essentially transactional rather than relational. Furthermore, the traditionally high levels of staff turnover within DSFs mean that providers remain vulnerable to loss of customers through the loss of staff, providing perhaps one of the simplest illustrations of the importance of employee satisfaction and retention as a contributor to customer satisfaction and retention (Clarke and Payne, 1993).

Thus, in the case of the DSF, although the integrated channel structure appears to present advantages in terms of closer customer relationships, it seems likely that these will be cancelled out by the disadvantages associated with commission-based remuneration structures and high salesforce turnover.

Authorized representatives

The term authorized representative is used to describe an organization which is authorized to sell the products of one provider only. Normally an AR is a separate corporate entity, engaged in a main business activity other than life and pensions sales, with several life and pension sales employees. Estate agents are perhaps the best example of small-scale ARs, while many of the large building societies held AR status until recent moves to establish in-house provision. Analytically, the AR is effectively a franchised direct salesforce. It is also the channel which is under most threat; sales through ARs have declined since 1991 and are likely to continue to do so as more major building societies (partly as a result of deregulation) look to establish their own life operations.

Considering the implications of this type of channel for customer relationships and customer retention, this decline is perhaps unsurprising. As a separate organizational entity, the AR channel does not offer the provider the same potential degree of closeness to the customer and, at the same time, as a representative of one provider only, the AR may be subject to the same public distrust as the direct salesforce. The degree to which ARs switch providers is rather less than the degree of mobility among the members of a direct salesforce and this may have some beneficial effects in terms of customer retention. Specifically, although the relationship with the final customer is at a distance, efforts by the AR to ensure client retention will lead to client retention for the provider because of the exclusive distribution arrangement. However, it would seem that for many providers this is small compensation for the loss of customer closeness and the poor public image. Consequently there are moves by the provider organization to internalize ARs where appropriate and bring them into the direct salesforce.

Bancassurance

A major development of the 1990s has been that banks and building societies have assumed ownership of production of insurance products. Rather than simply selling savings and investment products 'manufactured' elsewhere, banks and building societies have integrated backwards, forming their own life companies to provide a range of products to be sold through their own salesforces. This form of distribution is called bancassurance and tends to be of lower cost as the banks take advantage of the synergies of production and maintenance between insurance and more traditional forms of finance. Bancassurance has thus emerged as a specific distribution channel which is highly integrated and typically heavily reliant on salary rather than commission as the basis of salesforce remuneration. Customers in this channel are more directly linked to the provider and indeed in many instances will already have an established banking, saving or mortgage relationship with that provider. This provides the bancassurer with the opportunity to build strong and substantial relationships with customers through their ability to meet the full range of a customer's financial needs and to build on an established image and reputation in so doing. In addition, the salesforce are more likely to be in a position to develop relationships with customers because of the limited emphasis given to commission. In principle, the closer relationship between customer and provider should improve the opportunities for contract retention and the systems for managing the salesforce should improve the opportunities for client retention.

While it is clear that bancassurance (as a variant of the traditional direct salesforce channel) has many of the characteristics which suggest a relationship orientation, there are still a number of operational problems to address. Not all bancassurers organize their selling activities in the same way; in some cases, selling is closely integrated with the activities of the branch network, while in others the salesforce is a separate entity with only tenuous links to the branch. Morgan (1993) suggests that operational problems may be reduced and customer orientation increased through a high degree of integration of the salesforce. However, this is difficult to achieve and requires substantial structural and cultural change. Furthermore, the level of competition in these markets and pressures on profitability may lead to a less than customer-orientated approach to selling even from the bancassurers (Knights, Sturdy and Morgan, 1994).

Distribution channels can be seen as the key to the development of relationships between provider and customer, with those relationships being developed in the context of the relationship that is established between adviser and customer. The closer and more integrated the links between the parties involved in the delivery of savings and investment products, then the greater the opportunity to build effective relationships and encourage retention. While the nature of the marketplace is such that the development of a relationship is likely to be attractive to a large segment of the market, the extent to which this opportunity has been exploited may be open to some debate. The precise nature of customer relationships in this market has been relatively under-researched; nevertheless, there is some limited information on retention, which is perhaps one of the most tangible manifestations of effective relationship building.

The UK life-insurance market has received some severe criticism for its poor contract-retention record. Figures based on the termination and lapse data supplied to the Department of Trade and Industry regularly show that over 20% of new contracts sold are terminated within the first year, and a further 20% lapse in the subsequent two years. Recent figures announced for 1993 (*The Observer*, 29 January 1995) suggest that contract retention appears to be better for those insurers which rely on independent intermediaries. This seems to imply that an independent financial adviser is better at retaining customers than a direct-sales life office. Certainly this evidence is not inconsistent with the arguments presented earlier; IFAs were expected to have rather better contract retention as a consequence of the anticipated better quality of the initial product. The weaknesses associated with direct sales are again consistent with the concern expressed about the inability of commission to incentivize relationship building and the high level of salesforce turnover.

Following the 1992 survey by the Securities and Investments Board, a number of the largest life insurers commissioned research to investigate why so many contracts were terminated (Survey Research Associates, 1992). This research demonstrated that, in over two-thirds of cases, customers who terminated their contracts did so because of some unforeseen change in their personal circumstances (such as redundancy) and not because they were unhappy with the performance of the insurer or the advice or service they had received. Over 75% of all surveyed respondents were satisfied with their insurer, and would be quite happy to deal with that company again. However overall customer satisfaction and retention were substantially lower where the main reason for terminating the contract is the result of dissatisfaction with the insurer's service – particularly in relation to the advice given on the termination decision itself (e.g. alternatives, penalties, etc.). It appears therefore that insurers which are unable to retain a customer's contract may still be able to maintain a long-term relationship (i.e. client retention) so long as the termination arose for unforeseen reasons and the customer was properly advised.

From this survey evidence it would appear that the performance of financial advisers and product providers in building customer relationships has been reasonable, although the results should be treated with some caution given that this work was undertaken before some of the worst excesses of pensions mis-selling were disclosed. Furthermore, while the survey evidence may be optimistic with respect to contract retention, the position with respect to client retention is weaker. While there is little hard evidence on the extent of client retention, industry estimates suggest that the average customer holds around 1.5 products from the same supplier and that even the most effective providers only achieve a product holding of around 2 per customer.

Conclusions

RM is becoming increasingly important in the competitive financial services marketplace. In the specific case of savings and investment products, financial advisers are facilitating major purchases which are considered to be relatively high risk, complex and long term. Information problems are significant and the development of trust is crucial to the sales process. RM provides a mechanism for reducing perceived risk, mitigating feelings of dissonance and reducing search and transactions cost. Ultimately, a strong customer relationship should encourage repeat purchases and the performance benefits which result from improved retention rates. These strong relationships exist where the customers feel that they are treated as valued individuals and that customer service is critical in developing such feelings. Ultimately, these relationships are built through the delivery system, but the review in this chapter suggests that different types of channel structure have different implications for relationship development. Furthermore, because of the nature of distribution it is important to distinguish between provider–customer relationships and intermediary–customer relationships since this distinction may generate conflict between provider and intermediary. To some degree this type of problem may be resolved by a high degree of integration in channel structures of the form that is occurring in bancassurance. Alternatively, some providers may choose to concentrate on the IFA channel and in so doing de-emphasize their relationship with the final customer and concentrate instead on their relationship with the intermediary. Irrespective of how the industry develops, it is clear that although RM is important, there is still considerable progress to be made in developing a genuine relational orientation; recent scandals concerning the mis-selling of a range of financial products serve only to highlight the tendency for providers and intermediaries to adopt a short-term perspective on their business activities.

Notes

1. Figures from the Association of British Insurers (1994) suggest that for 1994, less than 3% of annual premium income (life and pensions) came from sales which were direct and did not use the services of a financial adviser of some sort.
2. This category covers the rapidly developing bancassurance channel which has the same basic structure of a provider with a direct salesforce. Some of the distinctive features of bancassurance will be considered in greater detail later.

3. Some would question whether a customer can have a relationship with a company or whether, in fact, that relationship will always be with an employee of a company (Barnes, 1994).

4. For example, Commercial Union has recently sold its commission-based salesforce to Abbey Life, and Guardian Financial Services has disbanded its salesforce. Legal and General has cut its salesforce in half and Norwich Union has reduced its salesforce to 150 from a peak of 800.

References

Barnes, J.G. (1994) Close to the customer: but is it really a relationship? *Journal of Marketing Management*, Vol. 10, pp. 561–70.

Berry, L.L. (1983) Relationship marketing. In L.L. Berry *et al.* (eds) *Emerging Perspectives in Services Marketing*, AMA, Chicago, Ill.

Burton, D. (1994) *Financial Services and the Consumer*, Routledge, London.

Clarke, M. and Payne, A.F.T. (1993) Customer retention: does employee retention hold the key to success? In *Emerging Issues in Marketing, Proceedings of the 1993 Marketing Education Group Conference*, Loughborough.

Devlin, J.F. and Ennew, C.T. (1993) Regulating the distribution of savings and investment products: retrospect and prospect, *International Journal of Bank Marketing*, Vol. 11, pp. 3–10.

Devlin, J.F. and Wright, M. (1995) The changing environment of financial services. In C.T. Ennew, T. Watkins and M. Wright (eds) *Marketing Financial Services*, Heinemann, Oxford.

Dick, A. and Basu, K. (1994) Customer loyalty: towards an integrated conceptual framework, *Journal of the Academy of Marketing Science*, Vol. 22, pp. 99–113.

Ennew, C.T. (1992) Consumer attitudes to independent financial advice, *International Journal of Bank Marketing*, Vol. 10, pp. 13–19.

Ennew, C.T., MacGregor, A. and Diacon, S. (1994) Ethical issues in the marketing of savings and investment products in the UK, *Business Ethics: A European Review*, Vol. 3, pp. 123–9.

Ford, D. (ed.) (1990) *Understanding Business Markets: Interaction, Relationships and Networks*, Academic Press, London.

Gower, L.C.B. (1982) *Review of Investor Protection: A Discussion Document*, HMSO, London.

Gummesson, E. (1994) Making relationship marketing operational, *International Journal of Service Industry Management*, Vol. 5, pp. 5–20.

Hogg, M.K., Long, G., Hartley, M. and Angold, S. (1993) Touch me, hold me, squeeze me, freeze me: privacy – the emerging issue for relationship marketing in the 1990s. In *Emerging Issues in Marketing, Proceedings of the 1993 Marketing Education Group Conference*, Loughborough.

Knights, D., Sturdy, A. and Morgan, G. (1994) The consumer rules: an examination of rhetoric and 'reality' of marketing in financial services, *European Journal of Marketing*, Vol. 28, pp. 42–54.

McAlexander, J.H. and Scammon, D.L. (1988) Are disclosures sufficient? A micro analysis of impact in the financial services market, *Journal of Public Policy and Marketing*, Vol. 7, pp. 185–202.

McKechnie, S. (1992) Consumer buying behaviour in financial services: an overview, *International Journal of Bank Marketing*, Vol. 10, pp. 4–12.

Morgan, G. (1993) Branch networks and insurance selling, *International Journal of Bank Marketing*, Vol. 11, pp. 27–32.

Morgan, R.E. and Chadha, S. (1995) Relationship marketing at the service encounter: the case of life insurance, *The Service Industries Journal*, Vol. 13, pp. 112–25.

OFT (1992) *Savings and Investments: Consumer Issues*. Occasional paper to the OFT based on reports by two consultants – Jeremy Mitchell and Helena Wiesner, OFT, London, June.

Palmer, A. and Bejou, D. (1994) Buyer–seller relationships: a conceptual model and empirical investigation, *Journal of Marketing Management*, Vol. 10, pp. 495–512.

Reichheld, F. and Sasser, W.E. (1990) Zero defections: quality comes to services, *Harvard Business Review*, September–October, pp. 105–11.

Rust, R.T. and Zahorik, A.J. (1993) Customer satisfaction, customer retention and market share, *Journal of Retailing*, Vol. 69, pp. 193–215.

Survey Research Associates (1992) *Persistency Research*, Survey Research Associates, London.

Zeithaml, V.A. (1981) How consumer evaluation processes differ between goods and services. In J.H. Donnelly and W.R. George (eds) *Marketing of Services*, AMA, Chicago, Ill.

10

Airlines

David Gilbert

Introduction

The marketing of airlines has evolved dramatically throughout the past 50 years. The early history of air transportation was one in which carriers emphasized security, safety and efficiency. We are often unaware that many of the early ventures of airline companies were unsuccessful owing to the superior benefits of railway transport systems especially with regard to safety. Early aircraft safety, speed and range offered few benefits over those of alternative means of transport. However, from the 1920s onward growth occurred for companies like Imperial Airways (the forerunner of British Airways) who were supported by subsidies from the government. This protection was an attempt to safeguard the airline against price cutting by French companies and such intervention became the pattern for flag-carrying airlines until just recently. Since earliest times the aviation industry has been a cyclical business. It is affected by recessions and other economic conditions and because of political intercession has been the subject of cartels, protectionism and hidden subsidies.

The 1990s witnessed the world airlines struggling for demand and market share on the basis of both discounted fares and promotional campaigns. This has led to a number of weaknesses linked to revenue generation and profitability. It is thought that the European airline industry is oversubscribed by airline operators and while this is the case profitability will remain a major problem. In order to address these problems airlines are adopting RM schemes which aim to

1. enhance the satisfaction of customers;
2. build greater customer loyalty and retention;
3. develop longer-term relationships; and
4. lead ultimately to increased sales and profits.

The attempt to become more competitive, as with all modern marketing, is based upon the segmentation of the airline market. This is of paramount importance to airlines as different promotional tools are required for each segment.

Air travel segments

Airline companies utilize market segmentation as a means of providing the right product (services) for different subgroups of customers. Once the relevant characteristics of consumer groups are identified they are treated as a target market. The demand for air travel can be divided into four broad customer segments (Gilbert, 1995) based on purpose of journey:

1. Business travellers (corporate, independent, conference, incentive).
2. Travelling for leisure purposes (holiday-makers or visiting friends and relations).
3. Travelling for personal reasons (student travel to place of study, visiting sick relations, migration).
4. In addition there is the revenue earned from the transport of mail and freight.

Each of the above sements can also be subdivided into *length of journey* as to whether it is short or long haul; *traveller characteristics* as to whether of a specific age, gender, occupation, income group; *flying experience* in terms of knowledge and background of previous flights; and *length of stay*, related to peak versus non-peak travel or any one day or combination of days of the week. The following sections describe the main segments in greater detail.

Business travel

Business travel by air is an important segment which can be defined as: 'A journey made for purposes which would be in conjunction with a person's employment and which is paid for by the employer not the individual.' While we tend to think of business travel as business meetings, other forms of business travel also exist. These are connected to attendance at a conference, workshop or seminar or as part of an incentive scheme for the employees.

Therefore business trips are related to a need for business activity and as such the purchaser of the ticket is the self-employed business person, the company or organization. The usual requirements for business travel passengers are those of a fast, comfortable journey with a high frequency of flights to enable travel plans to be altered as short notice. The total cost of business travel is substantial and represents on average about 5–6% of a company's total costs for different European countries (O'Brien, 1993) and 2.5% of the European gross domestic product (*The Financial Times*, 1993). The business traveller represents the most important area for profit as the ticket price normally represents a higher average value than that of the leisure traveller. Owing to the frequency and value of business travel it is this segment which is targeted for the building up of long-term alliances as part of RM initiatives.

Leisure travel

The second type of passenger segment is the one travelling for leisure purposes and paying from his or her own budget. This market is very important owing to its size and the ability of airlines to achieve bookings well in advance of departure dates. This is in contrast to the business travel market where there is a great deal more demand for last-minute travel. This segment is more price sensitive than that representing the business traveller. Economy prices made available through different booking schemes or last-minute offers are an important part of the airline marketing-mix offering rather than loyalty-building schemes.

There are other differences which characterize the leisure traveller. The leisure traveller is likely to stay for longer durations and to require less frequency of operation owing to this segment's flexibility regarding departure times. Demand from this segment is often seasonal with far greater demand occurring in school holiday periods.

Special reason travel

The final submarket relates to those who travel for personal reasons and pay from their own budget. The individual travelling for personal purposes is normally travelling at the last moment and has special reasons for travel such as urgent family matters or illness. Quite often the journey is in reaction to unpredicted circumstances. The trip is often taken with limited time availability and therefore schedule times and flight availability become important considerations. However, there is also price-sensitive travel such as that of students who journey to their place of study.

Competitive strategies

To be successful airline operators require a reduction in the level of costs and improvements in promotion. The growing trend is for airlines to seek as many efficiencies as possible for their operation. This is brought about in three ways:

1. *Association* Links between airlines through equity or co-operation arrangements, e.g. KLM and Air UK, BA and TAT, Air France and Sabena. Sometimes the links are forged as part of a longer-term strategy to provide for hub or even global domination. This limits rivalry and therefore price competition. It may also lead to the sharing of computer reservation systems (CRS) and shared costs for CRS and frequent-flyer development programmes.
2. *Efficiencies through scope and scale* Airlines have introduced less costly operations, e.g. Lufthansa Express and Condor owned by Lufthansa, or Iberia and Viva Air. The totality of the volumes of passengers carried by all the brands, in terms of scale, can lead to larger budgets being made available for travel-agent incentives or frequent-flyer programmes. This provides for specific competitive advantage.
3. *Overhead efficiencies* Cost saving achieved through the reduction of staff and the selling off of peripheral services such as catering so as to increase procurement power and have flexibility of purchasing for the non-core functions.

The airline industry has recently lost the cushion of support owing to deregulation in the USA and liberalization in Europe. The contemporary pressure on airline competitiveness has led to the need for sophisticated marketing, especially in relation to the customer. Even so, fewer airlines now exist, with many of the larger carriers needing to enhance demand from their higher-yield target segments such as business travellers. As part of this move there was the need for a sharper focus and an increasing use of sales-promotion techniques. One such recently developed marketing tool adopted by the airline industry is that of frequent-flyer programmes (FFPs). These are schemes which provide rewards for the frequency of usage of the airline and therefore build preference for one brand over another.

Frequent-flyer programmes

An FFP is a club concept with passenger rewards for loyalty. Members accumulate benefits in direct relation to their utilization of the airline or its affiliate services. High air-mileage passengers and those who fly on new routes or in low-demand periods may accrue progressively more attractive benefits. The power of this form of RM is that it offers benefits which can be redeemed in the air travellers' free leisure time and for their partners or family. If an airline offers initial credits and has a large enough network giving flight choice, the travel patterns of business flyers can be dramatically altered owing to the rewards offered. Enrolment is typically completed through the filling-in of a short application form which will capture details of the address for the promotional material and accumulated credit statements to be forwarded to at regular intervals. The airlines automatically follow the individual's booking patterns through the use of their CRS as members have simply to present their membership cards, when checking in for a flight, for the data to be captured.

The impact of deregulation of the US air transport sector in 1979 produced such a shake-out of the industry that it became essential to create cost-effective marketing promotions to persuade air travellers to remain loyal and provide consistency of demand. Given the drive towards safeguarding loadfactors, the airline business rapidly recognized and transformed otherwise underutilized capacity into a marketing tool for rewarding passenger loyalty. In a business where an empty aircraft seat flown on a scheduled sector represents irredeemable value, the advantage of developing this form of RM proved irresistible. RM was not accepted easily because at the time observers within and outside the industry thought FFPs to be a marketing gimmick of only peripheral importance (Levine, 1987). However, across the different airline brands FFP became successful because they appeal to the same instincts that induce people to save coupons or buy lottery tickets. Historically, in the evolution of airline marketing, FFPs are a direct link to Southwest Airline's 1970s' scheme of giving 'sweetheart stamps' for bookings which would allow the business traveller to collect benefits in order to take a partner on a free flight. Given the value placed upon free travel for a business person's family, or friends, the FFP promotions became an increasing compulsion to be sought out by millions of regular air travellers. Timing though was all important as the attainment of increased demand through FFPs took place at an appropriate moment. This is because the period of launch of the promotions took place after the introduction of deregulation. The notion of giving away flights in exchange for revenue passage on US airlines would not have been contemplated prior to deregulation as it would have created a serious violation of US anti-trust laws.

In 1980 Western Airlines introduced a $50 discount voucher for passengers who had completed five trips on its programme. This was the first attempt to reward a consumer for repeated loyalty. While the scheme had to be abandoned within a brief time, owing to the administrative problems of forgery, fraud and theft, it did sow the seeds for later relationship programme development. In fact the subsequent size and growth of the FFP schemes has been extensive, as is shown in the following quotation: 'More than one trillion miles – enough to take you to some of the planets and back – have been earned since frequent flyer programmes first made their debut back in the early '80s' (*IAPA World*, 1994).

The evolution of frequent-flyer programmes

Fierce battles to capture market share have produced a series of clever marketing initiatives within airline marketing departments. The development of relationship programmes can be traced to the application of the use of CRSs. American Airlines utilized the Sabre system to trawl its sales-history data in order to reveal the travel patterns of its passengers. The sales team identified the telephone numbers of those passengers who had flown more than twice in six-month periods. Once identified they were recruited to the 'Very Important Travellers Club' which provided recognition through such benefits as identifying baggage labels and improved menu choice. It did not take the sales team long to recognize the importance the passengers gave to free air-travel miles. American Airlines' AAdvantage programme, initiated in May 1981, became the industry standard to be copied as part of globalized market promotion practices centring around the frequent-traveller concept. American had no early worry that it could be copied owing to its belief that with such an extensive route system it could sustain a competitive advantage. However, within a short space of time the emulators were offering superior benefits to American which forced the airline's marketing people to alter their programme to match that of the competition.

Prior to RM schemes, if airlines required data on their passengers they could only utilize two sources. One was the travel agents, who jealously guarded information in the belief that airlines would bypass them if they could have personal data on their passengers. The other was their CRS which only held limited details of the customer base. The advent of RM schemes which compiled extensive databases expanded the range of options available for marketing departments to enable the larger carriers to gain advantage over the smaller airlines. In fact the strength of clubs has enabled current airline companies to produce a significant barrier to new entrants into the airline industry.

The very success of the early FFPs provided the basis for their retention and development. By the end of 1986, 24 out of 27 US carriers had devised similar programmes. Since their appearance they have grown rapidly into the largest promotional weapon of the major carriers. For example, American Airlines has 22 million club members (*EuroBusiness*, 1994). Once adopted, a 'club' basis for the flyer programme is developed which relies on the targeting of the right market for increases in member recruitment. The database developed for and from such clubs offers an abundance of information on travel patterns for which special promotional offers can be constructed. In addition benefits can be introduced tactically with increases in points or selected routes, and these being communicated to the club member base.

The programmes, created to build brand loyalty, offer concessions in relation to the level of usage of flights with the airline.

Extra credits can be gained for

- taking a flight with the airline within two months of joining the programme;
- booking a business-class or first-class cabin seat rather than economy;
- sending a parcel by air-freight utilizing the programme's airline;
- taking flights to any of those areas being specially promoted by the airline;
- booking a flight in identified periods of low demand; and
- leasing a car from affiliated car companies.

Through time, several modifications to the original FFP idea of providing free travel have occurred for US airlines (and increasingly their overseas imitators) to create new means by which their members could generate additional mileage credits, often from non-travel sources. Among the most popular of these have been the following:

- Non-airline travel services such as those offered by car rental companies, tour operators and hotel chains.
- Airline-affiliated credit-card purchases (i.e. mileage credits according to the volume of purchases processed through a particular card).
- Long-distance telephone calls through particular US telephone companies.
- Additionally, in some cases, credits for buying stocks and bonds through particular US brokerage houses.

Expansion of FFPs outside the USA

It took around ten years for the non-US carriers to introduce FFPs. Competition outside the US was related initially to European trans-Atlantic travellers who, although representing only a small proportion of the total market, found that they could accumulate attractive rewards on specific long-haul sectors. One turning point occurred when a survey of European passengers in the late 1980s revealed to sales and marketing personnel how many people had joined US FFPs. This brought home to the non-US airlines the effectiveness of relationship campaigns in capturing increases in the demand for high-yield, long-haul passengers.

Foreign carriers, having recognized the need to develop FFPs, were considerably slower than their US counterparts in integrating frequent-traveller programmes into their operations. In the 1980s this was in part owing to their underdeveloped CRSs technology – virtually a prerequisite for the movement and management of complex frequent-flyer travel arrangements, mileage awards and other benefits. Development was rapid in the light of the prospect of losing valuable high-yield traffic to US competitors and by the 1990s most European carriers, with British Airways in the vanguard, developed a variety of FFPs to counter this threat. BA was forced to launch Lattitudes in April 1991 owing to rising competition (*Travel Trade Gazette*, 1992). FFPs are currently also spreading rapidly to Asia and the Far East. It is quite clear, however, that Far East carriers are being drawn into the FFP culture with considerable reluctance. This reflects partly their relatively protected status, partly the buoyancy of their regional economy and partly a dislike of having the FFPs imposed on them by aggressive, revenue-hungry competitors from the USA and Europe. Verchere (1993) reported that Asia/Pacific carriers had to enter the FFP arena following the launch of the Qantas scheme which itself was an attempt to counteract US airlines operating trans-Pacific routes.

The business traveller and frequent-flyer programmes

Within the intensive and competitive airline market it has become clear that FFPs are having a considerable influence on travelling habits. It has been noticed that business travellers have increasingly been constructing their itineraries around the availability of promotional offers such as two-for-one tariffs or selecting an airline affiliated to their domestic FFP. Table 10.1 illustrates different reasons for the attraction of business travellers to join an FFP.

As with all promotions there is the need for innovation to compete against the wear-out factor of the scheme. Virgin Atlantic are offering action weekends and even a holiday on Richard Branson's private island in the Caribbean (Thomas Cook Travel Management, 1992). Whatever offers the airlines provide, the secret is for them to create biased behavioural responses expressed through time. Thus reward motivators act as a bias on decision-making and may replace existing brand loyalty. The demand which then exists is a specific form of preference buying behaviour which involves repeat commitment based upon the build-up of rewards being gained. Given an individual has a vested interest in gaining further credits for flights while the company pays for the flight costs, it is obvious there will be less price sensitivity of travel cost or the likelihood of defection to other airline schemes. Therefore FFPs currently are a very powerful marketing tool for airlines. However, a number of pressures are occurring which may prove as a warning signal to other highly competitive RM schemes.

Table 10.1 Reasons business travellers are attracted to FFPs

Feature	Importance of feature (%)
Waitlist priority	72
Mileage points	55
Lounge access	48
Upgrade available	46
Recognize status	36
Points from other schemes	25
Luggage tracing	25
Other rewards	12
Insurance schemes	12
Newsletters	3

Source: OAG, 1992.

The relationship marketing problems of frequent-flyer programmes

RM in the form of FFPs can be ruined if there is no due concern for the alienation of third parties and the overall cost and efficiency of expanding customer loyalty:

1. There is a growing hostility to the programmes by companies which fund business travel and cannot control their travel policies effectively owing to employee distortion of company guidelines.
2. Airlines have failed to recognize the heavy liability of unredeemed miles. This has placed a huge onus on replanning the rules and conditions of FFPs.
3. The failure to consider that when everyone offers similar rewards there is no competitive advantage and the cost of retaining existing, or winning new customers, may increase.
4. The government may introduce taxation on FFPs as a means of acquiring revenue benefits. There may also be tighter control of FFPs to re-establish a fairer market for smaller airlines or new entrants to the marketplace.

First strike: corporate antagonism towards FFPs

In the future the targeting of rewards may need to be reconsidered. Within the changes of administration of business travel is the emergence of the professional purchasing manager who wants to gain more for the organization and control the behaviour of the corporate traveller.

The changing 'corporate market' requires airline recognition of the shift from the demand-driven to that of a supply-driven environment. The need to direct RM to the corporate buyer and company, rather than the individual business traveller, is important owing to the power of the procurement professional in devising firm travel policies. Although FFPs have proved popular with passengers, particularly those travelling on business, they are seen to distort travel policies by the companies who actually pay for business travel. It is claimed that FFPs encourage unnecessary travel, travel at a higher fare than strictly required or travel by a circuitous route so as to use a particular airline. Many critics claim that the system of rewards offered to members has created a global travel frenzy by corporate mileage junkies more concerned with maximizing their travel perks than getting from A to B in the most cost-effective way. It is often noted that the relationship programmes have changed consumer travel habits with bizarre travel patterns emerging in terms of peculiar routeings and inefficient timings. Such a trend is a frustration to company travel managers who negotiate airfare deals on the basis of agreeing in advance a bulk number of travel arrangements with one or more leading carriers.

Wagonlits Travel confirmed that a growing number of senior company executives have concerns about airline incentive programmes. The majority felt that benefits such as upgrades, free tickets and frequent-flyer points should accrue to the company rather than individual travellers (*IAPA World*, 1994). It is argued that there is an ethical dilemma associated with employees' actions. There is a logical case for treating the incentive as a bribe rather than reward, in the same way that someone giving a company employee a free holiday in return for selecting a vendor would be offering a blatant bribe. As Stuller

(1992) has pointed out, it does not take much juggling of the business arrangements to ensure the chosen itinerary 'coincidentally' matches what the business traveller requires. Chandler (1986) had earlier categorized this as a form of employee embezzlement.

Some companies agree travel policies with their travel management company who then police company employees to take the lowest logical airfare – thus ensuring they are neither needlessly lengthening journey times nor paying full published fares when cheap excursion tickets are acceptable. Some companies are taking the view that any rewards should belong not to the individual but to the firm. Virgin Atlantic has been one airline which has recognized the importance of the corporate market and subsequently devised a package specifically for this market as well as the individual. Its programme has two levels. There is Individual Freeway, which any individual can join, and then there is Corporate Freeway, which is designed for quite small companies, e.g. those who fly 10–100 sectors in upper class a year.

Second strike: do airlines benefit from a relationship-orientated focus on FFPs?

While most airline publicity extols the virtues of the FFP concept, many privately question whether they actually enhance or erode yields. While reliance is placed on FFPs there is some evidence that FFPs do not displace carriers which dominate through a better service. Nako (1992) has shown that the competitive advantage of the larger airlines even with FFPs is significantly reduced when the smaller carrier has developed a successful hub. What is extremely worrying for the airlines has been the potential for FFP schemes to accumulate substantial quantities of unredeemed miles. Churchill (1993) has noted aviation experts have calculated that if all the unused air miles were redeemed on one day, 600,000 Boeing 747s would be needed to meet the demand. Fortunately, perhaps, most mileage never reaches the threshold where it can be used and a number of club members never redeem their miles. However, one

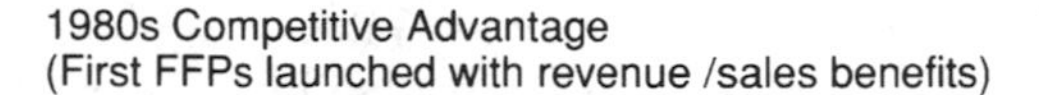

Figure 10.1 Cycle of FFP programmes

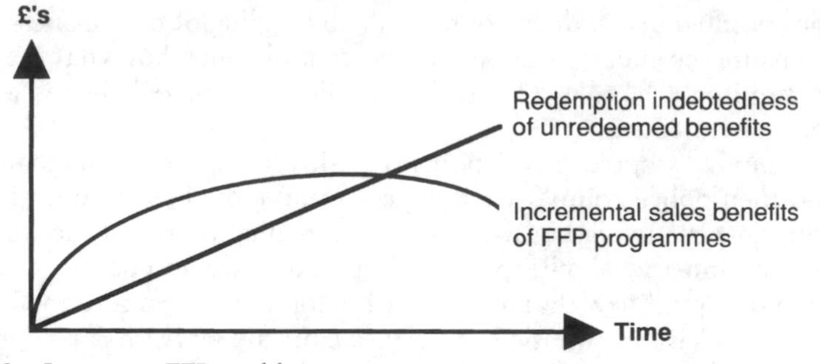

Figure 10.2 Long-run FFP problems

US airline is already giving away one in ten seats free. These are not always related to the FFP member as benefits are able to be brokered or sold on to others even though airlines outlaw the process (Mowlana and Smith, 1993).

The objective of any incentive scheme should be the reduction of the cost of the airline operation through incremental increases in demand which are cost effective. As the current schemes are offered by most major airlines and even consortiums are being forged between smaller carriers there is little competitive advantage to be found in their benefits. The rise and fall of competitive advantage is indicated in Figure 10.1 (Gilbert and Karabeyekian, 1995). This shows the cycle of the FFPs whereby it is now necessary to replan the conditions applicable to the airline RM programmes.

The current market position requires the need to replan the conditions of redemption as there is a growing risk of variable costs of airlines increasing so reducing the margin of safety between budgeted and break-even loadfactors. This may continue, as is shown in Figure 10.2 (Gilbert and Karabeyekian, 1995), where incremental sales are more difficult to achieve while the indebtedness to redemption of FFPs, is for ever increasing. Airlines operating flights on popular holiday routes oversubscribed with non-fare paying passengers from FFPs can dramatically affect a carrier's overall profitability. In a worst-case scenario if all FFP members were to redeem their miles at once fearing the end of such schemes, airlines could be catapulted into bankruptcy, rather like the run on a bank when all depositors rush to withdraw their money at the same time. The last evidence we had of the impact of redemption is when Pan Am insisted miles earned by 1983 had to be redeemed by mid-1984. Some 90% of miles were redeemed which created a massive loss owing to 11% of capacity being utilized (*Business Week*, 1984). Even those airlines who recognize the problems of ensuring no opportunity cost of a seat is lost realize there is still the cost of administration to be taken into account.

As a result of a fear of loss, ineligibility rules are now imposed on certain dates and sectors, often for periods of several weeks at a time, and the deadlines by which points must be redeemed have been shortened. Major US airlines have also reacted by raising the qualification for internal US flights from 20,000 to 25,000 miles flown and some have cut the bonus miles available for business and first-class travel. Protection is never as safe as airlines would hope. In one instance as airlines attempt to control the administration of FFPs a number of American travel agents discovered it was possible to book a ticket then turn up at the airport to check in and then cancel the ticket from the agency. This provided a refund on the tickets but allowed them the frequent-flyer miles (Hiscock, 1993).

On the subject of the treatment of allocating FFP seats, a recent study showed that the schemes are treated as neither a promotional loss nor an overall loss. In the case of Virgin Freeway this is not an issue since it is a financially separate company from Virgin Atlantic and consequently there is no loss or risk at all. Virgin Atlantic is just a customer, paying to participate in Virgin Freeway. It pays a set fee per month for the cost of miles issued for Freeway on their flights. This is then adjusted to redeem bookings on Virgin flights. Freeway does not have to pay at all. Virgin Atlantic just pays a lower fee compared to other partner airlines. For American Airlines, since the process is inventory controlled, frequent-flyer seats are allocated according to availability. Wherever there are no FFP seats available a member cannot redeem on the flight concerned. This overcomes Stuller's (1992) concern that the place passengers prefer is Hawaii not Cleveland. Demand for free places on the high-yield popular routes is always disproportionate and cannot be treated simply as a marginal cost. In April 1992 one in four passengers flew free to Hawaii, which culminated in a 20% reduction in yield per passenger and the displacement of paying customers (*ibid.*).

The benefits of RM programmes to the airline company accrue from the way the database is utilized. Given the company will have a record of its most important customers it can provide higher levels of customer satisfaction at every stage of the journey. Given it is known whether the customer smokes, his or her preferred drink, use of lounge, favourite magazines, paper, seat, and so on, there are ample opportunities to meet individual preferences. On boarding the plane a first-class passenger may be welcomed with the serving of his or her favourite drink and 'nice to see you flying with us again "Mr Loyal", we believe from our boarding notes you are a golfer and therefore would you like the latest golfing brochure to look at?' In addition information collected may mean various products and offers can be mailed out and details of response to these can also be monitored. The opportunity to make the customers feel a little more special by providing what they prefer ensures levels of expected service satisfaction are exceeded.

Third strike: the threat of taxing relationship club benefits

Several additional problems could arise in the near future regarding FFPs. One such predicament involves an interest by the collector. In Europe, some Brussels officials are already indicating that they believe it is necessary to ensure such personal benefits accrued by business travellers on frequent-flier schemes are taxed. This is a recent concern as the tax authorities have, in the past, taken the view that FFPs are not taxable for individuals because they are not a direct benefit arising from their employment.

One difficulty of any change if the Inland Revenue take a tougher line is related to how taxation should be applied. It is not possible to prove the benefits of the free flights are being taken and therefore it makes it difficult to apply taxation. Therefore, the only legitimate situation in which the benefit might be taxed is when the tickets are paid for by a business (where they are deductible as a business expense), with the rewards used by employees or owners for personal travel. The value of such rewards might be considered a type of 'in-kind' fringe benefit that should be subject to taxation. Furthermore, of the potentially taxable bonus awards, only those used for personal travel should be taxed. If companies insist that FFP benefits should accrue to them rather than individuals, and then they allocate those benefits to staff, they could be liable to providing tax on fringe benefits (Meade *et al.*, 1994).

Already in the USA, the Inland Revenue Service (IRS) has tried to tax participants on FFPs without any success. It would appear that the effort and organization of such an exercise were too difficult to mount and, as a result, the IRS dropped the idea. As Giertz (1988) reported, the taxation of bonuses may be beyond the administrative capability of the IRS.

Fourth strike: the question of distortion of the market

Owing to the highly competitive nature of the airline marketplace there is an underlying concern about anti-competitive marketing practices, particularly within the USA. It has been found that restrictive marketing practices associated increasingly with CRS and frequent-flyer offers make it more difficult for airlines to compete effectively in each other's markets.

The reason for FFPs to be considered as potentially anti-competitive is mainly because they favour larger airlines at the expense of smaller carriers. In the case of a flag carrier dominant in a particular city, its more extensive network of routes will encourage passengers wanting to collect FFP points. Cairns and Galbraith (1990) highlight that FFPs tend to result in barriers to entry on the demand side and this presents problems even for large carriers who want to start a new service on a route between two cities where it does not have a presence, and hence an inventory of FFP members. They argue entry at a competitor's hub will therefore only occur when an airline is extending service from its own hub.

With a consideration of unfair competitive practices both US and European regulators have recently focused their attention on aspects of anti-competitive influence that FFPs might have with the overall air-transport marketplace. In Europe, this could result in an EU code of conduct allowing smaller or weaker carriers to participate in bigger schemes and in rules preventing carriers from distorting market forces through overgenerous bonuses on selected routes. In the USA, on the other hand, steps to allow FFP benefits to become tradable and/or interchangeable between individuals via brokers could emerge as a means of lowering barriers to market entry. The background to discussions regarding unfairness is that the schemes in place cannot be easily replaced because they are increasingly regarded as an integral part of airline marketing.

The future

The situation in the USA over the past decade is one where the growth of frequent-flyer benefits has provided progressively less and less return owing to the number of similar programmes. The future may herald a return to more traditional choice criteria. In such markets the quality of the airline product may reassert itself as the primary governor of choice rather than the quantity

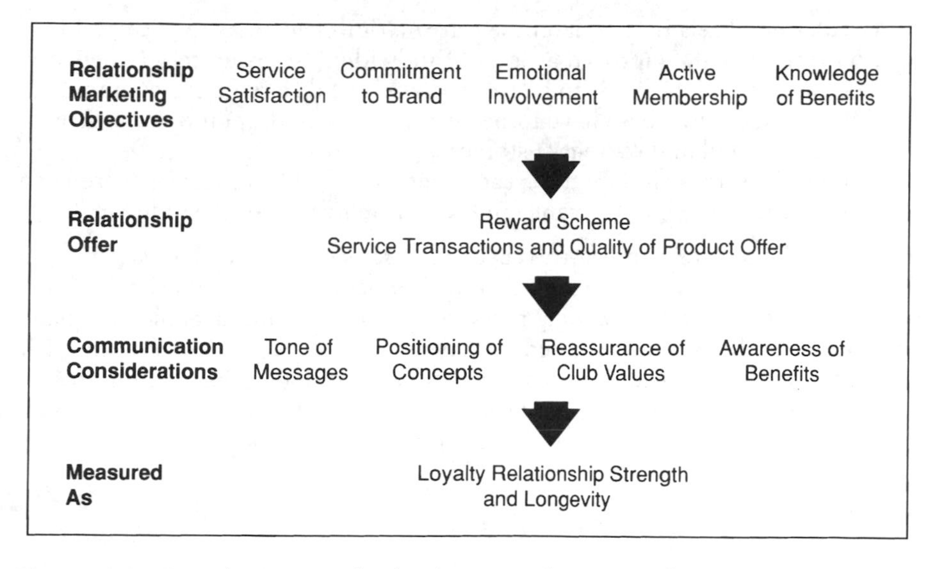

Figure 10.3 Considerations in the development of FFP RM schemes

of FFP rewards on offer. Moreover, the RM schemes may attempt to build affective or emotional commitment into the customer-service provider partnership. The future possibility exists of communicating with the club members where the emphasis is placed on the marketing literature sent out to members and the ways in which service expectations are met or exceeded. As stated previously, the CRSs of airlines are capable of allowing for more personalized service for passengers and of identifying the type of information they would value being sent to them. This could be a briefing document on business developments in countries they visit, changes in office technology which will affect their business or other areas of interest which correspond to the personal needs of the passenger. Figure 10.3 indicates some of the considerations for future RM schemes. These include communication considerations for all interfaces through literature and promotional material and advertisements. Such regard is important so as to ensure added-value and intangible benefits are associated with the company's RM offer.

Conclusion

It is clear that airline RM strategies differ between geographic areas. It has been observed that there are distinguishing features between FFP marketing in the US market and that of Europe. The American emphasis is on increasing frequency of use whereas in Europe there was a necessary reaction to compete and devise loyalty programmes. The rapid development of FFPs in Europe has more to do with the US marketing threat abroad and improving market competitiveness at home than with trying to dominate in markets through the use of RM axioms. This is disappointing because success can come from an improved approach to airline customers which incorporates three key elements of micromarketing:

1. Greater emphasis on the database information held so as to slice and portion it to provide improved aspects of individual or group service delivery.
2. The essence of RM needs to be the provision of differentiated communication and services. These have to be customized based upon the characteristics of potential and current customers.
3. The need to track and monitor each member of FFPs to ensure there is an assessment of the lifetime value and retention history of the individual.

However, the base of frequent-traveller programmes has become so general and led to such a build-up of rewards that such schemes are affecting profitability and effectiveness as well as adding pressure for constant product innovation and improvement. The schemes are here to stay as the evidence to date indicates that once FFPs are established, it is extremely difficult, if not impossible, for airlines to discontinue them. This is not a problem as long as the airlines adopt a more sophisticated RM approach than that demonstrated to date.

References

Business Week (1984) Does the frequent flyer game pay off for airlines? 27 August, p. 75.
Cairns, R. and Galbraith J. (1990) Artificial compatibility, barriers to entry and frequent flyer programs, *Canadian Journal of Economics*, Vol. 23, pp. 807–16.
Chandler, F.G. (1986) Will the airlines and corporations fight it out? *Official Airline Guide: Frequent Flyer*, November, p. 79.
Churchill, D. (1993) War in the air, *The Sunday Times*, 14 November, p. 8.
EuroBusiness (1994) Counting miles not money, October, pp. 8–10.
The Financial Times (1993) Business travel survey, 9 November, p. 5.
Giertz, F.J. (1988) IRS should steer clear of frequent flyers, *The Wall Street Journal*, 8 March, p. 8.
Gilbert, D. (1995) The air travel marketplace and customer. In P. Jones and M. Kipps (eds) *Flight Catering*, Longman, Harlow.
Gilbert, D. and Karabeyekian, V. (1995) The frequent flyer mess – a comparison of programmes in the USA and Europe, *Journal of Vacation Marketing*, Vol. 1, pp. 248–56.
Hiscock, J. (1993) Fly customers take airline for a ride, *The Sunday Telegraph*, 8 August, p. 32.
IAPA World (1994) Frequent flyer programmes, June.
Levine, M. (1987) Airline competition in deregulated markets, *Yale Journal on Regulation*, Spring, pp. 393–4.
Meade, E., Swenson, J., Lerner, H. and Fuller, J. (1994) Frequent flyer benefits analysed, *Journal of Taxation*, Vol. 80, p. 61.
Mowlana, H. and Smith, G. (1993) Tourism in a global context: the case of frequent traveller programs, *Journal of Travel Research*, Vol. 31, pp. 20–7.
Nako, S.M. (1992) Frequent flyer programs and business travellers: an empirical investigation, *Logistics and Transportation Review*, Vol. 28, pp. 395–414.
OAG (1992) *Business Traveller Lifestyle Survey*, Reed Travel Group, Bedfordshire.
O'Brien, K. (1993) The west European business travel market 1993–97. In *The Financial Times Management Report*, The Financial Times, London.
Stuller, J. (1992) Free ride, *Across the Board*, Vol. 29, pp. 16–21.
Thomas Cook Travel Management (1992) Airline reward schemes, *Air Matters*, November, p. 1.
Travel Trade Gazette (1992) BA to go it alone with US frequent flyer Plan, 13 February, p. 1.
Verchere, I. (1993) Frequent flyer programmes (Economist Intelligence Unit), *Travel and Tourism Analyst*, Vol. 3, pp. 5–19.

11

Hospitality

Suzanne C. Gilpin

The business of hospitality

The hospitality industry provides food, drink, accommodation and leisure facilities for business and leisure customers. Although the sector covers a variety of business types from small privately run fast-food outlets to international hotel and leisure chains, the emphasis in this chapter is on large hospitality organizations and hotel chains in particular.

'To be successful, the hotelier must keep the bar full, the house full, the storeroom full, the wine cellar full, the customers full, and not get full himself' (Garvey, 1986, p. 451). Garvey declares that the hotelier and his or her employees must be everything from quick thinkers, non-drinkers, mathematicians, to technicians, and at all times on the boss's side as well as the customer. He goes on to say that of the many skills an hotel operator is expected to master, the most important is marketing.

It is generally acknowledged that marketing is everything that touches the customer (Christopher, Payne and Ballantyne, 1991; McKenna, 1991; Grönroos, 1994). If it is the provider's role to supply what the customer wants, then it is up to that provider to understand the customer. Understanding customer needs in turn is the key to building longer-term relationships with customers themselves (Christopher, Payne and Ballantyne, 1991). But despite recognizing that the hospitality product is highly personalized with satisfaction being judged on individual experience (Lewis and Chambers, 1989, p. 46), the industry is still predominantly operations orientated. The traditional pattern of marketing evolution, as outlined in the introduction to this book and common to most consumer markets, has not occurred in hospitality. Indeed, according to Morrison (1989) it has been lagging behind manufacturing and packaged-goods firms in its use of marketing for perhaps as much as 10 or 20 years.

A historical reason for this slow development has been that many personnel, now holding key positions within the industry, have come up through the ranks, perhaps starting out as a chef or a waiter. One might have thought that such intensive 'hands-on' experience would have facilitated an exceptional understanding of the customer. However this has not been the case, with emphasis being placed on process rather than comprehension. Formal management education programmes available to managers today have to some degree overcome this traditional craft-orientated approach. Authors on the subject have claimed that the operations management and marketing are intrinsically linked within this sector (Chrissy, Boewadt and Laudadio, 1975; Lewis and Chambers, 1989; Reid, 1989). They argue that it is just as important for marketing personnel to understand the operational process and its limitations as it is for operations to understand and anticipate the customer.

As with many service industries common sources of conflict between hotel operators and their customers include the inability of some organizations to provide a consistent level of quality and service. In order to ensure product consistency, operational systems are often implemented seemingly for the convenience of the hotel rather than the customer. Recently operators have become increasingly preoccupied with the facilitation of opportunities for leisure and relaxation, in an effort to retain customer loyalty and increase product consumption. This increased emphasis on the requirements of regular customers and anticipating their future needs is intended to create a more positive and customer-friendly image.

Market structure

The hotel industry has rapidly developed from the large, often disjointed hotel groups of the 1970s to the uniform clearly branded portfolios of the 1990s. Where previously properties tended to be purchased or built according to their location or equity value, the hotel owners of the 1990s claim to place far greater emphasis on meeting the needs of the customer in terms of product specification. The result has been the evolution of multi- and family-brand portfolios, one of the most successful being the French Accor group. With a range of hotel types from the basic Formule 1 to the luxury of Sofitel they cater for business and leisure travellers on a wide range of budgets. The UK-based Forte group (recently acquired by Granada) underwent a well publicized rebranding and rationalization strategy in 1991 boasting a portfolio to suit nearly every type of customer – from the budget Travelodge brand to the luxurious individuality of the Grosvenor House Hotel, London. Thus there has been an evolution of hotel chains from a mixed portfolio of products under one corporate name to a rationalization that is based on customer rather than operator's needs. A clear brand positioning strategy offers customers an expectation of quality under the corporate umbrella but recognizes that not all have the same needs or indeed the same budget. This recognition has alleviated customer dissatisfaction and led to the building of stronger brand loyalty.

The hospitality market is segmented by purpose of visit and again into subsegments comprising leisure and business travel. Although most hotels target both leisure and business travellers, it is generally agreed that the business market is the more lucrative. The business market comprises not only travel and hotel accommodation but also conferences, training courses, incentive travel and special events such as private dinners and banquets. Bookings are made direct with the hotel group or through a specialist intermediary, usually a business travel agency. Local special events and banquets tend to be booked direct. Business travellers require accommodation and services throughout the year in contrast to the more seasonal leisure market. They tend to pay a higher tariff for their accommodation and consume a greater range of products and services. Price, location and suitability of the facilities are perceived to be key criteria. Unlike the leisure traveller, the majority of business travellers are restrained by some form of corporate directive as to how much can be spent and the quality and type of hotel to be used. Data from the annual National Opinion Poll (NOP) Hotel Guest Survey (1993)[1] confirm that 68–70% of UK business travellers either have no choice or are restricted in their business travel.

The marketing/relational evolution

When it comes to marketing there is a tendency within any business to concentrate almost the whole marketing and sales activity on gaining new customers. Traditionally profit driven, general managers within the hospitality sector were only reputed to be as good as their last month's sales. Consequently a short-term sales-orientated approach was the norm. Personnel responsible for corporate marketing activity usually held the title of 'Sales' or at most 'Director of Sales and Marketing', often reporting to the Financial or Operations Director. Sales and marketing, particularly within UK-based companies, was considered to be a secondary function to the all-important necessity of controlling costs. In times of recession, personnel, and particularly those predominantly responsible for sales, were the first to be shed as cost cutting became the rule. In recent years and as the industry begins to recover from recession a change has occurred with a clearer rationalization and marketing evolution occurring.

Many academics have argued the distinct differences between products and services (Berry, 1980; Bateson, 1989; Grönroos, 1990; Lovelock, 1991) and now this issue has been adopted by some hospitality specialists. They came to a similar conclusion that the traditional marketing approach of classifying marketing activity under the four Ps (product, price, promotion, place) was not appropriate for a service industry as highly intangible as hospitality. These hospitality specialists suggested several different approaches (Chrissey, Boewadt and Laudadio, 1975; Buttle, 1986; Lewis and Chambers, 1989, Reid, 1989). Nevertheless all agree that the hospitality product comprises predominately intangible features often easily copied by competitors, supplemented with tangibles. Renaghan (1981) pioneered this 'new' approach to a more appropriate marketing mix for the hospitality industry encompassing three submixes:

1. *Product service mix* comprising a combination of all the products and services offered by the hospitality operation.
2. *Presentation mix* incorporating all the more tangible elements that the customer recognizes in the product – physical location, atmosphere (light, decor, etc.), price and personnel.
3. *Communications mix* involving a two-way communication between the hospitality operation and the customer including promotion on the part of the supplier and marketing research conducted with the buyer.

Marketing theory has moved on once more. Grönroos (1994) talks of a further evolution, a 'paradigm shift' from the traditional four Ps, and the interaction/

network approach to industrial marketing used in the 1960s through to the services marketing of the 1970s and RM of the 1990s. While there is little empirical evidence of directly similar studies within the hospitality industry, parallels can nevertheless be drawn. The research by the IMP group (Ford, 1991) on the interaction of customers and suppliers in industrial markets is one such example. This model provides some means of explaining the interaction of hotel operators and their channel networks.

In the last few years concentration has increasingly being placed on the economics of long-term customer relationships (Heskett *et al.*, 1994) with customer information and database management forming key contributory activities of marketing in the 1990s. In their analysis of the international hospitality industry, Olsen, Crawford-Welch and Tse (1991) have identified several market trends that directly relate to the building of business-to-business and customer relationships. The growth of non-conventional marketing practices, through the increased use of technology and database analysis, has necessitated the need for a greater behavioural management approach. This is in direct conflict to the traditional operational approach, where branding has not evolved from market segmentation and understanding of customer needs but rather has been driven by product specification.

Lewis and Chambers (1989) and Reid (1989) suggest that RM is most applicable when there is ongoing and periodic customer demand, the customer controls the selection of the supplier, there is alternative choice, loyalty is weak with brand switching commonplace, and word of mouth is an especially potent form of communication. Levitt (1981) refers to RM as the consummation of a 'courtship' rather like a marriage. The hospitality industry conducts 'marriages' at all levels from the long-term investment by financial institutions, to mergers and acquisitions, management contracts, franchising and joint ventures. Major contracts are negotiated with corporate and travel-trade buyers for thousands of bed nights per year and all are built on trust. Trust that the company will perform well and produce a profit for the investors, trust that associated parties through channel agreements will profit and finaly trust that the end customer will be satisfied.

Whatever the guise, RM is increasingly being referred to and incorporated into hospitality marketing theory and practice. By the very fact that they are providing accommodation as a core product and obliged to collect certain information on their customers, hospitality managers are able through accurate data collection to identify who their customers are, where they come from, how frequently they come and how much they spend. Perhaps as Lewis and Chambers (1989) declared, nowhere is RM more apropos than in the hospitality industry.

One RM claim (although not identified through hospitality literature) is that it is less expensive to hold on to the customer base that is already in place than win new customers. The hospitality industry had always recognized the value of the repeat customer both for his or her past trade and his or her recommendation to other prospective customers. 'Word of mouth' is still one of the strongest promotional tools within the sector. Attracting new customers is merely the first step – everything else follows.

Customer retention

Traditional methods of customer retention used successfully by some airlines, for example British Airways, have failed to produce the same loyalty from hotel customers (Rivers, Toh and Aiaoui, 1991; Toh, Rivers and Weithiam, 1991; McCleary and Weaver, 1991; 1992), corporate buyers preferring to shop around and negotiate on price. The above authors suggest that the guest loyalty and frequent-flyer programmes developed and promoted from the late 1980s by the airline and hotel industries were not all successful, often proving too expensive to implement. Radisson Hotels, for example, terminated their programme in 1989 and Inter-Continental in 1993. In turn frequent-guest and loyalty programmes are generally expensive to the customer, the rationale being that the participant pays a relatively high tariff for receiving certain 'privileges', ranging from specific room allocation to accumulating 'points' thus enabling further discounts to be used at a later stage. The main criticism of the programmes described above is that incentives to customers do not constitute RM. This is because incentives do not solve customers' problems and wants. They provide something for nothing, often only if the participant pays an initial premium price, thus raising costs for both customer and supplier.

Effective price discounting

For the past few years discounting has been the industry norm, the rationale being that business is increased and customer loyalty built. Gimmicks include 'freebies' (for example, newspaper, wine in the room, etc.), room up-grading, preferential corporate rates, discount for volume and, more recently, face-to-face negotiation at the front desk.

Use of technology

The hospitality industry is rapidly transforming from a traditional craft orientation to an increasingly technologically driven one. The cumbersome billing machines of the early 1960s are now being replaced by highly sophisticated computer systems. How this technology has been implemented has varied throughout the industry ranging from a simple customer database run on a personal computer to worldwide central reservation systems (CRSs). These highly sophisticated systems facilitate extensive customer databases and more recently management decision-making through yield management systems. However, no matter the sophistication of the system or database, the majority are still operationally driven with the emphasis on maximizing profit rather than customer satisfaction.

CRSs

First conceived by American Airlines in 1963, CRSs have 1) allowed direct booking access for customers; and 2) enabled through-channel intermediaries and systems like Galileo, accommodation, travel and car hire to be reserved in one simple booking. Thus the business traveller benefits from a personally customized travel package. Today the majority of business travel is booked through some form of CRS, the implications of this being that if a particular product is not available on the system then customer choice is reduced.

Guest history databases

Using new technology to manage guest information should restore the personal touch that technology is often accused of destroying. An empirical survey conducted with hotel owners and operators (Dev and Ellis, 1991) indicated that hotel managers have not been taking advantage of this technology. Of the many reasons given the most prevalent were that hotel operators did not ask for information that customers could easily provide even though their research indicated that customers actually expect to provide quite substantial information. Often information was not stored for long enough to be useful. A guest history needs to be developed over several years. Finally, even if hotel operators did collect adequate information over a lengthy period of time, they did not use it.

Yield management

The implementation of yield management was heralded as one of the most revolutionary innovations to impact the hotel industry (Orkin, 1988). The technique matches supply with demand by fluctuating price levels depending on demand for that particular period. The system has the ability to enable pricing decisions that are claimed to be more marketing orientated than traditional methods. However, as stated earlier, in reality they offer an operational solution rather than customer satisfaction. Expensive to install, yield management systems are not feasible for the smaller hotel operator although collaboration with other organizations is possible through strategic alliances such as consortia.

Strategic alliance and managing distribution channels

The hospitality distribution chain can be divided into two parts: 1) the actual creation of the product through some predetermined method, for example, franchising, management contract or direct equity involvement; and 2) through intermediaries, for example, tour operators, travel agents, consortia, reservation networks, incentive houses and affiliations. The first is associated with the production of the product and provides opportunities for expansion into international markets through strong brand association and access to global reservation systems. The latter is associated with distribution itself. Agencies and operators bring the customer to the hotel through negotiated agreements normally involving some form of fee or commission. It is usual to offer a discounted rate for volume.

Short-term profit to relationships?

As most of the key hotel operators are targeting the same customer base in an increasingly competitive market, discounting and incentive schemes have become the expected norm. Traditionally one of the most common tools used to attract and maintain corporate business, discounting was based on the premiss that the customer was getting a better deal with one hotel group than another. These data were assessed on volume of business and although negotiated nationally were often discounted further locally where volumes were highest. Assuming that most customers would prefer to stay with one hotel who understands their needs and provides a quality service, customer loyalty has at times been poor within the sector. Reasons include the tendency for hotels to overbook by on average 15% per night. Thus the unfortunate customer who is paying a low rate or arrives later than expected, even if they are a regular guest and have booked through a reputable travel agent, may well find him or herself booked out to another hotel. Hotel rates can also fluctuate depending on the level of business for the day so that a regular guest who booked well in advance may well find him or herself paying a considerably higher tariff than the customer who arrives at the last moment and negotiates a rate over the front desk.

In the boom of the mid-1980s, overbooking in London was so common that some overseas visitors to the city found themselves staying in hotels at the airports and beyond. These situations rose out of a totally operational and profit-orientated approach by hotel management and their intermediaries. If a better deal manifested then hotel operators usually took it. Consequently travel intermediaries protected their interests by overbooking and then cancelling at a later date. Poor relationships between hotel operators and their intermediaries in turn led to customer dissatisfaction and even further mistrust and overbooking. Since the late 1980s demand for hotel accommodation has declined and a more stable professional approach has been adopted.

As we have seen the hospitality industry is just beginning to emerge from its traditional operational managerial style. Conscious of the value of customer loyalty, managers are seeking novel ways to attract and retain customers with discounting being the most preferred method.

So what constitutes good relational practice?

Every few months the Isle of Eriska Hotel, near Oban, Strathclyde, sends out a newsletter to former guests updating them on what has been happening in the hotel, any special offers available and news of the owners' pets. Although details are obviously derived from a database the former guests are still made to feel special. The personal letter of the proprietor essentially thanks them for staying at the hotel and invites them to visit again. Thus the basic commitments of RM are implemented: knowing the customer, listening to the customer, competing for the customer and finally thanking the customer. This simple example was given by Gordon (1994) in a hospitality trade journal, as typical of the personalized service that an individually owned hotel can offer its guests. But what of the larger organization with hotels distributed throughout the world?

Dev and Ellis (1991) use the example of a business traveller arriving at the airport, being met by the hotel courtesy vehicle and supplied with his favourite soft drink. On arriving at the hotel he is greeted by name at the front desk, has been preregistered and all details completed including method of payment. His room has been customized, from his preferred daily newspaper to a selection of the brands of drinks and snacks he consumed on his last stay. Tickets are booked for a theatre production he wanted to see that night. Excellent customer service or invasion of privacy? This example was only hypothetical but served to illustrate the power of the guest history system if used to its full potential.

Industry benchmarks of good practice

While no large organization can duplicate the personalization of the Eriska Hotel nor the detail of the hypothetical example given above, many organizations are practising good relations with their customers and intermediaries. Within the hotel sector one such example is the USA-based Marriott Corporation. Comprising four hotel divisions, the group owns, manages and franchises over 850 hotels worldwide with more than 170,000 rooms. Operating a tiered pricing system the organization provides a portfolio of products to suit leisure and corporate customers according to their budget, the period of their stay and the level of service that they require. As the corporation grew so did recognition that the culture of the organization would have to change to accommodate this growth. Employees at all levels are now consulted regarding everything from customer needs to training requirements. Implementation occurs through their total quality management programme (TQM) incorporating a highly effective internal marketing system.

This innovation and change was very much the initiative of Bill Marriott, son of the original founder of the corporation. As seems typical of many large groups within the industry the company founder traditionally influenced how the organization was seen by customers and employees. Other examples are Conrad Hilton, founder of Hilton Hotels, Lord Forte, founder of the Forte group and Sir Reo Stakis of Stakis Hotels: all charismatic figureheads with a clear personal association with the provision of quality hospitality. Today these large organizations are run by a team of professional directors often detached from customers and employees. Yet the personal touch is probably even more important in building sound relationships from financial investors to individual customers. There are several ways this can be achieved through the use of technology and quality systems.

Customizing the relationship

To customize the relationship is to understand customers' needs and the types of facilities most appropriate to them. The Marriott Corporation are in the forefront of the industry in terms of the market research they conduct. For example, their Courtyard brand was completely developed from the opinions and suggestions of business customers. Indeed Marriott have achieved the highest compliment through the number of similar or direct-copy products launched by their competitors – Holiday Inns' Garden Court and Stakis Hotels' Country Court are but two. Many of Marriott's competitors emphasize that their new product will be just like the Marriott concept.

Service augmentation

The hospitality product can be enhanced by building extras into the service repertoire. These extras are designed to differentiate the organization from that of its competitors and give a competitive advantage. They must not be readily available from others, and valued by the customer. Examples include concierge service, multilingual staff, 24-hour room service, laundry and other facilities, complimentary newspapers, mini-bars in the room, etc. Recently frequent-guest incentive programmes have enjoyed a resurgence. According to Marriott corporate directors the Marriott Honoured Guest programme (HGA), with 3.5 million members, is the largest, most popular incentive programme in the hotel industry. A highly effective marketing tool, it encourages guest loyalty and thereby maximizes repeat business for the branded hotels. In the UK the membership of the programme has grown to some 38,000 as of August 1994. Strategic alliances with other travel-service providers, for example airlines, have enabled Courtyard to offer Airmiles as a highly successful incentive.

Relationship pricing

As the relationship develops the prices offered to the customer can be reduced to provide a more favourable perceived price/value relationship. This can be accomplished in a number of different ways but historically has been handled with only a small degree of success. The main method adopted is to provide a discount directly related to the volume of business provided in a set time. It is used mostly with the travel trade, business-channel intermediaries and corporate customers booking conferences and other large events. Individual customers are often rewarded with an up-grade of room at no additional cost.

Internal marketing

Those individuals who come in contact with the guests are very important to the long-term success of any hotel or restaurant. The quality of the services provided is determined by these often low-paid employees who tend to have frequent customer contact. For this reason, it is critical to attract, train, retain and motivate high-quality personnel. Regular interaction with all service personnel is essential in order to monitor how satisfied they are with their position and therefore able and willing to provide an excellent service to the customer. There are many approaches currently being used in order to assist this employee motivation, from 'employee of the week' awards to the total commitment the UK-based Swallow Hotel group have made to the 'Investors in People' scheme.

Although this review of the literature has given some indication of the commitment to RM in the hospitality sector, there is little empirical evidence of good relationship practice.

Limitations to the implementation of relationship marketing within the hospitality industry

The literature presented above provides a comprehensive account of the methods of customer retention practised by hospitality operators. However, as previously stated, these activities alone do not constitute RM. The examples of good practice given by Dev and Ellis (1991) and Gordon (1994) were, in the case of the latter, an individual and highly personalized operation and, in the case of the former, merely hypothetical. In neither case nor indeed within the literature are we told what the customer actually expects.

Understanding the customer

Secondary empirical sources reveal that market research within the sector is often limited to national studies, for example, the annual NOP Hotel Guest Survey and guest comment cards distributed by some hotel groups. When directors are questioned about what their customers expect, they tend to quote from the findings of the NOP survey or, in the case of larger groups, for example the Marriott Corporation, data from their HGA programme. Only the larger more sophisticated chains have attempted serious customer surveys, often with the objective of implementing an operations-driven TQM system. One example is the successful UK Scotts/Marriott programme, the case history of which is provided in Teare (1994). Smaller hotel chains, for example the Swallow Hotels group, rely almost completely on the NOP survey for customer feedback.

An empirical study of the relationship practices of hotel companies, their intermediaries and their corporate customers revealed differences in individual customer expectations to that of corporate buyers purchasing multiple hotel products and services. Participants within the latter group expressed a desire to develop a more open relationship with their hotel suppliers than they currently enjoyed. The main grievance was the lack of understanding of customer needs by hotel operators, particularly when negotiating large long-term contracts. In contrast the individual traveller preferred to shop around, being predominately motivated by price (Gilpin, 1995). Customer expectations are difficult to evaluate but consumer research dedicated to understanding the customer rather than being operationally or systems driven could go some way to alleviate this.

Concern

If concern for the customer is key to practising RM then the hospitality industry is arguably well placed to apply it. One example comes from the Marriott Corporation who, having run a successful global CRS for many years, realized that customers prefer to talk to personnel directly at their chosen hotel. The group have managed to overcome this through 'personalizing' their CRS facility. If a customer calls the number of one of their hotels they are actually directed to the CRS office, who answer as though located at the actual hotel. If there is a query that the CRS staff cannot answer then they get the hotel to call the customer direct. Costs are reduced, expertise centralized through resource rationalization and the customer is still satisfied.

On occasions, despite the good intentions of the hotel company concerned, the customer can unintentionally be misled. Promotional campaigns tend to have a specific message often associated with a particular incentive or range of hotel facilities. The current Swallow Hotels' advertising campaign is one such example. The television commercial relies heavily on using hotel leisure facilities to target the business traveller. Unfortunately not all Swallow hotels have leisure facilities. Thus it could be argued customer expectations are being raised without hope of delivery.

The complexity of the hospitality product, demand for suitable properties, high capital outlay and the constant need to refurbish suggest that it is not always realistic to promise high-quality standardized facilities and services at every location. Consequently whatever message is conveyed, some customers will inevitably be disappointed. One way to overcome this is through a tiered pricing system that reflects the facilities and services available at a given hotel. Concern for the customer therefore is conveyed through a policy of communication using a realistic pricing system.

Trust, commitment and good service

Trust is one of the key criteria in building good long-term customer/supplier relationships through encouraging the marketer to work at preserving relationships, resist short-term alternatives and assume that partners will not act in an opportunistic manner (Morgan and Hunt, 1984). Trust involves all aspects of the marketing and operational function from the belief that the rate negotiated with the customer is the best available, understanding customer needs, being able to satisfy those needs and finally a willingness to help. Trust is broken when little things start to go wrong. The case of the customer, running a conference at a luxury hotel that she used regularly, is a typical example. On one occasion she had cause to request some last-minute photocopying for one of the speakers addressing the conference. Despite being heralded as one of the leading conference hotels in the area, with full 'business support services', there was a distinct reluctance to arrange for the photocopying and when it did come it was an hour late and the hotel charged a fortune (Gilpin, 1995). The price charged was not the contention, it was the reluctance to help. If a customer experiences a situation where he or she feels personally let down then it is unlikely that any form of incentive will win him or her back. Hospitality operators suggest that the implementation of TQM is one means of ensuring that customers receive the best possible service. However, it is up to that operator to understand the motives of the customer and the implications of bad service. In the case of the conference organizer it was her own credibility that was at stake, should the speaker not receive his papers on time, not that of the hotel.

Hospitality relationship marketing in reality

RM has been presented as an economic and viable marketing tool in that it arguably costs less to retain a customer than to recruit a new one. However there are limitations as to how successfully these marketing practices can be implemented within the hospitality sector.

First, there is no empirical evidence of individual customer demand for closer relationships with hotel companies. A simple telephone call or travel agent reservation is all that is required to complete the transaction between hotel and customer. Recent developments in technology, in particular the Internet, mean that in future customers will access a hotel CRS and book without the need for any human interaction. Secondly, while an individual hotel database is able to keep comprehensive records of a frequent guest, it is impractical to suggest that this information should be transported to all other hotels that he or she might use within a group. The individual customer is only a viable proposition to the hotel that he or she frequents regularly. In contrast the corporate customer is potentially worth considerable revenue to the hotel operator. However, customer data cannot always be easily collated from different hotels to give a true picture of an organization's loyalty.

Business travel is often the most expensive and least controllable expenditure that an organization is likely to incur. Consequently control mechanisms are essential. If hotel operators are unable to provide accurate information on that expenditure then the customer may have little alternative but to seek advice elsewhere. Managers at American Express, a leading business travel intermediary, realized that through their own customer database they knew more about what their corporate customers spent in terms of travel than they did themselves. By seizing the opportunity and offering their services in the form of a travel 'consultancy', a mutually beneficial relationship has evolved, providing the necessary cost control to the customer and a lucrative source of revenue to the agency. Indeed many large companies now have their own in-plant[2] to manage all travel arrangements within a given budget.

In contrast the relationship between hotel operators and their intermediaries has historically ranged from tolerable, where bookings were made and commissions paid, to a situation of retaliation. One example is the Swallow Hotel group who were blacklisted by Expotel, a leading booking agency, for refusing to pay increased commission rates. Hotel operators often perceive the intermediary as a strong power base because of the volume of business they provide but resent the additional costs involved. Equally, intermediaries are reluctant to deal with hotels because of the low revenue and high administration costs involved. The working relationship seemed to be purely operations driven, concentrating on keeping costs down and maximizing revenue.

If hospitality companies wish to compete with the service now offered by their intermediaries then technology must be directed at collecting data on the individual customer/organization loyalty, rather than forecasting revenues. The customers in turn must be confident that they are able to negotiate directly and secure the best deal.

Conclusions

Evidence from hospitality literature indicates the RM is still perceived to be associated with successful frequent-guest or incentive programmes. This confirms the findings of hospitality authors (Rivers, Toh and Aiaoui, 1991; Toh, Rivers and Weithiam, 1991; McCleary and Weaver, 1991; 1992). The main benefit of the programmes is that they gave operations management more control over the individual guests in terms of monitoring their product consumption.

The small hotel operator is able to maintain a relationship with their customer base through a personalized database and the stability of ownership and personnel. However this luxury is not an economic reality to an international hotel chain. RM only becomes viable where there is sufficient revenue to merit the investment in accurate customer databases.

Large international hotel chains are best able to meet customer expectations through the provision of consistent high-quality products and services that meet the needs of customers. Greater customer consultation is more likely to win loyalty than expensive incentive and loyalty programmes. The individual buyer above all requires easy access to these products and services via a flexible multiple booking service. A branded hotel chain with a portfolio of products positioned within clear pricing ranges can provide that.

RM is best implemented within business-to-business hospitality markets where risks are reduced through greater understanding of customer needs and the operator in turn receives guaranteed revenues.

In summary, although the hotel industry would appear to have all the right criteria for the implementation of RM it still requires a change in management attitudes to implement a more behavioural approach to understanding the hospitality customer and thus fully to exploit potential revenues.

Notes

1. The National Opinion Poll Hotel Guest Survey is conducted annually with participating UK hotel groups and their customers. The business sample in 1993 comprised 501 business travellers with 20% from the upper, 40% from the middle and 20% from the lower budget markets.
2. An in-plant is a travel agency providing an exclusive travel service on-site to organizations.

References

Bateson, J.E.G. (1989) *Managing Services Marketing: Texts and Readings*, Dryden Press, Orlando, Fla.

Berry, L.L. (1980) Services marketing is different, *Business*, Vol. 30, pp. 24–9.

Berry, L.L. (1983) Relationship marketing. In L.L. Berry, G.D. Shostack and G.D. Upah (eds) *Emerging Perspectives on Services Marketing*, AMA, Chicago, Ill.

Buttle, F. (1986) *Hotel and Foodservice Marketing*, Cassell, London.

Chisnall, P. (1986) *Marketing Research*, (3rd edn), McGraw-Hill, London.

Chrissy, W.J.E., Boewadt, R.J. and Laudadio, D.M. (1975) *Marketing of Hospitality Services: Food, Lodging, Travel*, Educational Institute of the American Hotel and Motel Association, East Lansing, Mich.

Christopher, M., Payne, A. and Ballantyne, D. (1991) *Relationship Marketing*, Butterworth-Heinemann, Oxford.

Dev, C.S. and Ellis, B.D. (1991) Guest histories: an untapped service resource, *Cornell HRA Quarterly*, August, pp. 29–37.

Ford, D. (ed.) (1990) *Understanding Business Markets*, Industrial Marketing and Purchasing Group/Academic Press, London.

Garvey, J. (1986) Outlook and opportunities in market segmentation. In R.C. Lewis, T. Beggs, M. Shaw and Croffoot (eds) *The Practice of Hospitality Management II*, AVI Publishing, Conn.

Gilpin, S.C. (1995) Relationship marketing and corporate buyer behaviour in the hotel industry. An empirical study. In *Interaction, Relationships and Networks, Proceedings IMP 11th International Conference*, Manchester Federal School of Business and Management, Manchester.

Gordon, R. (1994) The personal touch, *Caterer and Hotelkeeper*, 9 June, p. 26.

Grönroos, C. (1990) *Service Management and Marketing: Managing the Moment of Truth in Service Competition*, Lexington Books, Lexington, Mass.

Grönroos, C. (1994) From marketing mix to relationship marketing: towards a paradigm shift in marketing, Management Decision, Vol. 32, pp. 4–20.

Heskett, J.L., Loveman, G.W., Sasser, W.E. jr and Schlesinger, L.A. (1994) Putting the service profit chain to work, *Harvard Business Review*, March–April, 164–74.

Hotel Guest Survey (1993) *National Opinion Poll*, Market Research and Applied Research and Communications, London.

Levitt, T. (1981) Marketing intangible products and product intangibles, *Harvard Business Review*, May–June, pp. 94–102.

Lewis, R.C. and Chambers, R.E. (1989) *Marketing Leadership in Hospitality*, Van Nostrand Reinhold, New York.

Lovelock, C.H. (1991) *Services Marketing*, (2nd edn), Prentice-Hall, Englewood Cliffs, NJ.

McCleary, K.W. and Weaver, P.A. (1991) Are frequent-guest programs effective? *Cornell HRA Quarterly*, August, pp. 39–45.

McCleary, K.W. and Weaver, P.A. (1992) Do business travellers who belong to frequent-guest programs differ from those who don't belong? *Hospitality Research Journal*, Vol. 15, pp. 51–64.

McKenna, R. (1991) Marketing is everything, *Harvard Business Review*, January–February, 39–45.

Morgan, R.M. and Hunt, S.D. (1984) The commitment-trust theory of relationship marketing, *Journal of Marketing*, Vol. 58, pp. 20–38.

Morrison, A.M. (1989) *Hospitality and Travel Marketing*, Delmar Publishers, New York.

Olsen, M., Crawford-Welch, S. and Tse, E. (1991) The global hospitality industry of the 1990s. In R.Teare and A. Boer (eds) *Strategic Hospitality Management*, Cassell, London.

Orkin, E.B. (1988) Boosting your bottom line with yield management, *Cornell HRA Quarterly*, February, pp. 52–6.

Parasuraman, A. (1991) *Marketing Research* (2nd edn), Addison Wesley, New York.

Reid, R.D. (1989) *Hospitality Marketing Management* (2nd edn), Van Nostrand Reinhold, New York.

Renaghan, L.M. (1981) A new marketing mix for the hospitality industry, *Cornell HRA Quarterly*, August, pp. 31–5.

Rivers, M.J., Toh, R.S. and Aiaoui, M. (1991) Frequent-stayer programs: the demographic, behavioral and attitudinal characteristics of hotel steady sleepers, *Journal of Travel Research*, Fall, pp. 41–5.

Teare, R. (1994) Closing the gap between consumers and services. In R. Teare, J.A. Manzanec, S. Crawford-Welch and S. Calver (eds) *Marketing in Hospitality and Tourism*, Cassell, London.

Toh, R.S., Rivers, M.J. and Weithiam, G. (1991) Frequent-guest programs: do they fly? *Cornell HRA Quarterly*, August, pp. 46–52.

12

The advertising agency–client relationship

Paul Michell

The advertising industry adage that 'clients are won on (good) creativity and lost on (bad) service' is a useful starting point, since it stresses three of the major aspects of the agency–client partnership: creativity, service and relationship dynamics. Also helpful is a Mark Twain quotation that 'its a difference of opinion that makes horses run', since as a mainly subjective decision-making arena, robust discussion is another important ingredient in the relationship. In this chapter, we will first investigate the idea of the agency account life cycle and its dynamics, then selection of the agency in 'goodness of fit' terms, followed by an interorganizational team approach to working together, relationship maintenance strategies and, lastly, creativity training as an instrument for improving account-team cohesion.

An account life cycle?

One way of viewing the agency–client relationship is that it is analogous to the product life cycle, involving the four phases of prerelationship, development, maintenance, followed by termination (Wackman, Salmon and Salmon, 1986). However, while many accounts do go through stages that are arguably similar to the product life cycle (and might conceivably even be a direct result of it), there are many others that do not. In the UK, around half of all advertising accounts are switched from one agency to another in a seven-year period, and may therefore be seen to fit an 'account life cycle' hypothesis. Loyal, switch-prone and new accounts, conversely, typically fail to pass through all the stages of the cycle, and the concept does not therefore appear fruitful to the understanding of the dynamics of these relationships. An alternative idea is thus suggested, that of segmentation by degree of client loyalty towards the advertising agency.

Around 5% of advertising accounts may be termed switch prone, since advertisers will switch their agencies twice or three times during a five-year period. As it takes a minimum of two years to develop even a tenuous relationship with an agency (Newsome, 1980), such accounts by definition get no further than the development stage before abrupt termination occurs. Often, the agency acts as a scapegoat for the client's own failures, or the agency is in strategy or personality conflict with the client. More rarely, the agency itself resigns the account, for example when it is offered more attractive competitive business. 'New' accounts, comprising around 20% of all accounts, are principally new products, although a minority are relaunches of old products previously unadvertised. Unfortunately, over 60% of these new accounts fail during the following five years. Here, a wide range of market factors will have contributed to the failure as well as the product's advertising positioning. Clearly, new-product failure is a major source of dislocation for agents and clients alike, and the account relationship probably gets no further than the early stages of development before termination, thus leaving out the maintenance stage altogether.

Around 25% of clients may be termed loyal, since they will have retained their accounts with the same agency for a period of more than ten years. Characteristically, these are larger accounts, typically in mature-product categories, and almost invariably linked with the larger agencies, believing in a 'closeness of fit' view of the compatibility of larger accounts with larger full-service agencies. They tend to believe that the account is too large to take perceived high risks in changing agencies for the sake of it. These client managements thus tend to be loyal in the philosophical sense, believing in the benefits of continuity. The management challenge is to ensure that the account life cycle does not happen, by nurturing the relationship and providing a positive environment for the agency's work.

Do the policies of these exceptionally loyal advertisers contain attitudes and perspectives of value to switchers? Such customer support exacts a degree of potential sacrifice, for example, non-exposure to new customs and opinions, as well as potential benefits such as reduction in transaction costs, continuity of long-term thinking and a more effective and tailored service quality. Understanding why loyalty occurs in organizational relationships is a complex process, involving the need to investigate the whole decision-making context. While the reasons for break-ups in advertising agency relationships tend to be very specific, the reasons for loyal relationships are more general. Loyal advertisers tend to stress the relative importance of the business context, the organizational context, and the pervasiveness of their general attitudes and policies towards suppliers, as being of equal concern to the more situation-specific interpersonal and performance-related characteristics of the actual advertising account. It is apparent that advertisers engaged in long-term relationships do not simply treat agencies as reservoirs of creative talent but rather as equal business partners. Such advertisers gauge the benefits they gain from long-term relations as outweighing problems posed by short-term difficulties. Obviously, they have the power to change the agency personnel on the account when dissatisfied, and the agency is large enough to accommodate them. For the agency, there is the incentive to maintain quality based on the expectations of future business. Such attitudes have implications for 'disloyal' clients. More prolonged relationships are important because failure results in significant costs and anguish. The process of switching and the development of a new fruitful partnership can take several years. More loyal clients appear, therefore, to have identified many of the important policies, processes and attitudes an organization needs to have in place to increase their chances of building more durable agency relations.

Goodness of fit

A major determinant of agency–client success is obviously for the advertiser to have selected the right agency in the first place. A degree of polarization has occurred in client choice of agency type, with the largest full-service agencies showing a remarkable resilience within an industry exhibiting a relatively large percentage of account movements and some structural change. Within the large agency category, there has been a substantial movement towards agencies with higher creative reputations away from agencies with higher marketing reputations. A number of new agencies have also emerged which have managed to convince advertisers that they can offer fresh creative approaches. Creative consultancies have also developed, typically complementing rather than replacing conventional agencies. Both consultancies and the newer creative agencies have benefited from the striking success achieved by specialist media independents, which have become an accepted alternative to the full-service agency. Advertisers have also increased their need for specialist assistance, for example direct marketing and public relations, forcing agencies to look carefully at the mix of services they are offering, and stimulating the growth of specialist agencies. Advertisers' own in-house advertising departments are now almost non-existent, except in a small number of specialist cases. Advertising services may therefore be custom built to fit the particular needs of the advertiser, but the main types of relationship have been summarized and fitted to the continuum shown in Figure 12.1.

Full-service agency, where client takes all services on 15% commission basis

Full-service agency, but offering parts of service to client for fee (e.g. media buying)

Full-service agency, except for media, which is placed through media independent

Large creative consultancies, offering additional services, working with media independent

Small creative consultancies, specialists in creative work, often working anonymously for agencies and clients

Media independent co-ordinates account, using creative consultancies

Direct client co-ordination, using both media and creative consultancies

Figure 12.1 Continuum of advertising services available to clients

Importantly, a very strong link exists among the size of the client, the size of the account, the size of the agency and the degree of account loyalty. The bigger the client and account, and the bigger the agency, the higher the likelihood of the account being maintained with the agency for a longer period of time. The close relationship between the size of the account and the size of the agency holding it suggests that advertisers do take a 'goodness of fit' approach to the selection of agencies. The larger agencies are perceived by major clients to be the more creative agencies since they have tended to win the majority of creative awards. Major advertisers place emphasis on creative reputation and size because of the perceived value of the full range of services and the professional quality of management offered by these larger agencies. While there is an argument that clients should be seeking complementary agency relationships, it thus appears they actually choose agencies more in their self-image. Advertisers tend to select a relationship that is compatible with their size and level of professionalism. It is also clear that clients are also involved in other communications relationships, not in place of the main agency but in addition to it. The driving forces here appear to be the increasingly specialist demands of clients, and also their search for value and effectiveness.

Agencies also have their own personalities. Partly it is a matter of creative ethos, such as the Ogilvy and Mather 'brand image' philosophy or the Ted Bates 'USP' standpoint. Also, part of the agency ethos must concern the relative emphasis given to the creative department within the agency, and in particular the degree of involvement of creative personnel within all phases of the advertising process, including media planning. The attitudes of different agencies to the pursuit of advertising awards has also pointedly indicated a general divergence in agency philosophies. Some agencies, eschewing awards as an agency philosophy, would argue that their role is to sell clients' products rather than compete for creative elegance, while others are attracted by the potential visibility award-winning success can bring to the agency and the client. Moreover, stress should also be given to the 'people factor' in the selection of an agency: the visibility, reputation and integrity of key agency personnel, the likelihood of interpersonal compatibility and mutual understanding, and the opportunities for synergism (Cagley and Roberts, 1984). While prospective clients have very clear-cut perceptions of candidate agencies, the positive word-of-mouth recommendation of the satisfied clients is widely sought and considered highly effective in winning new business for the agency (Wills, 1992).

Successful account teams

As the relationship evolves, the agency in effect becomes an extended arm of the client's organization, and an interorganizational matrix develops. The basic objective of the matrix is to provide an informal organizational structure which optimizes integrative effectiveness with functional effectiveness in agency–client resource allocation and performance. Matrix organizations tend to institutionalize the conflict already present between integrators and functional specialists, and endeavour to harness it to the beneficial advantage of the organization. Clearly, then, conflict is a characteristic inherent in agency–client

Personal characteristics	Task characteristics: Integrative task predominance	Task characteristics: Specialist task predominance
Behavioural predominance	Account manager	Creative manager
Analytical predominance	Product manager	Account planner

Figure 12.2 The parts of the account team

relations, and it is only the dysfunctional element of conflict that is likely to lead to dissatisfaction and ultimate break-up. Indeed, healthy 'exchange' within the relationship appears to be directly related to the level of mutual respect between the parties.

One way of investigating functional relationships between agency and client account-team members is to consider the agency–client relationship as a channel and to allocate channel tasks to those members best suited to them. Each activity is shared by a different mix of members, represented as 'functional shifts' across the advertising system. Thus, the conventional advertising flow, from product manager to account manager to creative manager, back to account manager, back to product manager, is replaced by shared activities. The division of tasks and boundaries between agency and client now becomes blurred and arbitrary, since different situations require different functional mixes; and all aspects of the account become a shared responsibility. It is equally appropriate to study the agency–client relationship as a unit of its own confronting other competitive units instead of dwelling on the intricacies of the relations within an organization. The competitive environment includes competition for resources between accounts within the agency and between products at the client end, as well as perceiving it as a dual entity confronting competitors. In this broad view, it does not matter seriously which part of the relationship does the planning so long as effective planning does occur.

The effectiveness of account-team members can thus most sensibly be assessed in terms of members' perceptions of the team's professional compatibility. The account team is seen as a creative resource centre with very blurred boundary positions competing in the marketplace. In order to be successful, the account team needs to develop a blend of integrative and specialist task performances, with behavioural and analytical characteristics, as shown in Figure 12.2.

The model stresses that effective account teams are characterized by compatibility and cohesiveness through personal competencies; blurred job boundaries; integrated tasks; lack of functional conflict; analytical expertise; behavioural support; and flexibility to cope with uncertainty. Providing responsibilities in each of these quadrants are fulfilled effectively, responsibility allocation is a secondary consideration if the designated manager has sufficient talent and centrality to succeed. For example, creative consultancies could undertake the aspect involving specialist task (creative)–behavioural predominance (e.g. nurturing), and product managers could be responsible for the remaining three areas. However, wider responsibilities, combining analytical and interpersonal characteristics with integrative and specialist responsibilities, appear to be too multifaceted for the great majority of product managers.

Leadership, motivation and small-group task orientation appear to be key elements of high-performance account teams. Within the agency, the main roles include being a high standard setter, a motivator of enthusiasm and industry, a centre of prominence to attract highly talented people, and effective defence and presentation of the agency's work. In managing the account team, intrinsic rewards, such as the sense of professionalism, the exercise of competence, peer approval and appreciation, and longer-term career self-interest, appear to be the prime motivators. Viewed as an account team, 'creativity', in the broader operational sense, is not the sole prerogative of creative managers, since account planners especially, account managers and product managers can all contribute their perspectives to the account team's advertising solution. Nevertheless, personal relations within the account team also place stress on individual achievement, and any one member is likely to become intolerant of lower competencies among other team members.

Communications failures are serious obstacles to account productivity. The relationship between high interaction, frequent communication and the avoidance of competition within the team are characterized as developing positive 'behavioural linkage'. There also appears to be an inverse relationship between increased complexity in client and agency hierarchies and internal and external effectiveness in communications. Problems of communication are often symptomatic of more fundamental problems in the relationship, for example lack of trust, lack of interdependence and lack of common agreement. Further, organizations are sometimes forced to heighten the frequency of communication in order to overcome problems of co-ordination. Throughout the creative process, intensities of involvement can be developed for each team member. Task factors are characteristically high in intensity during creative development of the creative execution and low at early and late stages. Different mixes of tasks and roles during the creative process have implications for the effective management of creativity. The integrative contribution is highest in the early stages of development, during front-end planning of the task (inception and interpretation of research, development of concepts, strategic development, and developing the brief), and later in the process (progressing, presenting and decision-taking). Thus, product managers and account managers, conscious that different skills will be required at different stages of the creative process, will assume leadership when integration needs are high but will assume other roles, such as diplomacy, mediation and disturbance-handling, to motivate and maintain the pace of development at a time when integrative communication is characteristically low. Moreover, product and account managers will need to stimulate the climate most beneficial to each development stage, with formality high in the early analytical stages, but low with open communications in the middle of the process to nurture the actual period of creative execution. Interorganizational complexity thus places major importance on the role of communications within the account team.

Typically, product managers have very restricted authority in decision-making on advertising except on routine creative matters. The divorce of decision-making authority from day-to-day account contact is a major feature of agency–client relations, and places strong pressure on lateral account-team members. Since decisions are taken at high level, CEO attitudes to advertising and the leadership style taken in fostering a favourable creative environment are clearly important facets of the relationship. Creativity, as a relatively high-risk dimension, requires courage and adaptive qualities from top advertisers, and the desire to accept the tensions and stresses of creativity must come from top management. To quote John Sculley: 'Apple's passion in creating the product has to be captured in the way we create the message of the product, making it hard to tell where the reality of Apple ends and where the fantasy of the world of our creative advertising begins' (O'Toole, 1985).

Account maintenance

To maintain the account, agencies themselves need to have a strong marketing orientation towards their customers (clients), and to be very sensitive to signs of client dissatisfaction. Advertising agencies invest a significant proportion of their resources developing speculative presentations for new accounts but normally only a fraction of resources to speculating the strength of existing relationships. They have new business managers but not old business managers! Insight gained from the analysis of why account break-ups have occurred in the past is helpful in proposing a number of strategies for protecting established accounts more effectively.

First, vigilance to signals of vulnerability. Client dissatisfaction is often triggered by certain key events, including new marketing policies, dissatisfaction with campaign results and agency service, and changes in agency management. Such signals should alert agencies to active search for means of forestalling client disenchantment. For example, if there is a mismatch in the main personalities in the relationship, the advertising itself is likely to suffer and might even take on a secondary role. Failure to meet deadlines and poor communications are important indicators of slippage in service.

Next, constant informal contact. Very regular contact, almost day to day, appears necessary on all but the smallest accounts to maintain continuity in the relationship. A break-up is typically the result of accumulated incidents, none of which individually is sufficient to justify the decision. Switches tend to be based as much on misunderstanding as on lack of performance. Creeping disenchantment can only be overcome by total involvement with the client. Of course, frequent contact can sometimes be counterproductive, with the client interfering with the agency's work, and the agency thus losing total accountability. Moreover, clients may get resentful of agency participation in client matters not concerning the agency. Thirdly, regular formal review sessions. More formally, agencies should hold reviews with clients at least annually, probably more often. These should explicitly cover all the areas of potential disagreement and disaffection. Some agencies use the concept of a performance audit, which has a number of recommended guidelines, including objectivity, regular appraisal, partnership between agency and client, and confidentiality. Such an audit can be used to stretch the agency by creating commitments. A key aspect of genuine account-team management is that both sides share responsibility for productivity, and as such the regular review should include not only the agency's performance but also productivity on the client side. Much of the misapplication of agency talent might result from loose thinking and casual briefing by the client. This system should result in a firmer relationship with well defined roles and commitments agreed for both agency and client.

Again, tactical adaptation to the client organization. Changes in client management break existing ties and create new pressures for change. Rapid response is required of agencies to build up new personal relationships which emphasize that the agency is not associated with the old guard. More importantly, agencies should often take the initiative by developing and presenting new creative developments. This will emphasize the agency's enthusiasm for change and so pre-empt the natural inclination of the client to look elsewhere.

Fifthly, a whole-hearted commitment to new strategies. When clients initiate a major strategic change of direction on the account, they often complain of disagreement over objectives. If agencies fail to show a whole-hearted commitment to a new strategy the client is likely to switch agencies to implement it. For example, a movement to a more promotional emphasis will require adaptation by the agency in both structure and image to retain the account.

Next, agency account audits. Besides review sessions between the agency and client, the agency should also consider its own review of the operation of its major accounts and make recommendations on account development. One method is to preserve the committee's independence by excluding members of the actual account team from it. The function of the audit would be to take a comprehensive and systematic view of the effectiveness of the agency's performance for its major clients. This is particularly necessary in industries like advertising, where there are a number of factors contributing to a comparatively volatile environment. These audits should, however, not be too narrow in focus, examining operational problems; rather, they should investigate the positioning of the agency as a whole.

Seventhly, the agency–client independent counsellor. Independent arbitrators can be of particular assistance when agency–client personality problems are so acute that they permeate all areas of the relationship, with each side taking up hardened positions. More positively, freelance consultants can act as go-betweens to ensure strong links are maintained.

Lastly, an account portfolio approach. From the agency standpoint, the overall objective is to concentrate scarce creative and servicing resources on those accounts (current and potential) which will determine the long-term future of the agency. A portfolio approach is recommended with accounts placed in boxes according to their present and future potential net profits, as shown in Figure 12.3.

Accounts are then categorized into four types: 1) highly desirable accounts, with high present net profits and high future-growth prospects. Characteristically, these are high spending, fast-growing accounts, giving visibility to the agency. They should receive the primary attention of top management and top creative and account resources; 2) developed accounts, with high present net profits and low future-growth prospects. These are high spenders in stable markets, important to the continuity of the agency, and should receive an emphasis on good service to retain loyalty; 3) underdeveloped accounts, with

Future net profit growth	Present net profits: High	Present net profits: Low
High	Highly desirable accounts Focus of top management	Underdeveloped accounts Early identification of major prospects
Low	Development accounts Good service to retain loyalty	Undesirable accounts Early elimination or fee payment

Figure 12.3 Agency account portfolio

low present net profits and high future growth. These are characteristically small spenders with a big future. The management task is to identify and build such accounts through agency initiatives; and 4) undesirable accounts, with low present net profits and no growth potential. These are usually small accounts in mature industries, typically overdemanding of management time and deflecting resources from more important activities.

When an account is lost, the agency should initiate a formal and systematic post-mortem to identify the reasons. The objective should not be a witch hunt but rather to learn for the future and discourage the prevalent notion that its loss was the result of client perversity.

Training and the account team

Both clients and agencies regard creativity as a broad concept, placed firmly in the context of the agency–client relationship. Yet, there are also disagreements. Clients perceive the creative process itself and the agency's creative philosophy as the most important factors, while agencies stress the importance of the creative environment and personalities. There is a tendency for clients to view creativity as a more structured process compared with agencies who stress spontaneity. The differing perceptions lead to disagreements on a number of issues: intuitive versus analytical thinking; originality versus effectiveness; imagination versus hard work; and freedom versus control. Given the above recommendation for the development of interorganizational account teams, these are potentially difficult areas of discord. Team members working within the agency–client relationship therefore need to understand and identify with the advertising process much more sympathetically, and develop increased compatibility and cohesion with the creative department and the creative process. The meeting of analytical and intuitive thinking has been characterized as 'the clash of two cultures', with creative managers criticizing product managers, in particular, as information disseminators nevertheless unable to define the proper direction for creative strategy. The primary problem is the difference in approach and behaviour between the two cultures.

'Creativity' involves inventiveness, originality and open-mindedness across the multiphased creative development process, with product and account managers contributing to the creative thinking at the research, strategy, progression, decision-taking and evaluative stages. Thus, all account-team members must make broad creative imputs to campaign development for the team to be effective. Creative talent is, therefore, a broadly conceived aptitude rather than a narrowly defined trait, and combines aptitudes, abilities, special skills and knowledge with personality factors.

The Advertising Creative Circle has been running very successful creative role-reversal courses for a decade, with product and account managers spending a long weekend as competitive agencies working on an advertising brief, developing advertising strategy, detailed execution, finished roughs and presenting their proposals to a 'client' team. The course places product and creative managers in the role of creative managers and encourages them to gain direct experience, under pressure, of the creative process.

The creative role-reversal training courses have been shown to be an extremely powerful instrument for rapid improvement in the ability of product and account managers in the overall management of creativity and for building process and behavioural relationships with creative managers. Importantly, the beneficial effects of the courses appear to have been maintained into the longer term, with participants reporting improved effectiveness and greater confidence and cohesion with creative members of the account team (Michell, 1987). Creative role-reversal courses also offer the advertising agency a useful device for improving the quality of client input, particularly briefing and decision-taking, into the relationship.

Conclusion

Successful agency–client relationships depend on a 'goodness of fit' between the advertiser and selected agency and a 'goodness of fit' between account-team members. Creative leadership requires the integration of group effort to optimize the creative synergy of account-team members. Given the subjective nature of the activity, personal chemistry, compatibility and reference-group harmony are crucial at both the strategic and the account-team level. The account team is essentially a creative resource centre, with a blend of integrative and specialist tasks and an input of behavioural and analytical characteristics. Team members designated to tasks need to be perceived by other members as sufficiently competent and prominent to contribute to the account team's group success. Given the volatile nature of the agency–client relationship, and the problems experienced by product managers in particular, in the management of advertising, creative role-reversal training has been identified and shown to be an extremely powerful instrument for rapid improvement in the management of creativity.

Loyalty is related to campaigns that are strong in image and sales effectiveness, with high creative standards and good marketing advice. Conversely, break-ups occur when the actual account exhibits relative weakness in the campaign, dissatisfaction with the standard of creative work and concerns over the standard of the agency's marketing advice. Loyalty is also associated with clear-cut and compatible objectives, while disaffection is linked with changes in marketing objectives and a 'time for a change' feeling. Lastly, personal affinity, personnel continuity and 'closeness to our business' attitudes are related to loyalty, whereas personal conflict, changes in agency personnel and the agency 'not being close to the business' are associated with disloyalty.

Importantly, successful partnerships tend to have processes such as periodic reviews and shared co-ordination and responsibility, plus attitudes such as team spirit and shared values designed to be vigilant and to forestall signals of failure before they become critical incidents.

References

Cagley, J.W. and Roberts, C.R. (1984) Criteria for advertising agency selection: an objective appraisal, *Journal of Advertising Research*, Vol. 24, pp. 27–31.

Michell, P.C.N. (1987) Creativity training: developing the agency–client creative interface, *European Journal of Marketing*, Vol. 21, pp. 44–56.

Newsome, J.E. (1980) A basis for partnership: choosing an advertising agency, *Advertising*, Vol. 66, pp. 26–8.

O'Toole, J. (1985) CEOs say getting involved makes good ads, *Advertising Age*, 2 September, pp. 60–1.

Wackman, D.B., Salmon, C.T. and Salmon, C.C. (1986) Developing an advertising agency–client relationship, *Journal of Advertising Research*, Vol. 26, pp. 21–8.

Wills, J.R. jr (1992) Winning new business: an analysis of advertising agency activities, *Journal of Advertising Research*, Vol. 32, pp. 10–16.

13

Relationship marketing within the not-for-profit sector

Tony Conway

This chapter demonstrates that marketing is equally important for organizations pursuing motives other than profits. The differences between profit and not-for-profit are identified and, as a result of these differences, it is proposed that RM can perform an important role in the successful strategic direction of such organizations.

What is the not-for-profit sector?

In simple terms, this sector includes all those organizations where the pursuit of profit is not the predominant motive. However, in reality, there does seem to be some confusion as to what types of services should be included within this sector and also as to which terms should be used. In the USA, the economy is classified into three areas: commercial, public and non-profit. Here, the term non-profit is used to denote voluntary organizations and indeed is sometimes known as the voluntary or third sector. Fine (1990) combines the second and third elements of the US economy and uses the term 'social sector' in his work on social marketing.

In the UK, the term 'non-profit' seems to be less specific and tends to be used as a generic description for both public sector and voluntary organizations or what Kotler (1975) describes as public not-for-profit organizations and private not-for-profit organizations. However, in order to emphasize the fact that profit is not the major motive of such organizations, the term 'not-for-profit' is preferred.

The 'not-for-profit' sector in the UK, therefore, comprises government agencies and other organizations, some of which are voluntary, that provide individual and community services. Fine (1990) claims that these services are more likely to be 'ideational' in nature. They would seem to differ from typical profit-orientated services in that they consist as much of exchanging ideas (concepts, thoughts, feelings, etc.) as they do of providing a physical service. As a result of a variety of legislative changes that are taking place, however, an overlap is developing between the not-for-profit sector and the more commercial services sector of the UK economy.

The UK public sector employs approximately 6 million people in many diverse areas, which include transport and communication, public administration, education and health (*Employment Gazette*, 1995). The voluntary sector is generally included in the private sector statistics as charity, voluntary or trust organizations. They not only formally employ a large number of people but also incorporate many unpaid members/volunteers. Indeed in 1992 the top 14 voluntary organizations had over 1½ million volunteers (*Social Trends*, 1994).

In addition to the large degree of human participation of employees and volunteers within this sector, the value of revenue/expenditure is considerable. For example, the total real income of the top 200 charities in 1992–3 was £2,415 million with the top 25 bringing in £793 million (*ibid.*). The total expenditure on government services in 1993 was £116,948 million (*Economic Trends*, 1995).

The very size and importance of this sector, therefore, is worthy enough for specific consideration within any general marketing text and, as will be seen, the unique characteristics of such services lend themselves well to an RM perspective. However, given this size and importance, it is difficult to analyse the degree to which marketing in general and RM in particular can be applied without attempting some form of classification of the various types of not-for-profit organization/service that exist.

In his general classification of organization types, Kotler (1975) distinguishes between those organizations within either the private or public sectors which have or do not have profit as the major motive. As a result, he produces a fourfold classification:

1. Private for profit organizations.
2. Public for profit organizations.
3. Private not-for-profit organizations.
4. Public not-for-profit organizations.

Rados (1981) distinguishes between five different types of organization depending on the relationships between the firm's 'backers' and its 'clients'. Within the *business firm* 'backers' receive interest and profits in exchange for capital. 'Clients' receive goods and services in exchange for payment. He then identifies a number of other organizations which could be considered to be in the not-for-profit sector.

The *non-profit business* is similar to the business firm but rather than receiving interest and profits, backers/owners receive a surplus in exchange for their capital. Such a surplus, no doubt, is returned to the organization to ensure that the provision of the relevant goods and services continues.

Within *common benefit organizations*, clients are not outsiders but are considered as members of the organization. Such individuals receive services in exchange for fees and provide services themselves for other members. *Service organizations* are those organizations which are funded partly by clients and partly by backers, and *commonwealth organizations* are those which are funded by taxes to provide services which benefit society as a whole. Rados believes that these are stereotypes and that there can be various combinations of these in existence.

Using a broader, 'relationship' perspective, Wensley (1990) produces a taxonomy to characterize various ways of representing the relationship between suppliers and users. He distinguishes between relationships which are supplier driven ('supplier specified') and those which are user driven ('user specified'). He also distinguishes between those relationships where the user is generally a passive recipient of the product/service and those where the user has a more active role. As a result, he identifies four 'beneficiaries':

1. A 'consumer' who is user passive/user specified.
2. A 'customer' who is user active/user specified.
3. A 'client' who is user active/supplier specified.
4. A 'patient' who is user passive/supplier specified.

In attempting to classify various aspects of the public and non-profit sectors in the USA, Fine (1990) considers the type of output produced rather than the type of organization or the type of relationship with 'customers'. In his typology he identifies the motive (profit or otherwise) for the production of the output and the degree of tangibility of the output itself. For example, a blood donation could be a non-profit tangible product whereas higher education would be a non-profit service. Child abuse would be a non-profit issue or cause.

Scrivens and Witzel (1990) consider the nature of the relationship between the organization and its customers to produce a classification. They see there being three major types of context within which relationships exist: free trading within a market, enforced trading (frequently using an 'internal' market) and non-trading.

The major difference between free trading within a market as it exists in the not-for-profit sector and that within the commercial sector is in the ownership and accountability of managers to the owners. In the public sector there is a responsibility to government bodies or their representatives and thus there is likely to be a political scrutiny in addition to financial accountability. Scrivens and Witzel, however, believe that in terms of the relationships organizations have with their 'customers' in this situation, there seems to be little difference between the two sectors. The second context, the 'enforced trading' situation, has developed quite considerably over the last few years. Public services have rarely been totally transferred to a truly commercial, competitive environment. Instead, there has been a move towards competition within internal markets rather than organizations being subject to consumer market conditions.

These 'internal markets' exist where public interest is represented by government agencies. The main driving force behind this market approach is to improve the efficiency of the service in question. However, Scrivens and Witzel believe that, within this new 'market' environment, there is still little understanding of 'customer orientated' issues and the responsibilities of the various parties in market transactions.

Complex relationships develop in such markets but few purchasers require the provider to develop long-term close relationships. In many situations there are many potential purchasers, and providers have a choice of developing close relationships with a limited number or providing limited services to a larger number of purchasers. Public policy and legislation, however, mean that the organization's mission is more likely to emphasize the latter.

At first glance, there seems to be little role for marketing in those situations where non-trading relationships exist. However, there does now seem to be a general acceptance that marketing can be applied to those situations where there may indeed be no economic reward but some other form of mutually satisfying exchange. Scrivens and Witzel, however, see that the key difference between trading and non-trading is not in the marketing tools used, but in the different social agendas that can exist. If social policy determines that certain identifiable groups should receive services, then marketing techniques are applicable. In many cases, however, those eligible for such services may not be the people who actually desire them. Another difficulty within this non-trading context exists because many services are considered available to all. Marketing tools such as segmentation may not be appropriate in this context as they could lead to some groups being overlooked or stigmatized. Here, therefore, equity issues can conflict with marketing issues.

Hansmann (1980) classifies various organizations by source of funding and how the particular organization is managed, and distinguishes between:

- *donative* organizations which secure revenue mainly through donations/ government contribution or other;
- *commercial* organizations which charge users for the service;
- *mutual* organizations which are controlled by their users; and
- *entrepreneurial* organizations which are controlled by professional managers.

Various not-for-profit organizations are then identified as combinations of these elements. For example, charities would generally be donative but some would be managed by the membership and would therefore be classified as mutual organizations. Others who employ professional managers would be classified as entrepreneurial.

Not only are there differences between organizations using these dimensions but there are also differences within organizations. For example, within a university, many undergraduates would have their fees paid by the local authority whereas other students may very well have to pay full fees themselves. Two types of situation can be seen to exist here within one organization: donative/entrepreneurial in the first instance and commercial/entrepreneurial in the other.

Looking more specifically at the public sector, Smith (1988) identifies three types of organization:

1. *Quasi-public* organizations. These are those organizations which used to be public corporations. These now face extensive competition and maximization of revenues has become a major motive. Smith believes that the private sector model of organization would be the most appropriate here.
2. *Social* organizations. These are not driven by market forces and provide services which are obligatory. Tax and social security would be examples here. For Smith, it is unlikely that full-blown marketing would ever be appropriate for such organizations.
3. *Quasi-public/social mix*. This type of organization is unlikely to be at ease with either situation. Libraries and leisure services would be examples of these.

Table 13.1 Not-for-profit classification

Sector of concern	Key variables/dimensions	Resultant typology	Example
General classification	Sector profit motive or otherwise (Kotler, 1975)	Private for profit	IBM
		Public for profit	Commercial consultancy within a university
		Private not-for-profit	NSPCC
		Public not-for-profit	Inland Revenue
General classification	Relationships between backers and clients (Rados, 1981)	Business form	Marks & Spencer
		Non-profit business	Public school
		Common benefit organization	Golf club
		Service organization	YMCA
		Commonwealth organization	Social Services
General classification	Degree to which user is passive/active. Degree to which user or supplier is specified (Wensley, 1990)	Patient (user passive/supplier specified)	Hospital patient
		Client (user active/supplier specified)	Accountant's client
		Consumer (user passive/user specified)	Child and toy
		Customer (user active/user specified)	Parent purchasing toy for child
Public and non-profit (USA)	Profit-making nature; degree of tangibility of product (Fine, 1990)	Non-profit tangible	Blood donation
		Non-profit service	Local park
		Non-profit idea	Family planning
		Non-profit issue/cause	Drink/driving
		Profit tangible	Blood bank (paid)
		Profit service	Private health
		Profit idea	Fashion design
		Profit issue/cause	Recycling waste

Table 13.1 *Continued*

Sector of concern	Key variables/dimensions	Resultant typology	Example
'Non-profit' (Europe)	Nature of relationships between organization and its customers (Scrivens and Witzel, 1990)	Free trading within a market Enforced trading Non-trading	British Gas NHS Library
'Non-profit' (USA)	Source of revenue; type of organizational management (Hansmann, 1980)	Donative Commercial Mutual Entrepreneurial	Age Concern AA Local golf club NSPCC
Public sector (UK)	Degree to which subject to market forces (Smith, 1988)	Quasi-public organization Social organization Quasi/social mix	British Gas HM Customs and Excise Leisure centre
Public sector (The Netherlands)	Degree of contact with the public; degree to which price is paid (Van Der Hart, 1990)	High/high High/low Low/high Low/low	Theatre Education Government pension fund Local authority department

Van Der Hart (1990) looks specifically at government organizations within The Netherlands and identifies two key factors: the degree to which there is direct or indirect contact between the organization and the public; and the degree to which the customer pays for the service. For example, the education service would have high direct contact with the public but relatively low degree of customer payment. In comparison, a state pension fund has low direct contact with customers but direct customer payment.

To summarize, the term 'not-for-profit' is one of a number that is used to identify that part of the economy which does not rely on profit for its existence. Within this general category, however, there are a number of different types of organization which involve various types of relationship and produce many different goods and services, and there have been a number of different attempts to classify these. Table 13.1 summarizes some of these classifications in simple form.

Is marketing relevant to the not-for-profit sector?

Notwithstanding the above, the fundamental issue of the degree to which marketing is generally applicable to this sector of the economy needs to be addressed. This debate was opened by Kotler and Levy (1967) who proposed that the concept of marketing be broadened to apply to organizations other than profit seekers and this topic was the basis of a good deal of debate during the 1960s and 1970s (Kotler and Levy, 1969; Luck, 1969; Arndt, 1978). The key to the debate was that marketing was in essence about the process of exchanging mutually satisfactory values between two or more parties. Such mutually satisfying exchanges are not just the prerogative of profit-seeking organizations and, today, given the coverage of not-for-profit in the various marketing texts, there would seem to be a general acceptance that marketing can and should be applied to this sector.

Indeed, the public sector has recently become more interested in marketing owing to changes in funding and increased competition. This trend has been shown particularly among those organizations where privatization has taken place. Privatization itself can be of a number of extremes from the sale of shares on the stock exchange to merely making an institution a 'cost centre'. In the first case organizations join the private sector and have to make profits to survive. In the other case, the organization is given a level of self-government – the motivation being still to provide a public service but an increased emphasis is placed on costs. Public utilities such as gas and electricity and public corporations such as British Telecom and British Steel have all moved in the direction of complete privatization.

There have also been other growing links with the competitive environment. 'Customers' have been given greater freedom of choice about which institution/organization they wish to use (choosing between different secondary schools, for example). Such changes are not only taking place in the UK. Writing about The Netherlands, Van Der Hart (1990) identifies a number of developments which seem to mirror the UK experience:

- An increasing attention to quality.
- A growing realization that government institutions can also be considered as regular businesses.

- The delegation of managing authority to lower levels within the organization so that decisions can be made which are closer to citizens.
- The privatization of government services.
- The acceptance in some government services of the principle that the user pays.
- The deregulation, simplification/streamlining of rules, and an attempt at the general debureaucratization of government.
- An increasing attention to self-determination within the government.

The public sector is not the only element of the not-for-profit sector realizing a need for the role of marketing. Charities and other voluntary bodies have also come to understand that they must compete for donations, grants or other contributions and that they need to satisfy their customers' requirements more effectively, whoever their 'customers' might be.

Many organizations have introduced sections or programmes that are intended to be profit making – hospitals selling paramedical services to local industry, for example, or universities producing commercial courses.

In the USA, there has been a growth in non-profit marketing, and Kotler and Andreasen (1991) believe that this is the result of four developments. First, just as in the UK, there have been changes in the political environment which have led to the increased privatization of public services. Secondly, the social climate in the USA has tended to encourage a growth in voluntarism. Thirdly, international social agencies have started to give social marketing a central role, and the final development relates to changes in the traditional sources of non-profit support. In addition to the usual sources, such as government subsidies, grants, corporate and private giving, there are now sales of services which utilize further marketing approaches.

Differences between marketing in the profit and the not-for-profit sectors

It therefore seems to be the case that the application of marketing concepts, principles and approaches is appropriate to the not-for-profit sector. However, the straightforward transfer of product-marketing approaches to this sector may not be appropriate and indeed such a transfer could be quite counter-productive. It is therefore necessary to delve a little more deeply at the characteristics of not-for-profit organizations, their goods and services and their relationships with their 'customers'.

Lovelock and Weinberg (1990) utilize the terms 'business' and 'non-business' marketing, and identify five significant differences between the two.

Multiple publics

The major difference between profit-orientated and not-for-profit-orientated organizations is the identification and satisfaction of customer need. The not-for-profit organization has two different types of constituency/customer: the beneficiaries of the not-for-profit product/service and the donor/resource provider. In many cases these are not the same people.

The profit-making organization has the marketing function of facilitating direct two-way exchange. This simultaneously deals with both resource allocation (providing goods and services) and resource attraction (obtaining revenue). Within the not-for-profit organization, however, resource attraction and resource allocation are two separate tasks as they involve separate constituents with differing needs (Shapiro, 1973).

Although Kotler and Levy's 'exchange' concept has meant that there is now growing acceptance of multiple publics in any transaction, the not-for-profit situation still has the above differences regarding resource attraction and allocation. Within the profit-based firm, there are more likely to be some common needs found among the various constituents. This is less likely within a not-for-profit organization. Gwin (1990) identifies seven constituent groups within profit organizations: shareholders, management, unions/employees, customers, suppliers, community/public and government. In most of these cases (apart from customer and community), relationships are of a formal, contractual nature and therefore relationships are well defined and generally easy to understand and manage.

In contrast, Gwin identifies the following constituent groups within the not-for-profit context: resource generators (a large proportion of resources for operations is typically not a function of direct sales to customers); service users (non-revenue generating and revenue generating); regulators (those who constrain or define the ability of the not-for-profit organization to function); managers (professional and quasi-professional); and staff members (volunteers and paid professionals). The difficulty with the not-for-profit context is that one person may belong to several constituent groups simultaneously. Each constituent's role has different needs and demands on the organization. Gwin believes that each constituent group served by the not-for-profit organization requires a separate and distinct approach, based on the needs of the constituent group targeted.

A university student, for example, can be both customer and product of the education process simultaneously (Litten, 1980; Lovelock and Rothschild, 1980; Conway and Yorke, 1991; Conway, MacKay and Yorke, 1994). If considered as a customer, marketing strategies targeted towards potential and present students need to be considered. If considered as a 'product', strategies aimed at the employers need to be pursued. On many occasions the demands of each constituent grouping could be considerably different.

The non-financial objective

The second significant difference between business and non-business marketing identified by Lovelock and Weinberg (1990) is the non-financial objective itself. This in fact makes it difficult to choose between alternatives. Shapiro (1973) also notes that this leads to difficulties in the measurement of success or otherwise of the organization.

In a profit-seeking firm, profit would be the measurement of success. In the not-for-profit situation, the equivalent would be a measurement of revenue attracted (contributions from donors, etc.). This, however, would not be a very effective measure of success as there is no indication here whether the actual 'clients' of the organization are being satisfied. Alternatively, a situation could arise where clients are being satisfied and yet 'donors/contributors' are not.

Services and social behaviours

Another major difference highlighted by Lovelock and Weinberg (1990) is the fact that not-for-profit organizations tend to provide services and social behaviours rather than physical goods. However, as has been previously noted, this distinction may not in fact exist. All goods tend to have service elements and all services have degrees of tangibility (Shostack, 1977).

Non-market pressures

Not-for-profit organizations tend to have greater public scrutiny or have more non-market pressures compared to business organizations, although even business firms have legal requirements and constraints.

Conflict between mission and customer satisfaction

A final distinction highlighted by Lovelock and Weinberg is that there is likely to be a tension between the not-for-profit organization's mission and actual customer satisfaction. For example, a taxpayer is unlikely to be happy about the payment of taxes.

Rothschild (1979) considers non-profit marketing to be unique. He identifies the following specific characteristics:

1. Poor availability of good secondary data.
2. It is difficult to get reliable primary data.
3. Often payment/involvement is required from people who may not be particularly interested in the issue/cause/service.
4. 'Consumers' are often expected totally to change their attitude or behaviour.
5. It is often difficult to modify an offering to meet 'consumer' needs and wants more effectively. Thus it is difficult to be 'consumer orientated'.
6. Because of the complexities of the offerings involved, a large amount of information needs to be given.
7. Very often benefits resulting from payment/involvement are not evident.
8. In some situations people other than those who pay/get involved actually gain.
9. It is usually difficult to portray the true offering in the media owing to the intangibility of the social and psychological benefits.

A particular feature of not-for-profit marketing is the tendency to emphasize the tactical aspects of marketing and more particularly the communication function. Cousin (1990) has found this 'marketing mix' bias and believes that, in some instances (e.g. charities), the product is entirely separate from income and, in others, the product is partly connected to the flow of income. In no situation, Cousin claims, is there a direct exchange that typifies the marketing within the commercial sector.

Birks and Southan (1991) have a similar view. Within profit-seeking organizations, they see the success of the process of resource attraction being clearly linked to the success of resource allocation. This takes place through the application of specific marketing techniques addressed to specific target markets. This feedback does not exist in the not-for-profit organization. Resources are generated from a donor/contributor market and then reallocated to a separate beneficiary market.

Because receivers do not directly pay for the service, there is pressure for marketing to take on a 'selling' function in order to attract resources. The allocation of resources to the beneficiaries tends to be undertaken by people or departments not involved with marketing. Any marketing department or role tends to be one of communication. Indeed, the National Society for the Prevention of Cruelty to Children (NSPCC) does not have a marketing department as such but has a communication department instead.

The role of relationship marketing within the not-for-profit sector

Grönroos (1994, p. 9) defines RM as to 'establish, maintain and enhance relationships with customers and other partners, at a profit, so that objectives of the parties involved are met. This is achieved by a mutual exchange and fulfilment of promises'. Apart from the reference to 'profit' there would seem to be little difficulty in applying this to a not-for-profit context. If it is accepted that profit need not be of a financial nature but any 'gain' on the part of various parties, then the above could be a useful working definition.

Is RM relevant for this sector? As indicated, there are a number of major inter-related characteristics of the not-for-profit sector: multiple constituencies; the non-profit motive; the resource attraction and resource allocation split; and the overemphasis on tactical rather than strategic marketing. Of major philosophical importance is the overemphasis on tactical issues, i.e. the marketing mix. According to Grönroos (1994), the dominant marketing function of the marketing mix characterizes the more traditional, short-term transactional marketing perspective. In this context, there is little interface between market operations and personnel and there is little role for internal marketing.

However, for the types of organization that exist in the not-for-profit sector, there is indeed a need for a more long-term RM perspective. According to Grönroos such a perspective would utilize the marketing mix merely as a support for a broader interactive marketing where the quality of interaction with the customer is paramount. The interface between market operations and personnel is of strategic importance in this context and so also is the role of internal marketing.

With whom should relationships develop? There is therefore a need for not-for-profit organizations to move to a more strategic, planning perspective. Here the development of long-term relationship becomes important not only with resource providers but also with other 'customers'. Christopher, Payne and Ballantyne (1991) identify six markets that need to be addressed within an RM perspective: customer, referral, supplier, employee (recruitment), influencer and internal markets. Morgan and Hunt (1994) identify ten relational exchanges that exist within four 'partnerships' in RM: buyer partnerships, supplier partnerships, internal partnerships and lateral partnerships.

Who, however, are the not-for-profit organization's customers? It has previously been noted that such organizations have five key constituent groups that need to be considered: resource generators, service users, regulators, managers and staff members (Gwin, 1990). If competitors are included as another 'public' that needs consideration, Morgan and Hunt's classification could be utilized.

Resource generators (buyer or supplier partnership?)

A large proportion of the resources available for operations is not the result of direct sales to 'customers' but comes from a number of other sources such as taxpayers, donors, third-party providers and patrons. It has been claimed that this lack of direct economic link between resource attraction and resource allocation is the major cause of an overemphasis on the marketing mix. More particularly, there has been a tendency to overemphasize the 'selling' function aimed at raising funds.

There are, however, indications that RM is being applied within the not-for-profit sector. At first glance, the fact that charities are the third largest mailers in the UK after financial and mail-order organizations (Massey, 1995) would seem merely to reinforce the overemphasis on the tactical, communication aspects of marketing. This heavy use of the postal medium, however, is less important than the actual response rates achieved. An acceptable rate used to be 2% but now a rate of 25% in response to a warm campaign would be considered poor and 65% to be good.

This success has been the result of the increasing requirement for efficient financial management imposed by donors and independent watchdogs. Recruitment of funders is expensive and therefore charities with a long-term commitment and sufficient finance have built a database of supporters so that they do not have to continue to search for new donors. Some donors are more generous than others and therefore donor-based segmentation based on recency, value and frequency of gifts has been taking place.

Burnett (1992), when considering the relationship between resource generators and the organization, actually uses the term 'relationship fundraising'. Funders are represented in a hierarchy with each level representing a different funding type. The aim of relationship fundraising is to move funders up the hierarchy where there is greater commitment and greater gift-giving value. Thus the approach attempts to push individuals through the following stages:

Donors → Committed donors → Big gifts → Legacies

Burnett suggests that different communication strategies would be used for differing groupings.

Lindsay and Murphy (1994) take this further by considering in more detail the actual relationships concerned. For example, a 'customer/donor' who through deed of covenant becomes a 'committed donor' in fact performs the role of 'supplier'. This not only means more money for the organization but also a change in ideology on the part of the donor. In other words, the donor displays an ideological commitment. Lindsay and Murphy believe that the role of relationship funding is to facilitate the movement of customers up the hierarchy. This can only take place if the customer/donor, through effective two-way communications, has a clear understanding, agreement and commitment to the philosophy and vision of the organization.

A problem with this perspective, however, seems to be the rather single-sided view of 'tying in the customer'. Is this desire for a relationship mutually felt? Many services provided by organizations in this sector tend to involve very strong emotions. It is therefore important for there to be a mutual desire for such a relationship otherwise more harm than good can be done. High-profile funding campaigns, for example, can leave an impression of 'waste' if they are not publicly converted into hard cash (O'Sullivan, 1993).

Fine (1990), in considering organizational donors, believes that strategies for corporate giving have changed over the years and that corporations are now looking for new ways and places to give. Two successful 'relationship' approaches are identified:

1. *In-kind philanthropy*. An example of this could be an advertising agency donating services. In exchange, the agency gets others to see its work. Such donations can also be utilized for public-relations purposes.
2. *Cause-related marketing*. These are the activities a firm undertakes to benefit both itself and an assortment of social causes. Cause-related marketing refers to programmes that are mutually beneficial to a private firm and a selected social or charitable cause (Heinz and National Children's Homes, for example).

Another reciprocal fundraiser is the affinity card (see Chapter 8). In this situation a social cause receives a small percentage of every credit-card transaction.

Service users (buyer partnerships)

For whose purpose were organizations founded? In most cases within this sector, organizations have been set up to provide goods and services to individuals and groups who have particular needs.

These are the charity's beneficiaries or clients, the hospital's patients, the university's students, the local authority's citizens. A true marketing perspective would ensure that these constituents' needs were identified, anticipated and met. Lindsay and Murphy (1995) believe that there should be a movement away from being 'funding orientated' towards being 'need orientated'. In other words there is a need for a strategic response focused on resource allocation. If successful, revenue-raising activities would be subservient to the servicing of the identified beneficiary but such fundraising would emphasize a long-term commitment on the part of funders and a greater flow of information from the organization.

Some elements of the public sector are starting to display a broader awareness of marketing generally and are starting to demonstrate a commitment to building relationships. In local government, for example, the arrival of compulsory competitive tendering has meant that there has been a need to develop close relationships with client departments in order to maintain the ability to provide the service.

In higher education, there is a growing awareness that a student can be recruited to undertake an undergraduate programme of study. Once completed, the graduate acquires a job, and can then be recruited to study for a professional qualification. Once successful, the individual could then follow a part-time postgraduate qualification. Even having left the institution, communication would continue through an alumni association and revenue could come from this source and/or through affinity cards, etc. As has been noted on many occasions in this text, it is far cheaper to maintain relationships than it is continually to develop new ones and, in this particular example, the student has moved from being a beneficiary of resource attraction to being a source of that resource at a later date.

Although there does seem to be some indication that RM is being pursued in the not-for-profit sector, there are still some difficulties. In the exchange relationship with many charitable beneficiaries and those of local and central government services, there is normally no competition among suppliers with demand usually exceeding supply. A recommended solution to this 'overfull demand' (Kotler, 1984) is 'demarketing'. This involves demand reduction techniques aimed at certain or all consumers. Demarket segmentation may be a valid application of the marketing concept and here RM is typified by the identification of a particular target customer in which the relationship needs to be built.

McCort (1994) considers both resource generators and service users and believes that non-profit organizations have unique characteristics that are congruent with an RM strategy. Individual donors/contributors provide resources, i.e. time and money, in exchange for either personal psychological or normative external benefits. However, the 'output' of the organization is distributed to service users in exchange for the intrinsic rewards from fulfilling its mission and possibly extrinsic benefits such as favourable publicity. This structure creates unique difficulties for non-profit organizations. It is these issues which McCort believes RM addresses.

For example, long-term support is needed from donors. RM fosters the long-term committed relationship. Although the goods and services produced are intangible, McCort believes that the relationship can become a tangible benefit that ties the donor to the organization. Such a relationship can also foster a sense of mission on the part of the donor and thus once again link the particular donor to the cause/organization.

Regulators (lateral partnerships)

Another constituent or public with whom relationships should be built is that grouping which has an influence on how the organization is allowed to function. These 'regulators' can either be government bodies or advisory boards which comprise private individual volunteers empowered by law to oversee the operations of the firm. The needs of such groups need to be identified and anticipated and where possible satisfied. Two-way channels of communication need to be utilized and common issues of mutual benefit must be identified.

Competitors (lateral partnerships)

In some instances, it may be prudent to build relationships with other organizations in order to gain considerable advantages. Wiesendanger (1995), for example, has discovered that when an entire industry or sector falls on hard times, competitors often become collaborators. The American Heart Association, along with the Multiple Sclerosis Society, has teamed up with the Arthritis Association in order to share resources. Although they still compete for donor funds, they have found that they can help each other in terms of administrative costs.

Managers and staff members (internal partnerships)

There seems to be general acceptance that RM should also involve the development of relationships with employees or the 'internal market' (Arndt, 1983; Berry and Parasuraman, 1991; Christopher, Payne and Ballantyne, 1991;

Morgan and Hunt, 1994). Internal marketing involves the attraction, development and motivation of qualified employees through the philosophy of treating employees as customers. Thus managers and staff members are another constituent with whom relationships need to be developed. Successful internal marketing depends a good deal on the organizational culture. Such a culture must include a commitment to RM from the very top of the organization and should include a commitment to employee empowerment, teamwork, rewarding good performance and effective training.

Managers in not-for-profit organizations are invariably professionals or at least quasi-professionals. They are likely to be qualified in particular professions rather than be trained as managers, e.g. environmental health officers, social workers, etc. Such individuals will therefore perhaps have differing motives for involvement within the organization. Staff members within such organizations are either trained and paid professionals or volunteers. Once again, each type is likely to have differing needs that require identification and satisfaction.

Drucker (1989) notes that there has been a considerable increase in productivity within the sector. Among a number of aspects, Drucker identifies an increase in the number of volunteers and a fall in the number of paid employees. Through a combination of job satisfaction and training, staff members tend to be retained within the organization and enjoy their work.

Recommendations for action

There therefore seems to be a role for RM within the not-for-profit sector, despite the sector's unique characteristics.

Given the many and varied constituent groups which are likely to have different needs and various demands on the organization, Gwin (1990) proposes the following strategies to attempt to overcome such difficulties:

1. Identify and list each of an organization's constituent groups and carefully explore the needs of each group *vis-à-vis* the organization itself.
2. Individual needs should be carefully considered and research should take place where appropriate to discover whether or not common wisdom about the needs of these groups is accurate.
3. As a result of this analysis, strategies often become apparent that can simultaneously satisfy the needs of more than one group.

An important characteristic of intangible products, particularly in the not-for-profit sector that requires special attention for retaining customers is that the customer is seldom aware of being served well (Levitt, 1981). It is only when things do not go well that the customer becomes aware. Therefore customers tend to be more aware of failure and of dissatisfaction and this makes them vulnerable to competition and other constraints. Levitt recommends service providers regularly to remind customers what they are getting to show them that they are in fact satisfied. This can be done through letters, telephone calls, newsletters, regular visits, etc.

Cross (1992) identifies five degrees of customer bonding: awareness, identity, relationship, community and advocacy. All involve different levels of trust and interaction in the relationship with customers.

Awareness

This involves creating the right impression. The customers/citizens/donors are anonymous and nothing is required of them. This is a very expensive stage and results are not easy to measure. There is also no customer dialogue and therefore it is the weakest form of relationship. A more persuasive message from elsewhere can break the relationship as can a change in the environment. As has been noted, this environmental flux is a feature of the not-for-profit sector in the UK and therefore a rapid development on to the next stage would seem to be recommended.

Identity

Here, the customer starts to identify the service as fulfilling high-level needs such as belonging, status and/or self-fulfilment. Interest, desire and action may all be encompassed at this stage. There needs to have been a successful implementation of the previous stage to get to this level of relationship.

Relationship

This is where there is the direct exchange of benefits that may go beyond the delivery of the basic product/service. Each customer is now recognized as an individual and packages can be tailored to specific needs. Customers respond with more information about themselves, greater loyalty and eventually more sales/donations/contributions, etc. Frequency-marketing programmes and loyalty schemes are examples of this stage. The importance of the database is clearly demonstrated at this level.

Community

At this stage a common bond develops among fellow customers and common interest groups are formed. Such groups can also be organized by the not-for-profit firm itself. Throughout this phase two-way communication is vitally important.

Advocacy

This is the most sought-after level. Here there is word-of-mouth recommendation and 'customer get customer' schemes can be developed. There is an element of risk here, however, as the relationship is now visible to others.

Massey (1995) believes that in general the charity element of the not-for-profit sector can already teach general marketers about developing relationships. Such organizations track and score their donors and think up new ways of identifying different types of donor using traditional techniques. For example, the St Thomas Blood Transfusion Service tracks whether donors respond at the first, second, third, up to the ninth call, to give blood. In other words, those who respond most promptly are not called upon again and this saves on mailing costs.

Each person's generosity is triggered in different ways: relief from guilt, the need for self-esteem, fear of contracting a disease or concern for humanity. It is only by finding out about the people who have given that organizations discover which triggers work with each type of person. Massey believes that lifetime value needs to be used to measure success rather than cost per response or cost per thousand.

Conclusion

Not-for-profit organizations, whether they be within the public or voluntary sectors, now exist within a more competitive environment than hitherto. There seems to be growing acceptance that marketing in general can play a valuable part in such organizations' effectiveness. With an improved understanding of what marketing actually entails (and not what people *think* it entails) will come a growing commitment to a more long-term strategic approach. This will emphasize the development and maintenance of mutually satisfying relationships rather than the single, individual buyer–seller interaction. There is a particular difficulty experienced by not-for-profit organizations, however. The lack of a direct economic link between resource generation and resource allocation does seem to direct organizations down a path of short-term tactical decisions aimed more at the resource generators than any other 'customer'. It would seem to be the case that those organizations which are aware of this dilemma, and that propose strategies to overcome it, are more likely to be the most successful in the future.

References

Arndt, J. (1978) How broad should the marketing concept be? *Journal of Marketing*, Vol. 42, pp. 101–3.

Arndt, J. (1983) The political economy paradigm: foundation for theory building in marketing, *Journal of Marketing*, Vol. 47, pp. 44–54.

Berry, L.L. and Parasuraman, A. (1991) *Marketing Services*, Free Press, New York.

Birks, D.F. and Southan, J.M. (1991) The potential of marketing information systems in charitable organizations, *Marketing Intelligence and Planning*, Vol. 8, pp. 15–20.

Burnett, K. (1992) *Relationship Fundraising*, White Lion Press, London.

Christopher, M., Payne, A. and Ballantyne, D. (1991) *Relationship Marketing*, Butterworth-Heinemann, Oxford.

Conway, A., Mackay, S. and Yorke, D.A. (1994) Strategic planning in higher education: who are the customers? *International Journal of Educational Management*, Vol. 8, pp. 29–36.

Conway, A. and Yorke, D.A. (1991) Can the marketing concept be applied to the polytechnic and college sector of higher education? *International Journal of Public Sector Management*, Vol. 4, pp. 23–36.

Cousin, L. (1990) Marketing planning in the public and nonprofit sectors, *European Journal of Marketing*, Vol. 24, pp. 15–30.

Cross, R.H. (1992) The five degrees of customer bonding, *Direct Marketing*, October, pp. 38–58.

Drucker, P.E. (1989) What business can learn from nonprofits, *Harvard Business Review*, July–August, pp. 88–93.

Economic Trends (1995) HMSO, London.

Employment Gazette (1995) May.

Fine, S.H. (1990) *Social Marketing*, Allyn & Bacon, Boston, Mass.

Grönroos, C. (1994) From marketing mix to relationship marketing: towards a paradigm shift in marketing, *Management Decision*, Vol. 32, pp. 4–20.

Gwin, J.M. (1990) Constituent analysis: a paradigm for marketing effectiveness in the not-for-profit organization, *European Journal of Marketing*, Vol. 24, pp. 43–8.

Hansmann, H. (1980) The role of nonprofit enterprises, *The Yale Law Journal*, April, pp. 835–901.

Kotler, P. (1975) *Marketing in Nonprofit Organizations*, Prentice-Hall, Englewood Cliffs, NJ.

Kotler, P. (1984) *Marketing Management: Analysis, Planning and Control* (5th edn), Prentice-Hall, Englewood Cliffs, NJ.

Kotler, P. and Andreasen, A. (1991) *Strategic Marketing for Nonprofit Organizations*, Prentice-Hall, Englewood Cliffs, NJ.

Kotler, P. and Levy, S.J. (1967) Broadening the concept of marketing, *Journal of Marketing*, Vol. 33, pp. 10–15.

Kotler, P. and Levy, S.J. (1969) A new form of marketing myopia: rejoinder to Professor Luck, *Journal of Marketing*, Vol. 33, p. 57.

Levitt, T. (1981) Marketing intangible products and product intangibles, *Harvard Business Review*, May–June, pp. 94–102.

Lindsay, G. and Murphy, A. (1994) NSPCC: marketing the 'solution' not the problem. In J. Bell *et al.* (eds) *Working Paper, Marketing Education Group Annual Conference: Unity in Diversity*, University of Ulster, Coleraine.

Lindsay, G. and Murphy, A. (1995) A systematic approach to the application of marketing theory for charitable organisations. In D. Jobber *et al.* (eds) *Proceedings of the Marketing Education Group Annual Conference: Making Marketing Work*, University of Bradford, Bradford.

Litten, L.H. (1980) Marketing higher education – benefits and risks for the American academic system, *Journal of Higher Education*, Vol. 51, pp. 40–59.

Lovelock, C.H. and Rothschild, M.L. (1980) *Uses, Abuses and Misuses of Marketing in Higher Education. Marketing in College Admissions: A Broadening of Perspectives*, The College Board, New York.

Lovelock, C.H. and Weinberg, C.B. (1990) *Public and Nonprofit Marketing*, Scientific Press, San Francisco, Calif.

Luck, D.J. (1969) Broadening the concept of marketing too far, *Journal of Marketing*, Vol. 33, pp. 53–5.

Massey, A. (1995) Information exchange, *Marketing Business*, March, pp. 35–8.

McCort, J.D. (1994) A framework for evaluating the relational extent of a relationship marketing strategy: the case of nonprofit organizations, *Journal of Direct Marketing*, Vol. 8, pp. 53–65.

Morgan, R.M. and Hunt, S.D. (1994) The commitment-trust theory of relationship marketing, *Journal of Marketing*, Vol. 58, pp. 20–38.

O'Sullivan, T. (1993) Goodwill gestures, *Marketing Week*, 26 November, pp. 30–1.

Rados, D.L. (1981) *Marketing for Nonprofit Organizations*, Auburn House Publishing, Dover, Mass.

Rothschild, M.L. (1979) Marketing communications in nonbusiness situations or why its so hard to sell brotherhood like soap, *Journal of Marketing*, Spring, pp. 11–20.

Scrivens, E. and Witzel, M.L. (1990) Editorial, *European Journal of Marketing*, Vol. 27.

Shapiro, B.P. (1973) Marketing for nonprofit organizations, *Harvard Business Review*, September–October, pp. 123–32.

Shostack, G.L. (1977) Breaking free from product marketing, *Journal of Marketing*, Vol. 41, pp. 73–80.

Smith, G. (1988) Applying marketing to the public sector: the case of local authority leisure centres, *International Journal of Public Sector Management*, Vol. 1, pp. 36–45.

Social Trends (1994) HMSO, London.

Van Der Hart, H.W.C. (1990) Government organizations and their customers in The Netherlands: strategy, tactics and operations, *European Journal of Marketing*, Vol. 24, pp. 31–42.

Wensley, R. (1990) The voice of the consumer? Speculations on the limits to the marketing analogy, *European Journal of Marketing*, Vol. 24, pp. 49–60.

Wiesendanger, B. (1995) Profitable pointers from nonprofits, *Journal of Business Strategy*, Vol. 15, pp. 33–9.

14

Where do we go now in relationship marketing?

Francis Buttle

The previous 13 chapters have described, analysed and critiqued RM practice in a number of organizational settings (supply-chain relationships, principal–agent relationships, business-to-business relationships, intraorganizational relationships) and industries (hospitality, air travel, retail banking, corporate banking, credit cards, financial advisory services, advertising agencies, not-for-profit organizations). This chapter explores some of the common themes and issues. It is organized around a number of questions raised in the introductory chapter.

Is there evidence of a shift from short-term to a longer-term marketing focus?

Historically, marketing has been very short-termist, concerned with today's sales and this year's top and bottom lines. Under an RM regime, the focus becomes more long term. Is there any evidence of this? There is evidence in both for-profit and not-for-profit sectors.

In the not-for-profit sector, the long-term perspective afforded by RM is of paramount importance. Charitable fundraisers, for example, want to develop long-term relationships with resource generators, and to move known individual donors from casual gift-giving to legacy status. Also, the creation, development and maintenance of corporate donors are particularly advanced forms of RM. Equally, beneficiaries of not-for-profit organizations are the subject of long-term RM strategies. Students in higher education, for example, may be targeted for undergraduate, diploma, postgraduate and executive education over many years. Long-term RM efforts are also directed towards regulatory bodies such as government agencies and advisory boards.

Evidence of a long-term RM perspective is found in high-street banking. Retail banks know that many of their customer accounts take up to six years to break even. Banks have therefore begun to take a longer-term view of account retention. Despite this, only half the banking institutions in a recent survey claimed to have strategies in place to prevent customer defection.

In corporate banking, however, there appears to be a structural impediment to the formation of long-term relationships with customers. Because banks need to develop a balanced credit portfolio across sectoral and geographic divisions, they are inhibited from forming long-term relationships with clients who might upset an established equilibrium.

Is there any evidence of mutual interests being served?

Relationship marketers value win–win relationships with their customers. They have concern for the welfare of their customers. Is there any evidence that RM practices are serving mutual interests? Evidence from the credit-card, financial services, retail, airline and hospitality industries is mixed.

Affinity credit cards offer benefits to three parties: the card issuer, the affinity organization whose membership is targeted for the offer and the card user. The card issuer earns fee and interest income. The affinity organization (e.g. university alumni association) receives a payment based on the number of cards issued and/or the volume of spending on the cards. In turn these payments enable the organization better to serve the needs of its membership. It has been observed that this last relationship between organization and member, is the weakest in this ostensibly win–win–win triangle.

In the financial services market, both customers and suppliers benefit in a very broad sense from RM. For the customer, a long-term relationship can help to reduce the level of perceived risk associated with purchase of financial services. For the supplier, RM is seen as a means of enhancing customer retention rates in the face of bad publicity and regulatory concerns about the sales of inappropriate financial products, undisclosed commissions earned by salespeople and poor contract retention rates.

In the supply chain, the key issue is: How is the profit margin earned from customer spending to be split between manufacturer and retailer? In the 'old paradigm' view of relationships between channel members, the distribution of profit was regarded as the outcome of power imbalance. Multiple retailers and buying consortia exerted power over manufacturers, demanding lower purchase prices, slotting allowances, own-brands, advertising monies, pre-pricing and rapid-response delivery, thereby transferring inventory costs to manufacturers. Major manufacturers, equally, were seen as able to exert power over the weaker independent retailers. The 'new paradigm', or 'partnership' model of channel relationships, is gaining momentum. For example, retailers and manufacturers are increasingly collaborating in product development. Those retailers who do develop close relationships (e.g. Marks & Spencer) can offer their suppliers significant benefits: guaranteed production and distribution, and assurances that margins will be maintained, for example. Equally, they make significant demands of their suppliers: strict quality controls, financial penalties for customer complaints and returns, and exclusivity of supply which precludes sales of product through competing channels, even if rebranded. However, there is very little evidence that profit is being redistributed. Elsewhere in business-to-business marketing (B2BM), the perspective offered by the Industrial Marketing and Purchasing (IMP) group has redirected attention away from a focus on buyer *or* seller, to a joint focus on buyer *and* seller in interaction, producing outcomes beneficial to both parties. IMP adherents believe that the old 'transactional' view of marketing has never been adequate to the task of describing B2B relationships.

Frequent-flyer programmes (FFPs) are clubs which offer significant advantages to frequent travellers as well as benefiting the airlines. Travellers may enjoy improved menu choice, special lounge facilities at airports, preferred rates with partner organizations such as car-hire firms and hotels, class upgrades, and mileage points redeemable in free flights or merchandise. The airlines have found that FFPs have reduced the price sensitivity of travellers and have been a useful tool for filling unused capacity. They are, however, concerned about the substantial amount of unredeemed mileage points; airlines do not want to displace fare-paying passengers on popular routes with an FFP beneficiary. This could seriously impact their profitability. Like frequent-guest programmes in the hospitality industry, FFPs are better characterized as sales promotions. They provide added benefits to the customer. However, they are not focused on better solving customers' accommodation or travel needs.

Do companies understand the concept of lifetime value?

Do relationship marketers pursue the goal of customer retention? Whereas market share and sales volume are typical objectives in transactional marketing, the success of longer-term marketing strategies can be better measured in customer retention/defection rates, share of customer, economies of scope and customer loyalty. These objectives would indicate that the concept of the lifetime value of a customer is understood. Is there any evidence that this is so?

Some evidence does exist. Credit-card issuers such as MBNA are fully aware of the lifetime value of a customer. American research has shown that it costs on average about $50 to recruit a new credit-card customer. It is not until part way through the second year of the relationship that these costs are recovered through fee and interest income. Thereafter, annual profits rise. The research showed that a reduction in the defection rate from 20% to 10% meant that the average lifespan of an MBNA customer doubled from 5 years to 10 years, and the lifetime value more than doubled. Similarly, a 5% increase in retention had a downstream effect on raising profits by 60% in the fifth year of the relationship.

About 20% of respondents to a survey of banking institutions reported that they were able to define the lifetime value of a customer; another 70% claimed to be working towards this goal. Retail banks are aware that not all their customers are profitable. Customer retention strategies are directed at those customers who contribute most to fixed costs and profit. As defection rates decline with account tenure, accounts retained in the short and medium term are less likely to defect in the long term. Identifying accounts to target with retention strategies is problematic for the first three years since practically all accounts are unprofitable during this period. Indeed, they may not break even for six years.

Banks' efforts to cross-sell multiple services is evidence of their desire to obtain a larger share of customer. The telephone banking service First Direct now offers current accounts, savings accounts, mortgages, personal loans and insurances. Since current account operations are generally loss-makers for high-street banks, they frequently seek cross-subsidization from profitable lines such as credit cards to ensure corporate success.

Advertising agencies, too, are aware that not all clients are equal. The most attractive accounts to whom agencies (should) direct their retention efforts are those producing high present net profit and having great future potential. The least attractive are those at the opposite ends of both scales.

Is there evidence of trust and commitment between relational partners?

The purpose of much academic research into RM has been to conceptualize, operationalize and measure trust, commitment and related variables such as honesty, helpfulness and benevolence. Is there any evidence in practice that efforts are made by RM partners to develop trust and demonstrate commitment? Some evidence is found in supply-chain relationships, corporate banking and financial advisory markets. Supply-chain relationships are becoming more open and trusting. Information judged to be of mutual benefit is being shared by both parties.

Corporate banking is typified by an asymmetrical informational relationship: the bank knows much about customers' credit history and requirements, but customers know little about how the bank's credit decisions are made. The same asymmetry is found in the relationship between financial adviser and client. Since financial services can be very complex, clients become dependent on vendor or agent expertise. Furthermore, customers find it very difficult to assess the quality of a decision to purchase a financial service. This is partly because the benefits may not be experienced for some time (e.g. with-profits endowment policy), and partly because the outcome is at least in part beyond the control and knowledge of the vendor. Such informational imbalance and uncertainty is bound to increase the client's sense of vulnerability and to impose on the marketer (bank or adviser) the requirement to develop a sense of trust in the client. Full disclosure of commissions earned from product sales is one means of developing trust.

Is endorsement of relationship marketing reflected in high-quality customer service?

Having the welfare of relationship partners at heart can be expressed through excellent service. Is there evidence of this in practice? Indeed, there is. Electronic data interchange (EDI) has enabled manufacturers to deliver better service to retailers and they, in turn, to serve better their customers. EDI has produced fewer stock-outs and fewer billing errors in manufacturer–retailer relationships.

Retail banks are finding that their customers are demanding higher service quality in their financial transactions. Surveys have identified that one of the chief reasons for customers' switching banks is dissatisfaction with service. Banks are increasingly recognizing that there is a link among high-quality service, customer loyalty and profitability. However, evidence indicates that, although there is considerable dissatisfaction with service performance, defection rates are remarkably low. Why? One reason is that relationship termination costs, or switching costs, are very high. The temptation for banks, and other organizations with similar experiences, is to interpret inertia as customer satisfaction, or as evidence of customer loyalty and commitment. It may not be.

Inadvertently, banks may be encouraging customers to defect by offering better service to new accounts than they do to established accounts. Corporate bankers, for example, commonly charge their more established customers a higher rate of interest on borrowings. Lower rates are used to attract business, not to keep it. Perhaps it should come as no surprise that client companies often have a major relationship with a single corporate bank and additional minor liaisons with secondary banks. To apply the marriage metaphor, this is rather like having a spouse and several lovers.

In the airline industry the most visible evidence of RM is the FFP. Essentially, FFPs are loyalty schemes offering enhanced customer service standards to members, as detailed earlier: wider menu choice, terminal lounge facilities, discounts from partner organizations, upgrades and redeemable mileage points. The key for the airlines is to identify customer service improvements which incur low costs (thereby preserving margins) but are perceived by flyers as offering high perceived value. Alternatively, airlines must identify customer service improvements for which travellers are prepared to pay a price premium.

Long-term clients of advertising agencies tend to enjoy superior, tailored service. It does take a long time for interorganizational relationships to mature and produce benefits for both parties. Agencies needs time to understand the client's business and the affordances and limitations of their brief; clients need to give agencies the time for advertising positioning strategies to take effect. Strategies can only be judged (in)effective over the long run. Building a strong consumer franchise for a brand requires long-term investment in brand development. Not only are these account-specific measures important in determining whether an agency–client relationship will endure but so are the general attitudes and policies of the partners. Advertisers, particularly those with more experience, are likely to treat agencies as equal business partners, rather than simply as pools of creative talent and media-buying muscle. Therefore, as might be expected, large clients with big budgets are more prone to commission advertising through large agencies and are less likely to move accounts. However, as the recent Saatchi and Saatchi affair proves, some clients are more loyal to individual persons than they are to an agency.

All these examples are of improved service being offered to external customers. There is evidence too of RM being associated with improved service to internal customers. Both external and internal service quality have been found to be measurable. Evidence from the hospital context suggests that there are nine components of internal service quality: helpfulness, reliability, promptness, communication, tangibles, professionalism, confidentiality, preparedness and consideration. Internal relational partners are able to assess the quality of service provision in terms of these dimensions.

Is internal marketing necessary for relationship marketing to prosper?

Internal marketing is widely viewed as a prerequisite for successful RM. Evidence from the Post Office, banking, hospitality and not-for-profit contexts suggests that organizations are likely to be less effective externally if the expectations of internal relational partners are not met. What remains unproven is whether it is necessary and/or sufficient cause of RM success.

RM as it has been explored in this book is largely seen as an interorganizational or organization–customer phenomenon. Conceptually, however, RM can be both internal and external to an organization. Internal supplier–customer relationships are endemic in any flow process or multidepartment organization (e.g. IT/management and R&D/marketing relationships). These relationships tend to prosper and benefit the parties mutually when there is clear goal congruence, or when both parties subscribe to a superordinate mission or vision. In the not-for-profit sector, for example, RM can contribute much to the development of a supportive and enthusiastic culture among volunteers, and can help bind professionals of different disciplines to the organizational mission, thereby ensuring that the goals of the organization are accomplished.

Some of the major causes of sub-postmaster dissatisfaction are the lack of co-ordination and consultation with Post Office Counters Ltd (POCL) in policy-making, and the production of performance targets and operational standards. They believe that POCL imposes top-down authority without due recognition of their requirements. Sub-postmasters want to have more say in policy and strategy decisions. This description can also apply in an inter-organizational RM context. Extraorganizational partners are likely to seek and enjoy mutual benefits when goals, mission or vision are shared.

Banks are investing in employee development in the belief that well trained, customer-orientated, satisfied employees generate more effective, long-term relationships with customers. However, it seems that the UK is behind many other countries in terms of the sums invested. In the hospitality industry the Marriott Corporation has declared that its primary target market is the internal customer. Bill Marriott believes that it is first necessary to satisfy the employee. An employee who feels valued at work is much more likely to give excellent service to guests. In turn the guest is likely to return, establishing over time a personal relationship with employees, and a sense of loyalty towards the organization.

Are sophisticated information systems employed, enabling managers to meet or exceed customer expectations?

It is claimed that managers cannot deliver goods and services which match or exceed customer expectations unless they have customer information that is in an accessible and usable form. RM places heavy demands on the acquisition, storage, dissemination and use of customer information. Flexible IT systems are said to be vital for RM success. The banking, credit-card, airline and hospitality cases reported here provide evidence that IT is playing a significant role in RM practice.

In retail banking, it is commonplace for banks to hold information on product holdings and the duration of a relationship. However, it is unusual for banks to have the type of information on customer needs and preferences which would enhance their RM strategies. In corporate banking, marketers accumulate an abundance of customer information which is inaccessible to competitive banks. Clearly this should provide a competitive advantage in identifying and meeting customer needs. All banks find it relatively easy to compete on the supply and cost of credit; relationships, in contrast, should be induplicable.

Credit-card issuers require applicants to supply information on their personal circumstances and family commitments. This enables the issuer to credit score the application. If successful every card-based transaction is then logged against the customer's account, providing a wealth of useful marketing information to the issuer. These data are used to make further offers to the customer.

FFPs and frequent-guest programmes depend on computerized reservation systems and customer information for their successful operation. Both airlines and hotels use central reservations systems to manage yield, that is, to generate the highest possible revenues from a fixed capacity.

The danger, however, in all these cases, is that IT and customer information will simply enable a more sophisticated form of database marketing to emerge, and that RM, charged with developing long-term mutual benefits and corporate profitability, will become subordinated to short-term sales and profit.

In B2BM, the exchange of information is critical to the development of successful interorganizational relationships which benefit both parties. The claim made in this book is that B2BM is best characterized as the management of information.

In the supply chain, EDI is becoming more widespread. Essentially, EDI automates the order-billing cycle, delivers improved customer service and eliminates much of the paper chase that has characterized this function. Although more efficient, it is also associated with fewer personal contacts between channel partners, making it more difficult to forge interpersonal relationships.

Do organizational structures and reward systems facilitate the achievement of relationship management goals?

RM theory indicates that common sales and marketing organizational structures (territory or product-centred organizations) are potentially incompatible with RM goals. Equally, performance-based systems which reward short-term sales performance and customer acquisition may not elicit the behaviours which are best suited to achieving RM goals. Have companies made changes to organizational structures and reward systems in an effort to bring about mutually beneficial long-term relationships? Some sectors have made changes.

Both retail and corporate banks have introduced relationship managers who are given the responsibility of managing the bank's relationships with specified clients. Corporate relationship managers may be responsible for up to 15 firms. Despite this organizational innovation, the primary motivation for switching corporate banks has been dissatisfaction with the manager who is often thought to have little understanding of the client's business. In addition, the centralization of credit functions and the disempowerment of branch managers have been counterproductive in promoting RM goals. Furthermore, it is a widespread practice for managers to be rewarded on a series of transactional measures rather than relational criteria.

Elsewhere in the financial services sector, high salesforce turnover and commission-based selling have been counterproductive in developing trust and demonstrating commitment. The recent requirement for advisers to disclose to customers commissions earned on sales is a conscious move to eliminate one of the sources of mistrust. Many financial services organizations are presently replacing their commission-based salespeople with salaried salespeople. These initiatives appear to be facilitating the achievement of RM goals.

Advertising agencies spend significant sums pursuing new accounts. Most agencies have new account, or new business, managers. Account directors/managers have the responsibility for managing existing accounts, but rarely are they rewarded for account retention. More often than not they act as liaisons, linking the requirements of clients to the capabilities of the agency.

A final comment

Where does this lead us? RM theory is both mirror and tutor. Certainly theory reflects practice in many ways. There are worthy examples of long-term marketing orientation, mutuality of interests, customer retention management, trust, the centrality of customer service, internal marketing, astute IT management and adaptations to organizational structures and reward systems.

RM theory has also taken a normative turn. Not only does it describe how RM is but it also specifies how RM should be, drawing heavily on the analogy of interpersonal relationships. While there is plentiful evidence that some organizations in some sectors are applying some of the principles, the cases and contexts discussed here suggest that finding a single exemplary instance of best practice is at best contestable, perhaps even impossible.

What is clear is that many organizations are retreating from the transactional view of marketing which has been shown to be relatively costly and ineffective compared to RM. Retreat does not imply surrender. Companies are taking on some RM practices but have yet to commit themselves to the full philosophy and strategic repertoire of RM. It remains to be seen whether there will be a reinvention of marketing practice across all sectors and industries.

Index